PATENTS AND INNOVATION IN MAINLAND CHINA AND HONG KONG

How do patents affect innovation in Mainland China and Hong Kong? How can two patent systems operate within one country, and how is innovation affected by the "one country, two systems" model? For the first time, this book links these challenging issues together and provides a comprehensive overview for government officials, lawmakers, academics, law practitioners and students to understand the patent systems of Mainland China and Hong Kong. Themes examined include the interaction between the two distinctive patent regimes, the impact of patents on innovation in China's specific industries such as green tech, traditional Chinese medicines and telecommunications, the role of utility models in inflating low-quality patents and the application of good faith principle in enforcing FRAND in Mainland China, patent system reforms in Hong Kong, and the impact of these changes on innovation in the two vastly distinctive yet closely connected jurisdictions.

Yahong Li graduated from Stanford University with a doctorate in Science of Law. She teaches and researches intellectual property law extensively, in particular on the intersection of IP and innovation. Her major publications include *Imitation to Innovation in China: The Role of Patents in Biotechnology and Pharmaceutical Industries* (2010); *International and Comparative Intellectual Property: Law, Policy and Practice* (2005); and "China" in L. Bentley (ed.) *International Copyright and Practice* (2015). She is Associate Professor and Director of the LLM Program in Intellectual Property and Information Technology at the Faculty of Law, the University of Hong Kong; a member of ATRIP; and Honorary Advisor of the Hong Kong Institute of Patent Attorneys.

T0371519

Patents and Innovation in Mainland China and Hong Kong

TWO SYSTEMS IN ONE COUNTRY COMPARED

Edited by

YAHONG LI

The University of Hong Kong

CAMBRIDGE
UNIVERSITY PRESS

CAMBRIDGE
UNIVERSITY PRESS

University Printing House, Cambridge CB2 8BS, United Kingdom

One Liberty Plaza, 20th Floor, New York, NY 10006, USA

477 Williamstown Road, Port Melbourne, VIC 3207, Australia

314-321, 3rd Floor, Plot 3, Splendor Forum, Jasola District Centre, New Delhi - 110025, India

79 Anson Road, #06-04/06, Singapore 079906

Cambridge University Press is part of the University of Cambridge.

It furthers the University's mission by disseminating knowledge in the pursuit of education, learning and research at the highest international levels of excellence.

www.cambridge.org
Information on this title: www.cambridge.org/9781108707107
DOI: 10.1017/9781108163583

First published 2017
First paperback edition 2019

A catalogue record for this publication is available from the British Library

Library of Congress Cataloging in Publication data
NAMES: Li, Yahong, 1963– editor.
TITLE: Patents and innovation in Mainland China and Hong Kong : two systems in one country compared / edited by Yahong Li.
DESCRIPTION: Cambridge [UK] ; New York : Cambridge University Press, 2017. | Includes bibliographical references and index.
IDENTIFIERS: LCCN 2017026225 | ISBN 9781107194649 (hardback)
SUBJECTS: LCSH: Patent laws and legislation – China. | Intellectual property – China. | Technological innovations – Law and legislation – China. | Patent laws and legislation – China – Hong Kong. | Patent laws and legislation – Singapore. | BISAC: LAW / Intellectual Property / General.
CLASSIFICATION: LCC KNQ1194 .P387 2017 | DDC 346.5104/86–dc23
LC record available at https://lccn.loc.gov/2017026225

ISBN 978-1-107-19464-9 Hardback
ISBN 978-1-108-70710-7 Paperback

Contents

Figures

Tables

Contributors

Yifu Chen
PhD (The University of Hong Kong), LLM (The University of Sydney).
Assistant Professor, School of Law,
Shanghai University of International Business and Economics, China.

Li Gao
PhD (The University of Hong Kong), LLM (China University of Political Science and Law).
Yong Pung How Research Fellow, School of Law,
Singapore Management University.

Jyh-An Lee
JSD (Stanford University), LLM (Harvard University).
Associate Professor and Director of the Centre for Financial Regulation and Economic Development (CFRED), Faculty of Law,
the Chinese University of Hong Kong.

Yahong Li
JSD and JSM (Stanford University).
Associate Professor and Director of LLM Program in Intellectual Property and Information Technology, Faculty of Law,
the University of Hong Kong.

Jeffrey Mclean
Master of Industrial Property (Sydney University of Technology),
Master of Information Technology (Queensland University of Technology),
BS (University of Queensland). Senior Associate at Deacons and Registered Patent Attorney (AU).

Dan Prud'homme
PhD (MGSM, Macquarie University).
Visiting Scholar, Oxford University;

Senior Researcher, GLORAD Center for Global R&D and Innovation, Tongji University, China.

Leslie Shay
LLB (University of London), BS in Pharmacy (University of British Columbia). Legal Officer of the Intellectual Property Department of the Government of the Hong Kong Special Administrative Region of People's Republic of China.

Frank Charn Wing Wan
JSD (City University of Hong Kong). Director of Hong Kong Policy Research Institute; Director of the Board of the Versitech Ltd of the University of Hong Kong; and the Chairman of the Life Science Group, Business and Industrial Club of City University of Hong Kong.

Limeng Yu
PhD Candidate (Technology Management Institute, National Tshinghua University), MPhil (The University of Hong Kong), LLB in IP and Mathematics (Peking University). Former Patent Engineer of Huawei Technologies Co. Ltd.

Ronald Yu
JD (The Chinese University of Hong Kong), LLM (The University of Hong Kong). US Patent Agent; Board Member of International Intellectual Property Commercialization Council.

Winnie Yue
BA, MA (University of Cambridge), Dipl. In Intellectual Property Law and Practice (University of Bristol). Professional Support Lawyer, Deacons.

Foreword

The "one country, two laws" principle was a key part of the 1984 Sino-British Declaration that led in 1997 to the handing back to China by Great Britain of Hong Kong, its then Crown Colony. In the 20 years since the return of Hong Kong to Chinese sovereignty and its transformation into a self-governed Special Administrative Region (SAR) under Article 31 of the People's Republic of China (PRC) Constitution, it has thus provided a living and evolving case study of the challenges and opportunities offered by the coexistence in one country of two different systems of law.

As they do in many areas of law and practice, the challenges and opportunities present themselves in the field of patents. This is a youthful subject in Mainland China where the first patent law after the foundation of the PRC in 1949 dates only from 1984. Of course, as the contributors to the first part of this work describe so well, the pace of development and change since that time has been dizzying, and today's patent law and practice is very different to that initial law. As Dr. Yahong Li notes in her introduction to this fascinating examination and explanation of multifarious aspects of the laws both on the Mainland and across the border in the SAR, the PRC is now in the process of transitioning from an imitation economy to one based on its own innovative activities, with varying degrees of success and speed across the diverse reaches of the massive country.

Hong Kong too is in a state of transition as it tries to position itself as one of the hubs of the Greater Pearl River Delta region, while at the same time moving up the value chain and starting to play the IP game in all its manifestations (Frank Charn Wing Wan sets out in his chapter the role of patents in the development of Hong Kong's economy).

Just one of many initiatives was the introduction, in June 2016, of its own "original grant" patent system (described by Leslie Shay in his chapter on the new regime). Previously, Hong Kong SAR patents were obtained merely by re-

registering after having patents granted in other countries (or in the supranational European Patent Office in Munich) that have search and examination capabilities. However, as occurred earlier in Singapore (described in an excellent chapter by Ronald Yu), the Hong Kong authorities decided after considering the pros and cons (the arguments are enumerated by Jeffrey Mclean and Winnie Yue in their contribution, which also reveals the somewhat surprising fact that only six patent cases have reached court in Hong Kong in the past 20 years) that the importance of innovation to the territory's future necessitated sending a strong message that patents were being taken more seriously than they were before. That strong message was embodied in part by the move to the "original grant" system and away from re-registration.

Obviously, it is far too early to make any evaluation as to whether the HKSAR Government's initiatives to encourage and foster innovation are bearing fruit, although without doubt there is much room for improvement: Dr. Li observes that, of the more than 12,000 patent applications made in the SAR in 2015, fewer than 250 were filed by local residents. Although I endorse wholeheartedly Dr. Li's cautionary note that it is quality and not quantity that counts in this area as in many others, there is no doubt that the process of altering a society's mindset from one focused on short-term gain to one prepared to invest for the longer term is a slow and arduous one that many countries are engaged in.

While Hong Kong tries to up its game in innovation and creativity, on the Mainland the number of invention patent filings have exploded, as each year's World Intellectual Property Organization (WIPO) figures testify. But here again, all may not be what it seems: filing a patent may be a measure of an individual's or business's innovation that is beloved by many bureaucrats, but in the real world it is quality patents and ease of enforcement and commercialization that count. This can be seen too in the contributions both on utility models (where Dan Prud'homme addresses on a comparative basis the perennial problem of reconciling the aims of accessibility of the right with the need to ensure quality) and the invention patent scene in the PRC for green technology (where Li Gao describes the industry as "big but not strong"), Traditional Chinese Medicine (TCM) (amongst many other startling facts, Yifu Chen draws attention to the statistic that there were nearly 27,000 patents granted for herbal medicines in the PRC by 2011 compared to a mere 21 in the US Patent Office) and telecoms (where Limeng Yu sets out examples of the increasing resort to litigation in a field in which there are large numbers of invention patents granted every year).

As its editor, Yahong Li must be congratulated on gathering together in one volume a collection of contributions of such high quality on many of the areas in the patent field that bear comparative study. Of course, what makes unique the subject matter of this book is that the comparison is possible within one country where two systems with different roots, imperatives and influences coexist.

David Llewelyn
Professor of Intellectual Property Law, Dickson
Poon School of Law, King's College London;
Deputy Dean & Practice Professor, School of Law,
Singapore Management University

Foreword

On 1 July 1997, China resumed sovereignty over Hong Kong under the 'one country, two systems' framework. Although voluminous literature on the transition of this former British colony exists, very few books or journal articles have examined the parallel intellectual property developments in these two jurisdictions. This volume is therefore a delight to read. It is also very timely in light of the twentieth anniversary of Hong Kong's handover.

This book brings together policymakers, legal practitioners and academic commentators to discuss a wide range of patent issues, including innovation models, patent system designs, green technology, traditional Chinese medicines, telecommunications equipment and services, and enforcement of FRAND licences. The chapters draw on the contributors' expertise and experience in intellectual property law and policy in Mainland China, Hong Kong and often both. Although the topics vary from chapter to chapter, all the chapters centre around three important sets of stories, the study of which will greatly enhance our understanding of intellectual property developments in China.

The first set of contributions concerns transformation and transition. Since its promulgation in 1984, the Chinese Patent Law has been revised three times: in 1992, 2000 and 2008. These amendments responded to both the rapidly changing internal conditions and the continued external pressure from the United States and other developed countries, especially before China joined the World Trade Organization (WTO) in December 2001. In the mid- to late 2000s, China also underwent a dramatic transformation from an imitation economy to one relying on innovation – a phenomenon that is well captured by the editor's earlier monograph, *Imitation to Innovation in China: The Role of Patents in Biotechnology and Pharmaceutical Industries*.

Today, there is no denying that China is an emerging intellectual property power, even though pirated and counterfeit goods remain widely available in many parts of the country. Based on the 2016 statistics compiled by the World Intellectual Property Organization, China now ranks third in terms of international patent applications under the Patent Cooperation Treaty (PCT), behind only the United States and Japan. Among corporate PCT applicants, ZTE and Huawei also rank first and second in the world, respectively. In addition, China has the world's fourth largest volume of international trademark applications filed under the Madrid system.

Compared with Mainland China, Hong Kong has not experienced as dramatic a transformation. Nevertheless, intellectual property protection in this special administrative region has still improved considerably. When I was a kid growing up in Hong Kong, pirated cassette tapes and counterfeit clothes were widely and openly sold. If one were to pay for computer games, such payment would often have been for copying floppy disks, rather than buying genuine software. Even when I was studying in the United States in the 1990s, it was quite common to see people buying pirated computer games, video CDs and DVDs in select shopping malls.

Today, however, many people in Hong Kong have acquired at least some basic understanding of intellectual property law. In the recent public debate on the Copyright (Amendment) Bill 2014, for example, many youngsters and university students were amazingly well versed in concepts and terms used by intellectual property lawyers. Because pirated and counterfeit goods are no longer sold as frequently, many people in Hong Kong have also changed their attitude towards these goods. To be sure, there is still widespread piracy in the digital environment, but there is no evidence that the level of online piracy is much higher in Hong Kong than in other parts of the world.

The biggest transformation Hong Kong has seen, however, has to be the change of the intellectual property system from one serving a British colony – or, worse, its mother country – to one tailored to the needs and interests of a somewhat autonomous administrative region. In the patent area, no policy change has better exemplified this transformation than the introduction of the original grant patent system in June 2016, which is discussed in several chapters of this book. Until the introduction of this full-fledged system, Hong Kong reregisters the patents granted by the State Intellectual Property Office of China (SIPO), the UK Intellectual Property Office and the European Patent Office. The Hong Kong Intellectual Property Department did not undertake any substantive examination at all.

The second set of contributions pertains to positioning and interrelationship. For China, a big question concerns the country's role in the regional and international intellectual property regimes. In its National Patent Development Strategy (2011–2020), SIPO set out a 2015 target of at least two million patent applications for inventions, utility models and designs. Although this target seems highly ambitious – and, for many, mind-blowing – China had already surpassed this target by 2012. In 2016, China received close to 3.5 million patent applications – 1,338,503 for inventions, 1,475,977 for utility models and 650,344 for designs. The total of patents granted alone exceeded 1.75 million.

Another area that has received considerable attention is China's emergence as the world's most litigious jurisdiction in all three branches of intellectual property law. With over 12,000 patent lawsuits in 2016, as reported by the Supreme People's Court, China is now one of the world's preferred venues for patent litigation. That Chinese courts have attracted such a high litigation volume is ironic – and, for many, surprising – considering that foreign businesses continue to complain about the lack of rule of law and the under-development of the judicial system in China. Such juxtaposition therefore leads one to wonder whether the significant increase in intellectual property lawsuits could eventually strengthen the country's overall protection and enforcement of intellectual property rights. The growing litigiousness has also sparked concerns about an unprecedented ligation explosion that will eventually backfire on foreign rights holders, making it more difficult to do business in China.

Like China, Hong Kong faces similar questions about positioning and interrelationship, but these questions are different. They are not about the jurisdiction's role in shaping intellectual property developments in the Asia-Pacific region or the world. Hong Kong is just too small a place to take on such a role. Instead, the questions are about the role this special administrative region can and will play in China in view of the country's exciting and fast-paced intellectual property developments. Will the new original grant patent system provide the much-needed boost to reposition Hong Kong vis-à-vis other provinces and municipalities in China? Or should this special administrative region turn to other niche areas, such as the establishment of a hub for intellectual property trading? Ultimately, what will be Hong Kong's intellectual property identity?

A related and oft-raised question concerns Hong Kong's relationship with the Guangdong Province. Such a relationship is important considering that many Hong Kong businesses have production plants and marketing outlets in the Pearl River Delta. With Huawei, Tencent and ZTE, the Guangdong province has also been home to many intellectual property–intensive businesses, especially in the area of telecommunications services and electronic goods.

Moreover, Guangzhou now has one of the three newly established specialized intellectual property courts, alongside Beijing and Shanghai. This court has been explicitly empowered with cross-territorial jurisdiction over intellectual property cases in the Guangdong province. The province also constantly has to address difficult intellectual property challenges, including the notorious *shanzhai* (copycat) activities which critics have widely cited as illustrations of the continued inadequacy of intellectual property protection in China.

The last set of contributions captured in this book relate to divergence and discontent – or, to be more precise, the uneven distribution of the benefits derived from the intellectual property system. After all, this system does not provide the same benefits throughout the country or across the varying economic sectors. Compared with the first two sets of chapters, this final set is more subtle. Yet, these chapters are just as important, as they reveal a key policy dilemma confronting intellectual property policymakers in China and other parts of Asia.

It is nothing new to lament the uneven economic developments in China or its enormous gap between the rich and the poor. According to the National Bureau of Statistics, last year China had a Gini coefficient of 0.465, one of the highest in the world. Although economic inequality has received growing attention from policymakers and academic researchers both in China and abroad, inequality in the intellectual property context has been rarely explored.

Out of the three main branches of intellectual property law, the patent regime has been the most revealing about the highly uneven developments in China. Based on the 2016 SIPO figures on invention patents, Jiangsu, Guangdong and Anhui provinces – the provinces with the three largest volumes of applications – had a total of 184,632, 155,581 and 95,963, respectively. Meanwhile, Yunnan, Jilin and Gansu provinces had a total of only 7,907, 7,537 and 6,114, respectively. If one counts provinces and autonomous regions with fewer than 4,000 patent applications, such as Xinjiang, Inner Mongolia, Ningxia, Qinghai, Hainan and Tibet, the statistical contrasts will become even starker.

Like China, Hong Kong has experienced a similar – and arguably more longstanding – gap between the rich and the poor. Emblematic of economic Darwinism and generally reluctant to introduce policies to combat economic inequality, this former British colony has lately been filled with widespread citywide discontent, never-ending public protests and incessant political stonewalling.

Although similar disparity can be found in the intellectual property arena, such disparity is less about people than about economic sectors. To begin with, few individuals in Hong Kong can develop inventions out of their garages.

Garages are just too expensive for most local citizens to own. Furthermore, the patent system seems to have benefitted only a select group of industries, leading to the continuous debate about whether Hong Kong should continue to offer protection for short-term patents, which are granted without substantive examination. With the recent establishment of the new original grant patent system, it is therefore fair to question whether the new system will privilege certain industries at the expense of the others.

A related question about the differential impact of the intellectual property system concerns the ownership of patent-intensive industries. Are they based in Hong Kong, originated from China or merely subsidiaries of gigantic multinationals headquartered abroad? If the industries are located outside Hong Kong, should local policymakers start undertaking a deeper analysis on the costs and benefits of stronger intellectual property protection?

Policymakers frequently note, with little or no reflection, the need for stronger intellectual property protection to attract foreign investment. Yet, economists have repeatedly documented the ambiguous linkage between the two. The people in Hong Kong have also begun to realize the significant economic, social and cultural costs incurred by an out-of-balance intellectual property system, as shown in the recent protests against increased copyright protection in the digital environment.

Indeed, the concerns about striking an inappropriate balance were a primary cause for China's resistance to the external push for stronger intellectual property protection in the first place. The challenges confronting Hong Kong policymakers, to some extent, have brought us full circle to the historical debate on intellectual property law and policy in China.

Thus, when all of these three sets of chapters are taken together, this timely and important book has provided a rare window to examine the patent developments in both Mainland China and Hong Kong. Although the patent systems in these two jurisdictions are rarely discussed together – and even more rarely under the context of the 'one country, two patent systems' framework – the discussion in this volume has been highly insightful and especially instructive. By linking together the parallel developments of these two interrelated yet distinctive systems, this book has greatly enhanced our understanding of intellectual property developments in China.

Peter K. Yu
Professor of Law and Director,
Center for Law and Intellectual Property
Texas A&M University School of Law
April 2017

Acknowledgments

The publication of this book would not have been possible without the collective effort of the chapter authors, who share a passion for patent law and contribute to this book amidst their busy professional lives. We are fortunate to have been able to secure two forewords from Professors Peter Yu and David Llewelyn, whose profound understandings of the complicity between patent and innovation in relation to Mainland China and Hong Kong have shed much light on this pioneer book. The book was originated from an Intellectual Property Forum on Patent and Innovation back in January 2015, in which many people took part and made great contributions: the former Chief Judge Randall R. Rader of the US Court of Appeals for the Federal Circuit; Dr. Jasmine Chambers of Wilson Sonsini Goodrich & Rosati; Ms. Ada Leung and Mr. Thomas Tsang of the Hong Kong Intellectual Property Department; Professor Paul Cheung, Dr. Sun Haochen, Ms. Alice Lee, and Dr. Marcelo Thompson of the University of Hong Kong; Professor Bryan Mercurio of the Chinese University of Hong Kong; Mr. Tim Hancock of Asian Patent Attorneys Association; and Ms. Charmaine Koo of Deacons, just to name a few. I am very grateful for the support, insightful comments and suggestions of all anonymous reviewers, and for the research and editorial assistance of my PhD students, Mr. Anlei Zuo and Miss Weijie Huang. Last but not least, it has been my privilege and pleasure to work with Mr. Joe Ng, CUP Acquisition Editor, and his great team: Ms. Karen Oakes, Ms. Mary Catherine Bongiovi and Ms. Srilakshmi Gobidass, among others, and to be impressed by their professionalism in the production of this book.

Introduction

Patents, Innovation and "One Country, Two Patent Systems"

Yahong Li

I.1 BACKGROUND AND QUESTIONS

In 2015, China topped the world in invention patent applications, exceeding one million within a single year.[1] Its patent grants also scored a historical high of 359,000, ranking number one in the world.[2] However, its ranking of 25th in the Global Innovation Index (GII) is far from impressive.[3] In comparison, Hong Kong, China's special administrative region (SAR), is placed at 14th in the GII 2016, while ranking 16th in patent applications with 12,212, of which only 239 are from local residents.[4] The figures show that Hong Kong's ranking in patent applications is much lower than that in Mainland China, but its innovation status is 11 ranks higher. The reversing ranks raise interesting questions: what has made Hong Kong more "innovative" than its mainland counterpart with its incredibly low patent filing rate, particularly from local residents? What does "innovation" really mean in the context of Hong Kong and Mainland China having two distinctive patent systems within one country? Can the two regions learn from each other, given that one seems to be doing better in patenting and the other in innovation?

As a latecomer of economic and technological modernization, China has developed a sense of urgency in catching up with the Western countries. In the more than 30 years since 1984, China has built a comprehensive patent system from scratch, brought patent protection level to international standards with several patent law amendments, and formulated a series of patent and

---

[1]   To be exact, 1,101,864 applications, of which 968,252 are from local residents. See WIPO, "World Intellectual Property Indicator 2016" (Economics & Statistics Series, 2016), p. 5, www.wipo.int/edocs/pubdocs/en/wipo_pub_941_2016.pdf.

[2]   Ibid.

[3]   The Global Innovation Index 2016, www.globalinnovationindex.org/gii-2016-report#.

[4]   WIPO, "World Intellectual Property Indicator 2016," p. 67.

innovation plans with specific numerical targets, which have been proven to be effective in making China a world leader in patenting in less than one decade. Recently, China has realized that the "great leap forward" in boosting patent numbers and getting top scores in the world patent scoreboard will not turn China into a truly innovative country, and hence it has shifted its strategic focus from being a "big" IP country to a "strong" IP country, with a more holistic view in patent law reform, including promoting patent commercialization and trading, as well as effective patent protection. However, the question is, can China's innovation status be moved up by merely perfecting patent system without a broader reform in other innovation indicators used in GII such as a political system, education infrastructure, and business environment that are conducive to innovation?

On the other hand, as a former British colony and presently China's SAR, Hong Kong has been struggling to find its own identity and the right balance between dependence and independence. Such an identity-seeking mentality is demonstrated not only in the recent uproar in opposing the Central Government's political intervention into the chief executive election and other political freedom, but also in the process of its patent law reform. After about 150 years of colonial history, Hong Kong finally had its own patent system in 1997, but it was only a "registration system," allowing Hong Kong patents granted by other patent offices to be registered in Hong Kong. Although this "registration system" had been effective in accommodating the low patent filings in Hong Kong, the SAR government changed it to an "original grant patent" (OGP) system in June 2016 to allow SAR patent office to examine and grant patents. The rationale for this change, according to the SAR government, is to "facilitate the development of Hong Kong into a regional innovation and technology hub."[5] The question is, however, can this grand mission be achieved through reforming the patent system? Will the new system further enhance the connection between the two different patent systems, one from common law tradition and the other civil law, within one country so that they could function together to promote innovation in each side, and in one country ultimately? Or on the contrary, will it further alienate the already estranged two sides to harm innovation of each other?

The above questions had never been comprehensively and seriously discussed inside and outside of Mainland China and Hong Kong. The reality is that many people do not even know that Hong Kong, although returned to its

---

[5] Hong Kong Legislative Council, Panel on Commerce and Industry, "Updated Background Brief on Review of the Patent System in Hong Kong," April 21, 2015, p. 2, www.legco.gov.hk/yr14-15/english/panels/ci/papers/ci20150421cb1-743-4-e.pdf.

motherland almost 20 years ago, has maintained its own distinctive patent system that was inherited from the UK but has been operated under a registration system that does not provide substantive examination to its own patent applications. Even fewer people know that the majority of applications for Hong Kong patents had been substantively examined by the SIPO, and such practice will be continued under the new OGP system, only under the different name of "outsourcing." It is thus imperative to fill the gap by having a comprehensive academic and practical investigation into this unique arrangement of "one country, two patent systems." This study is also timely in the midst of vast confusion and uproar surrounding Hong Kong's role and identity within China, an authoritarian state with amazing speed in economic growth while striving to transform itself from an imitation-oriented nation to an innovation-oriented nation. Is Hong Kong willing to, or can it, play a role in this transformation? Or is its OGP designed to make the SAR more independent or alienated from this transformation process? Furthermore, can Hong Kong become a "regional innovation and technological hub" without the participation of the Mainland's patent system and technological innovation?

This introduction intends to address some, if not all, of the above questions by first taking the readers through the historical development of patent systems in Mainland China and Hong Kong respectively, and then by empirically examining how patents and innovation interacted in China and Hong Kong, and lastly focusing particularly on future interplay of the two distinctive patent systems in Mainland and Hong Kong under the unique political arrangement of "one country, two systems" (OCTs). This introduction also identifies and links the essential points of each subsequent chapter in this book. It is hoped that, through reading this book, the audiences will have a better understanding that, although hailed as a genius design of China's chief architect for economic reform, Mr. Deng Xiaoping, the OCTS could be very complicated and difficult in implementation, not only politically but also legally, and that the complication could have either a negative or positive impact on innovation in both Mainland China and Hong Kong, depending on how the two sides respond and interact with each other.

I.2 THE TWO SYSTEMS IN ONE COUNTRY: ORIGIN AND DEVELOPMENT

Before tackling the more challenging issue of patents and innovation in China and its SAR, it would be helpful to have a historical survey of the origin and development of the two patent systems. Since a whole chapter of this book,

Chapter 7, has been devoted to the development of Hong Kong's patent system, but no chapter is on that of the mainland, this section will fill the vacuum by giving a relatively detailed account of the historical development of the patent system in Mainland China.

I.2.1 The Origin, Development and Reform of PRC Patent System

Prior to 1903, there had been no legal regulation of intellectual property rights (IPRs) in imperial China. The 1903 US and China trade treaty provided limited patent protection only to US citizens in China,[6] which were made available beginning in 1912 and yielded less than 700 patents in the subsequent 30 years.[7] The Nationalist government, with a vision to modernize China's IP system after taking power in 1928, issued a provisional patent measure in 1932[8] and enacted a patent law in 1949 which was abolished immediately by the Chinese Communist Party when it established the People's Republic of China (PRC) in the same year.[9]

The PRC did not enact a formal patent law until 1984. During the 30-year gap, the government issued a few regulations governing patent matters. For instance, a *Provisional Regulations on the Protection of the Invention Right and the Patent Right* was issued in 1950, adopting the former Soviet Union's two-track system, under which either the state owned the patents while inventors received modest rewards, or inventors owned patents from five to 15 years. In 1963, the PRC government adopted the *Regulations to Encourage Inventions and the Regulations to Encourage Improvements in Technology*, which changed the former two-track system to a one-track system under which only the state enjoyed exclusive patent ownership.[10]

The first PRC Patent Law was enacted in 1984, a few years after the end of Cultural Revolution. It was drafted based on extensive study of western patent

---

[6]   The limited term of patent protection is provided "to citizens of the United States on all their patents issued by the United States, in respect of articles the sale of which is lawful in China, which do not infringe on previous inventions of Chinese subjects, in the same manner as patents are to be issued to subjects of China." The 1903 Treaty between the United States and China, Art. 10, reprinted in J. V. A. MacMurray (ed.), *Treaties and Agreements* (New York: Oxford University Press, 1921).

[7]   W. P. Alford, *To Steal a Book Is an Elegant Offence: Intellectual Property Law in Chinese Civilization* (Stanford: Stanford University Press, 1995), p. 42, note 79; some estimated 360, while others put the figure at 692.

[8]   "Measures to Encourage Industrial Arts."

[9]   See Yahong Li, "Transplantation and Transformation: 30-Year Development of China's IP System," in G. H. Yu (ed.), *The Development of the Chinese Legal System: Change and Challenges* (London and New York: Routledge, 2010), pp. 138–156.

[10] Ibid.

laws, but the following aspects were criticized by the West as nonconforming to international standards: *inter alia*, the 15-year patent protection term for regular invention patents (five years for utility model patents and design patents); the lack of protection for chemical and pharmaceutical products and process patents; and the state designated patent agents handling all patent applications. Therefore, in 1992, a "Memorandum of Understanding on the Protection of Intellectual Property" (MOU) was signed by the United States and China requiring the latter to raise its IP protection standards. Pursuant to the MOU, China amended its Patent Law in 1992 to (1) expand protection to include pharmaceutical products, food and beverages, flavorings and substances obtained via a chemical process; (2) extend the protection term for invention patents from 15 years to 20 years, for utility models and designs from five to 10 years; (3) narrow the grounds under which a compulsory license may be granted; and (4) specify the burden of proof in litigation relating to method patents and adding a provision for domestic priority.

The second amendment to the PRC Patent Law came in 2000 when China was trying to gain entry into the WTO. Major changes were made in accordance with the minimum requirements of the Trade-Related Intellectual Property Rights (TRIPS) Agreement, which include: ownership of "service invention" can be decided by agreement; the "offer for sale" of a pirated product can be deemed as an act of infringement for inventions and utility models; judicial review of decisions in re-examination and invalidation processes is allowed; preliminary injunctions and property preservation are permitted; more conditions are imposed on using compulsory licensing; and damages can be calculated by multiplying the royalties of licenses.[11]

To implement national IP strategies formulated by the government in the 2006–2008 period, which aimed at promoting China's indigenous innovation,[12] PRC Patent Law was amended for the third time in 2008 and the following changes were adopted: (1) replacing the mixed test to an absolute novelty test for all patent examinations;[13] (2) imposing higher standards for granting patents to industrial designs;[14] (3) requiring a security check for filing foreign patents for the inventions completed in China; (4) adding

---

[11] Ibid.
[12] China's State Council issued the Outlines of National Intellectual Property Strategies in 2008.
[13] Previous publication anywhere in the world and use of the invention within China prior to the filing date constitute "prior art" and destroy novelty, which was called a mixed test of novelty. Under the amended law, prior art (publication and use) found anywhere (in/out of China) will destroy novelty.
[14] Industrial design: (1) no patent for 2-dimensional printing matter; (2) "clear difference" from "prior art."

a requirement to disclose the genetic resources used for an invention in patent applications; (5) adopting an exception similar to the US Bolar exception to patent infringement, that is, using a patented invention without authorization for marketing approval; (6) allowing parallel importation; and (7) increasing the statutory damage up to one million RMB.

In 2013, the State Intellectual Property Office (SIPO) drafted the Fourth Patent Law Amendment with an objective of further strengthening the enforcement of patent rights in China.[15] The draft amendment includes the following proposed changes: giving the patent administrative agencies a semi-judicial power to handle the patent disputes; holding ISPs jointly liable for patent infringement over the Internet; imposing legal obligation on local patent bureaus to promote patents' marketization; allowing the inventors of a state-funded project to negotiate a right to use the invention; and increasing punitive damage awards to five million RMB.[16]

All of the above patent law reforms are aimed at promoting indigenous innovation by strengthening patent protection. Whether this goal has been achieved is a question to be further explored in Section I.3 of this chapter and subsequent chapters of this book.

I.2.2 *The Origin, Development and Reform of Hong Kong's Patent System*

Under the British ruling from 1843 to 1997, Hong Kong did not have an independent patent system, although it had a Registration of Patent Ordinance (Cap 42) (1932, amended 1977) allowing UK or European patents to be registered in Hong Kong. Those patents were not Hong Kong patents and were not enforceable in Hong Kong courts.[17]

The Sino-British Joint Declaration concerning Hong Kong's handover to China, which was signed in 1984, allows Hong Kong to maintain its own legal system under the unique political arrangement of "one country, two systems."[18] Hence, after 1997, Hong Kong has established its own independent patent system under the Patent Ordinance (Cap 514) that is totally separated from the patent system in Mainland China. This new patent system covers two

---

[15] At the time of this writing, the draft amendment is still pending for the approval from the State Council.

[16] See "Draft Amendment of the Patent Law of the P.R.C." (Draft for deliberation), www .chinalawtranslate.com/scpatentdraft/?lang=en#oldnew.

[17] For details, see Chapter 7 of this book.

[18] Paragraph 3.3 of the Joint Declaration on Question of Hong Kong provides, "The [HKSAR] will be vested with executive, legislative and independent judicial power, including that of final adjudication. The laws currently in force in Hong Kong will remain basically unchanged."

types of patents: short-term patents with an eight-year duration that are subject to only formality examination; and standard patents with a 20-year duration that are subject to substantive examination. The standard patents are examined and granted by one of the three designated patent offices: China's SIPO, UK Intellectual Property Office (UKIPO) and European Patent Office (EPO), and then registered in Hong Kong. The registered patent is a Hong Kong patent that is enforceable in Hong Kong courts.[19]

The registration model was adopted largely because Hong Kong did not have sufficient resources and expertise in conducting patent examination at the time. Although the system has been functioning very well since its inception, the SAR government initiated the patent law reform in 2011, recommending the establishment of an original grant patent (OGP) system that allows Hong Kong patents to be granted by Hong Kong's Intellectual Property Department (HKIPD). After four years of public consultation and deliberation, the Patent (Amendment) Bill 2015 was passed by Hong Kong Legislative Council (LegCo) on June 2, 2016.

The new OGP system is to coexist with the registration system, which means that, while some standard patent applications are locally examined and granted, some can still be examined and granted by the three designated patent offices. This is deemed necessary because Hong Kong lacks manpower and expertise in conducting patent examination. In fact, even for those patents examined and granted locally, the examination will be outsourced to other patent offices such as the SIPO. In addition, the HKIPD signed a cooperative agreement with the SIPO in December 2013, under which the SIPO will provide technical assistance to IPD in patent examination and manpower training.[20]

The short-term patent system has also been reformed to solve the low-threshold and easy-to-get problem that had led to the abuse of the system. Under the new system, substantive examination of short-term patents are required in cases where (1) an enforcement action is commenced; and (2) the patent holder is concerned about the validity of his patent. It is also required that the person threatening to sue for infringement of a short-term patent shall furnish all particulars to the alleged infringer.[21]

---

[19] For the constitutional foundation of the 1997 Patent Ordinance, see Chapter 7 of this book.

[20] "Legislative Council Brief," Patents Ordinance (Chapter 514), File Ref.: CITB 06/18/23, p. 4, www.ipd.gov.hk/eng/intellectual_property/patents/Patents(Amendment)Bill_2015_LegCo_Brief.pdf.

[21] Ibid., p. 5. For discussion of abuse of the short-term patent system, see Yahong Li, "Hong Kong's Short Term Patent through the Lens of the Case *SNE Engineering Co. Ltd. v. Hsin Chong Construction Company Ltd*," in Kung-Chung Liu (ed.), *Annotated Leading Patent Cases in Major Asian Jurisdictions* (City University of Hong Kong Press, 2017).

The purpose of introducing the OGP system is to help develop Hong Kong into a "regional innovation and technology hub."[22] However, very little, if any, theoretical justification and empirical evidence has been provided to explain why there is a link between the OGP system and innovation, and how the adoption of the OGP system can help Hong Kong become more innovative. The discussion below and in Chapters 6, 7, 8 and 9 in this book intend to fill this gap.

I.3 THE ROLE OF PATENTS IN INNOVATION: TWO SYSTEMS COMPARED

As mentioned above, in 2015, China topped the world in both patent applications and grants, while it scores fairly low (25th) in the Global Innovation Index (GII). On the other hand, in the same year, Hong Kong ranked fairly low in patents (16th and 15th in applications and grants respectively), but its innovation status ranked 14th, which is 11 ranks higher than China.[23] These data seem to suggest that patents are not very relevant, or at least not too crucial, to innovation. On the other hand, as a comparison, the US ranked high in both patents and innovation in 2015 (2nd for both patent applications and grants, and 4th for innovation),[24] and has been consistently leading in both patents and innovation for several centuries, which indicates a strong correlation between the two. These data raised the following questions: what is the true relationship between patents and innovation? What are other factors behind or in addition to patents that affect innovation in a given jurisdiction? What lesson, if any, can China and Hong Kong learn from the US in making patents a genuine tool for promoting innovation?

I.3.1 *From a "Big" to a "Strong" IP Country*

Before answering the above questions, we first examine the implications and possible causes for the disparity in China's patent scores and its innovation status, as well as the recent policy changes in government's patent strategies.

From 2006, the Chinese government has adopted a series of initiatives in an attempt to transform China into an innovation-oriented country. In the first few years, the government's main strategy and top priority was to boost patent

---

[22] "Legislative Council Brief," p. 1.
[23] See www.wipo.int/edocs/pubdocs/en/wipo_pub_943_2016.pdf and www.globalinnovationindex.org/gii-2016-report#.
[24] Ibid.

numbers, making China a "big" IP country. To achieve this goal, the government set specific numerical targets for patent filings and grants, e.g. ranking China in the top five in the world in invention patents and SCI papers,[25] increasing the numbers of overseas patent filings,[26] ranking China in the top two in annual patent number for inventions granted to domestic inventors, bringing the total patent applications to two million in 2015, and increasing the number of invention patents owned per 10,000 habitants from four in 2013 to 14 in 2020.[27] Guided by these targets, China has experienced an exponential growth, or a "great leap forward," in patent filling and granting, and has been leading the world in patents for six consecutive years since 2010.[28] However, as the number one patent country, China ranks only 25th in GII in 2016. How to explain the discrepancy? What other factors in addition to patents have dragged China down in innovation?

I.3.1.1 Quality of Patents and Government Subsides

To answer the above questions, we may use the US as a reference point, as it has been leading in both patents and innovation scoreboard. Although the US had been surpassed by China in the total numbers of patent applications and grants in recent years, it still leads in other categories such as the number of patentees per 10,000 people, foreign patents, PCT filings, the number of top 100 global innovators, and patents in high tech fields, which are normally

---

[25] Article II(2) of the National Medium and Long Term Plan for Science and Technology Development (2006–2020), www.google.com.hk/webhp?sourceid=chrome-instant&ion=1&e spv=2&ie=UTF-8#q=National%20Medium%20and%20Long%20Term%20Plan%20for%20S cience%20and%20Technology%20Development%20(2006–2020).

[26] Article II.2(7) of the Outlines of National Intellectual Property Strategy 2008 (IP Strategy Outlines) states that "China will rank among the advanced countries of the world in terms of the annual number of patents for inventions granted to the domestic applicants, while the number of overseas patent applications filed by Chinese applicants should greatly increase." www.wipo.int/edocs/lexdocs/laws/en/cn/cn021en.pdf.

[27] Article III of the National Patent Development Strategies (2011–2020); see http://graphics8 .nytimes.com/packages/pdf/business/SIPONatPatentDevStrategy.pdf.

[28] Specifically, the number of its patent applications (including invention, utility models and designs) increased from 573,178 in 2006 to 3,464,824 in 2016 (2,798,500 in 2015, exceeding the target in patent development strategy); see www.sipo.gov.cn/tjxx/tjyb/2016/201701/P020170124 439120249793.pdf. Patent grants increased from 268,002 in 2006 to 1,753,763 in 2016; invention patent applications from 130,384 in 2004 to 1,101,864 in 2016 (more than US and Japanese invention patent applications combined); see www.wipo.int/edocs/pubdocs/en/wipo _pub_943_2016.pdf. Resident patent applications increased from 470,342 in 2006 to 1,628,882 in 2016, and PCT applications from 3,910 in 2006 to 29,846 in 2015; see "PCT Yearly Review 2006," www.wipo.int/pct/en/activity/pct_2006.html#P58_3586, and "PCT Yearly Review 2016," www.wipo.int/edocs/pubdocs/en/wipo_pub_901_2016.pdf.

considered to be indicators of high patent quality and genuine innovation. For example, in 2012, out of 10,000 people, 35.6 American, but only 2.4 Chinese, own patents;[29] American filed 98,617 patents abroad, while Chinese filed only 13,258;[30] the US is the biggest PCT user (57,121) while China comes in 3rd (29,837);[31] in 2016, among top 100 global innovators, there are 49 US companies, but only one Chinese company (Huawei);[32] and vast majority of US patents are filed in high and emerging technological fields such as medical, computer and digital communication, in which Chinese patents have a very small share.[33] A study found that China's PCT applications achieve only 34 percent of the quality level of international PCT applications, and that "China's expansion of international filings was achieved to the detriment of quality."[34]

One of the factors causing the inflation of low-quality patents in China is the explosion of utility model patents, which are granted to trivial inventions without going through substantive examination.[35] Prud'homme found in Chapter 1 of this book that the over-filing of utility model patents were caused by the easy-to-get procedure, low cost and government subsidies:

> China's patent subsidies have encouraged behaviour that maximizes patent quantity at the cost of quality, namely: repeated patent applications; splitting inventions into smaller inventions just to boost the number of applications; filings for products that are already published or otherwise disclosed (in some cases for a significant amount of time) and thus are not patentable; and filing applications only to get an application number in order to claim subsidies but not even paying official patent fees.[36]

[29] SIPO, "Patent Statistics," No. 17, 2012, p. 6, www.sipo.gov.cn/tjxx/zltjjb/201509/P020150911515335919602.pdf; but this figure increased to 6.3 out of 10,000 Chinese in 2016, p. 3, www.sipo.gov.cn/tjxx/zltjjb/201601/P020160122404593275916.pdf.

[30] SIPO, "Patent Statistics," No. 17, 2012, pp. 6–7.

[31] WIPO, "WIPO IP Facts and Figures 2016," p. 16, www.wipo.int/edocs/pubdocs/en/wipo_pub_943_2016.pdf.

[32] Clarivate Analytics, "2016 Top 100 Global Innovators Report," http://top100innovators.stateofinnovation.com/sites/default/files/content/top100/L178%20Cvt_Top%20100%20Innovators%20Report_FA_20.01.2016.pdf.

[33] WIPO, "World Intellectual Property Indicator 2016," p. 51.

[34] Philipp Boeing and Elisabeth Mueller, "Measuring Patent Quality in International Comparison – Index Development and Application to China," Discussion Paper No. 15-051, July 2015, p. 26, http://ftp.zew.de/pub/zew-docs/dp/dp15051.pdf.

[35] Utility model patents constitute about 50 percent of all patent applications and grants in China. For example, 1,475,977 utility model patents out of 3,464,824 total patent applications and 903,420 out of 1,753,763 total patent grants, in 2016, respectively, www.sipo.gov.cn/tjxx/tjyb/2016/201701/P020170124439120249793.pdf.

[36] See Chapter 1 of this book, p. 50.

In addition, the explosion of utility model patents might have also been caused by the "dual filing"[37] strategy allowing the inventions to be protected earlier by utility model patent, and then by invention patent when it is granted later. Prud'homme argued that, although many studies show utility models can be used as an "accessible instrument of appropriability" in innovation, particularly incremental innovation in developing countries,[38] "the proliferation of low-quality utility models can hamper innovation."[39]

Chinese government has recently come to realize the harmful effects of the proliferation of the low-quality patents and has adopted measures to tighten the use of subsidies in utility model applications.[40] Notably, the State Council issued an Action Plan for Further Implementation of the National Intellectual Property Strategy (2014–2020) (hereafter, "Action Plan") in December 2014, shifting the focus of building a "big" IP country to building a "strong" (or "powerful") IP country.[41] The Action Plan declares that the state "will place more focus on IP quality and benefits, optimize industrial layout, guide industrial innovation and accelerate the quality/efficiency enhancement and upgrading of industries."[42] It is hoped that the trend of proliferating the patent numbers can be halted by these initiatives, and the numbers of patents will represent true status of China's innovation.

I.3.1.2 Capacity in Patent Commercialization

Another possible factor affecting China's innovation status is its weak capacity in IP commercialization. Innovation means how many patented inventions are commercialized into useful products, not how many inventions are patented.[43] In this respect, the US has been the world model. To promote technology transfer and commercialization, the US congress passed

---

[37] Under Article 9 of the Chinese Patent Law, one invention can be filed for both invention patent and utility model patent simultaneously.

[38] See Chapter 1 of this book, p. 39.

[39] See Chapter 1 of this book, p. 40–42.

[40] For example, SIPO issued Several Opinions of the State Intellectual Property Office on Further Improving Quality of Patent Applications on December 18, 2013. See Chapter 1 of this book, p. 52.

[41] Article 1(1), entitled "Guideline," mentioned, ". . . carefully plan the development path for China to build a powerful nation of IP, . . ."

[42] Action Plan for Further Implementation of the National Intellectual Property Strategy (2014–2020), Art. 2(1).

[43] Marshall Leaffer states that innovation "involves a multifaceted effort: the discovery, development, improvement and commercialization of new processes and products." Marshall Leaffer, "Patent Misuse and Innovation," 10 *Journal of High Technology Law* 142–167, p. 142 (2010); See generally Richard R. Nelson and Sidney G. Winter, *An Evolutionary Theory of Economic Change* (Harvard University Press, 1982).

Bayh-Dole Act in 1980, allowing federally funded research institutions to retain patent rights and to commercialize the inventions through exclusive licensing. In 1986, the Federal Technology Transfer Act was passed to make technology transfer a responsibility of federal laboratory scientists and engineers, and a part of their performance evaluation. Before the Bayh-Dole Act, the commercialization rate in the US was fewer than 5 percent,[44] and only about 1,000 licenses were granted by American universities in the period of 1974–1984. After the Bayh-Dole Act, 10,510 licenses were granted in the period of 1989–1990, indicating that more patents being commercialized after universities using federal funds were given patent ownership.[45] In comparison, patent commercialization rate in China has always been fairly low. A *Rule of law Blue Paper* published by China Academy of Social Science in March 2017 disclosed that only 2 percent of patents had been licensed during the period of 2012-2014.[46] A 2015 statistic reveals that only 2.1 percent, 1.5 percent and 1.7 percent of university patents were licensed, transferred or resulted in marketable products, respectively.[47] The low rate of patent commercialization in China indicates a need for a Bayh-Dole style legislation since most research in Chinese universities is state-funded and their patents are owned by the state.[48] In 2006, a provision drawing on the Bayh-Dole Act had been included in the draft of Patent Law Amendment, but it unfortunately disappeared from the passed 2008 Amendment.[49] In the 2013 Patent Law amendment draft, "promoting and encouraging" IP commercialization is imposed as a responsibility on patent administrative authorities;[50] however, no specific scheme has been formulated to enforce this responsibility. On the other hand, the above study focuses mainly on IP patent licensing, rather than other types

---

[44] Relecura, "Insights from Successful IP Commercialization Activities in Academia," p. 2, www .relecura.com/reports/Relecura%20Whitepaper%20-%20MIT.pdf.

[45] Yahong Li, *Imitation to Innovation in China: The Role of Patents in Biotechnology and Pharmaceutical Industries* (Edward Elgar, 2010), p. 138.

[46] "High Number but Low Utility Rate of Chinese Patents in Comparison with Other Countries," *China News Net*, April 5, 2017, www.chinanews.com/cj/2017/04-05/8191587 .shtml.

[47] SIPO, "2015 China Patent Investigation Statistic Report," pp. 11, 13 and 14, www.sipo.gov.cn/tjxx /yjcg/201607/P020160701584633098492.pdf.

[48] Article 14 of the PRC Patent Law.

[49] For the thorough discussion of the history of Patent Law amendment and its conflict with the Science and Technology Advancing Law on the Bayh-Dole style articles, please see Yahong Li, Imitation to Innovation in China, pp. 138–140.

[50] Article 79 of the Patent Law Amendment draft 2013 provides, "Patent administrative departments at all levels *shall* (emphasis added) promote the implementation and application, encouraging and regulating the marketization of patent information and patent application activities." www.chinalawtranslate.com/scpatentdraft/?lang=en#oldnew.

of commercialization such as self-implementation, which is predominantly adopted by Chinese enterprises. According to a report by SIPO, the rate of IP "industrialization," that is, transferring patents into marketable products, has reached about 40 percent, which is comparable with the US, Europe, and Japan.[51]

I.3.1.3 Scope of Patentable Subject Matter

Statistics show that majority of Chinese patents have not been filed in the strategic and world competitive technology areas such as medical, digital communication, optics, semiconductor, engine, and audio and video technologies.[52] China is particularly weak in medical and digital technology.[53] Besides the fact that China is a latecomer to economic modernization, the problems of patent law itself, that is, the restricted patent scope and incompatibility between patent criteria and innovation characteristics, may have also contributed to low filing in those areas. Unlike the US, which allows virtually "anything under the sun that is made by man" to be patentable,[54] Chinese patent law excludes the following subject matter from patent protection: computer program and business methods as such,[55] transgenic animals and plants, methods of diagnosis and treatment of human diseases, inventions against public interest and social morality. This is exactly the subject matter allowed to be patentable in the US and the technological areas in which the US has become a world leader. The denial of these areas from patent protection may stifle the innovation of the technologies in these fields because inventors will not invent, and investors will not invest, in the

---

[51] The Intellectual Property Development and Research Center, SIPO, "Summary of the Study on Patent's role in Business Strategies: Research on Chinese Companies' Patenting Motives, Patent Implementation and Patent Industrialization," p. 1, www.wipo.int/meetings/en/doc_de tails.jsp?doc_id=273436.

[52] Statistics show that foreign inventors filed 1.5 times the patents for optics and engine technologies in China than their Chinese counterparts. See SIPO, Patent Statistic Report, 2016, No. 1, p. 4, www.sipo.gov.cn/tjxx/zltjjb/201601/P020160122404593275916.pdf.

[53] The top three technology areas in which patents filed at the SIPO are (1) electrical machinery, apparatus, energy; (2) computer technology; and (3) measurement. In comparison, the top three technology areas in which patents are filed at the USPTO are: (1) computer technology; (2) medical technology; (3) digital communication. WIPO, "IP Facts and Figures 2016," p. 15.

[54] *Diamond v. Chakrabarty*, 447 US 303, 309 (1980). For a more detailed discussion of the scope of patentability under US patent law, see Yahong Li, "Intellectual Property and Innovation: Case Studies of China's High-Tech Industries," *Oregon Review of International Law*, 13, 2 (2012), 263–304, p. 279.

[55] Article 25 of the PRC Patent Law. But under Section 2, Chapter 9, § 2 of SIPO's Guidelines for Patent Examination, a computer program consisting of technical features or solutions that can solve technical problems and achieve technical effects can be patentable.

areas that are not protected by patents.[56] As I argued earlier, and I believe that the argument still hold true, "whereas that US patent system has become too aggressive and has created so-called 'the tragedy of anti-commons' and the impediment of public access to medicine, the patent system in China is comparatively still young and has hardly reached its full potential."[57] One of the potentials is to consider allowing the excluded subject matter to be patentable. Unfortunately, this seems to be the most ignored issue in all of China's patent law amendments. As a consequence, China has been lagging behind in the area of computer hardware and software, pharmaceuticals and medical treatment methods and equipment, and biotechnologies, among others. Without breakthrough technologies in the strategic high-tech areas, China will not be considered as an innovative country no matter how many patents are filed.

I.3.1.4 Compatibility between Patentability Criteria and Technology Characteristics

Another problem with Chinese patent law is the compatibility between patentability criteria and innovation needs of specific industries. Although this is a universal problem without a universal solution, it is particularly acute in China due to its more rigid construction of the law and the inflexibility of the patent prosecution and litigation system. Chapters 2, 3 and 4 of this book are the effort of multiple years of research devoted just to finding the cause and solution to this problem. Specifically, Gao in Chapter 2 discovered that, being the world's top manufacturer of solar panels and wind turbines, China actually lacks some core technologies and therefore bottlenecks the sustainable development of its green-tech industry.[58] Gao proposes to stimulate green-tech innovation through the "greening" of the Chinese patent law, that is, "to offer better incentives to green technological change by preventing the patenting of the environmentally harmful inventions and giving the environmentally beneficial inventions priority over others."[59] In Chapter 3, Chen found that traditional Chinese medicine (TCM) has not been well accepted and protected in the Western world, which is not beneficial to TCM innovation.[60] He proposes to introduce an industry-tailored patent policy to make the patent practice more compatible with TCM invention, such as adopting product-by-process claims and the doctrine of equivalence to remedy the problem in identifying and constructing TCM patent claims; allowing secret TCM

---

[56] Yahong Li, Imitation to Innovation in China, pp. 104–105.   [57] Ibid., p. 177.
[58] See Chapter 2 of this book, pp. 80.   [59] Ibid.   [60] See Chapter 3 of this book, pp. 107.

formulae to be patentable without requiring a full disclosure.[61] In Chapter 4, Yu argues that, Chinese patent law offers broad discretion to be applied to the characteristics of Chinese telecommunications industry (CTI), however, these discretions have been overlooked by the rule-makers, patent examiners and judges in formulating CTI-related rules, examining CTI-related patent applications and deciding CTI-related patent disputes, to the extent that innovation of CTI has been seriously affected.[62] Yu proposes to enhance patent prosecution and litigation procedure to allow a greater discretion for examiners and judges to interpret the concepts such as prior art and persons skilled in the art, and allow such judicial interpretations to bind future decisions.[63]

I.3.1.5 Patent Prosecution and Litigation System

Indeed, China's patent prosecution and litigation system are in want of further reform to foster technological innovation. China's patent prosecution system is fairly rigid in procedure but relaxed in substantive standards. For example, on one hand, China does not have inventor-friendly patent prosecution processes such as US' one-year grace period and provisional patent application providing inventors more chances of filing patents and additional time to further develop their inventions, determine the marketability, acquire necessary funding, and seek licensing and manufacturing opportunities.[64] On the other hand, the high number of patents granted might mean relaxed and speedy examination, which renders many immature and low-quality patents. As to patent litigation, China has made great strides in reforming its court system, particularly in creating three specialized IP courts, which has resulted in a remarkable growth in patent litigations in recent years, e.g. 13,000 cases reported in 2015, witnessing a 22 percent increase from a year before.[65] Research shows that foreign companies filed 10 percent of the patent lawsuits in China and won 70 percent of the actions.[66] China is now being perceived as "a reasonable and fair place to resolve patent disputes"[67] and has increasingly

---

[61] Ibid. [62] See Chapter 4 of this book, pp. 129. [63] Ibid.
[64] For the discussion of the benefits of US patent prosecution and litigation systems, please see Yahong Li, "Intellectual Property and Innovation," p. 279.
[65] Steven Brachmann and Gene Quinn, "China Increasingly a Preferred Venue for Patent Litigation, Even for US Patent Owners," *IPWatchdog*, November 10, 2016, www.ipwatchdog.com/2016/11/10/china-increasingly-preferred-venue-patent-litigation/id=74585/.
[66] Brian Love, Christine Helmers and Markus Eberhardt, "Patent Litigation in China: Protecting Rights or the Local Economy?" *Santa Clara Law Digital Commons*, February 23, 2016, 1–25, p. 25, http://digitalcommons.law.scu.edu/cgi/viewcontent.cgi?article=1920&context=facpubs.
[67] Steven Brachmann and Gene Quinn, "China Increasingly a Preferred Venue."

become a preferred venue for foreign patent holders due to the low court costs and fast return of verdict.[68] For example, in November 2016, a Canadian company, WiLAN Inc., sued Tokyo-based Sony Mobile Communications in Nanjing, signaling a trend of foreigners using China as a new venue for IP litigations.[69] However, is this a healthy development for China's innovation? In other words, does filing more patent litigations have an effect of promoting technological innovation? To some extent, the answer might be "yes," because more patent litigations, particularly those brought by foreign plaintiffs, may force Chinese companies to stop copying and to start innovating.[70] More patent litigations may also mean higher awareness of rights protection among Chinese citizens, and more confidence of foreign litigants in the Chinese judicial system. However, the explosion of patent litigations may also stifle those genuine incremental innovations, particularly when the law-suits were brought by patent trolls or patent assertion entities (PAE) who profit mainly from asserting patents. The situation might be worsened by the inexperience of the specialized IP courts that function as the first instance courts on all IP matters, rather than an appellate court specializing in patent lawsuits like those in the US, the UK and Japan.[71] With 13,000 patent cases a year,[72] it is hard to be optimistic about the quality of the court judgments,[73] particularly when there is no specialized appellate patent court exercising quality control.

The Chinese government is aware of the importance of the enforcement of patent rights to national innovation, and it has tried to find different solutions. For example, the fourth patent law draft amendment increases the statutory damage to RMB 5 million, and gives administrative agencies semi-judicial

[68] The average time from filing the suit to verdict at Beijing IP Court is 125 days. See Cao Yin, "Foreign Disputes Surge at Capital's IP Court," *China Daily*, April 15, 2016, http://europe.chinadaily.com.cn/business/2016-04/15/content_24583017.htm. In early November 2016, Canadian IP licensing firm WiLAN filed a patent lawsuit in Beijing against Tokyo-based Sony Corp. alleging that smartphones marketed by Sony infringed WiLAN's wireless communication technology. See Steven Brachmann and Gene Quinn, "China Increasingly a Preferred Venue."
[69] "Sony Sued in China for Patent Infringement," *Financial Times*, November 6, 2016, www.ft.com/content/f7e8690a-a3e8-11e6-8b69-02899e8bd9d1.
[70] Similar view concerning pharmaceutical innovation was expressed in Yahong Li, *Imitation to Innovation in China*, p. 90.
[71] For example, US Court of Appeals for the Federal Circuit (CAFC); UK's patent court within the Chancery Division of the High Court; and IP High Court in Japan.
[72] See note 63 above.
[73] According to personal interviews conducted by the author, some Chinese IP courts' judges have to deal with four patent cases a week, and a growing number of judges are resigning from their post due to the work pressure.

power in handling patent infringement disputes and in deciding damages.[74] On November 29, 2016, the SIPO published "Opinions on Tightening Patent Protection," which calls for a holistic improvement of the patent enforcement system including building online trading platforms to curb patent infringement and counterfeits, and improving the rules in the mediation and arbitration of patent disputes.[75] In practice, courts have also adopted other civil law principles to deal with the growing patent disputes involving foreign patent trolls. For example, the case *Huawei* v. *IDC*[76] discussed by Lee in Chapter 5 of this book demonstrates that Chinese courts have adopted a flexible approach in handling patent disputes by applying civil law principles such as good faith that suit China's own innovation needs. Specifically, the court in *Huawei* held that the patent troll (or PAE) company, InterDigital Communications Corp. (IDC), is bound by the good faith principle under the Chinese General Principle of Civil Law and Chinese Contract Law to provide a FRAND (fair, reasonable and non-discriminatory) rate for Huawei to license IDC's SEPs (standard-essential patents).[77] Lee concludes that, "In the long run, good faith doctrine may become an important part of China's innovation policy that fits its own needs because the application of this doctrine will reflect local business practices, norms, or even moral standards."[78]

I.3.2 From Re-registration to OGP System: More Innovation in Hong Kong?

As mentioned above, Hong Kong's landscape for patents and innovation is opposite to that of Mainland China in the sense that Hong Kong ranks relatively low in patents but fairly high in innovation. Hong Kong ranked 15th, 15th and 16th in 2008, 2012 and 2015, respectively, for patent applications, but ranked 12th, 8th and 14th in the same years in the GII, which are very impressive considering Mainland China ranked only 37th, 34th and 25th in GII in those years. These rankings may not be consistent with the popular perception about Hong Kong, an international financial center and a city dominated by service and real estate sectors without much technological innovation. The question arises then: What does "innovation" mean in the

---

[74] Article 61 of Patent Law Amendment Draft (2014), www.chinalawtranslate.com/scpatentdraft /?lang=en#oldnew.

[75] "SIPO Proposes to Tighten Patent Right Protection Comprehensively," https://hk.lexiscn .com/latest_message.php?id=205347.

[76] *Huawei Tech. Co.* v. *InterDigital Communications, Inc.*, No. 305, Guangdong High People's Ct. 2013.

[77] See Chapter 5 of this book, p. 172.   [78] Ibid.

context of Hong Kong? What has made Hong Kong more "innovative" than the mainland? Or in other words, what is Hong Kong's major strength that Mainland China lacks? Is that strength sufficient to make Hong Kong an "innovation hub"? In the discourse of patents and innovation, what, if anything, can Hong Kong learn from its mainland counterpart?

In its 2016 exercise, GII used, the following factors to assess innovation: (1) political situations; (2) education; (3) ICT access; (4) business environment; (5) knowledge intensive employment; (6) patents; and (7) trademarks and copyright industries.[79] It is obvious that the GII's criteria of "innovation" stretches beyond "technology" to encompass political, social, economical and cultural aspects of a society. It is in this sense that Hong Kong has been rated more "innovative" than its mainland counterpart. According to Wan, who provides an overview of Hong Kong's economic development in Chapter 6 of this book, Hong Kong has a strong IP system, an independent judiciary, effective law enforcement, a clean government, high business integrity and ethical standards, a well-established financial system and capital market, an advanced technology and information system, and excellent research universities and institutions.[80] However, when assessing "innovation" in relation to patents, the focus is normally on technological advancement. In this respect, Hong Kong has not been faring very well. In fact, a commentator remarks that in Hong Kong "so few companies here foster innovation or technology-oriented. Hong Kong's economy remains reliant on its traditional pillar industries of retail, property, financial services and shipping."[81] Taking biotech as an example, a study conducted 15 years ago shows that Hong Kong was lagging behind not only Western countries but also its neighbors such as Singapore, Taiwan, Mainland China and India, even though biotech was identified by the HKSAR government as a significant industry.[82] The situation with the biotech has remained unchanged today. Digital technology and e-commerce have also been significantly dwarfed by the remarkable development in Mainland China, despite the SAR government formulated the Digital 21 Strategies as early as 1998 and last updated in 2013,

---

[79]   The GII 2016 Indicator, www.globalinnovationindex.org/gii-2016-repor.t#.
[80]   See Chapter 6 of this book, pp. 178 and 188.
[81]   Jesse Friedlander, "Four Ways for Hong Kong to Become a Leader in Technology, Instead of Always Playing Catch-Up," Insight & Opinion, *South China Morning Post*, February 21, 2017, www.scmp.com/comment/insight-opinion/article/2072634/four-ways-hong-kong-become-leader -technology-instead-always.
[82]   Yahong Li, "An Overview of Patent Protection for Biotechnology in Hong Kong," *Law Lectures for Practitioners* (Hong Kong: Sweet & Maxwell Asia, 2003), 27–47, p. 28.

which called for establishing a world-class information and communication technology (ICT) infrastructure.[83]

Hong Kong's disappointing performance in technological innovation is reflected its very low patent applications from local residents. For example, in 2015, out of 12,212 patent applications, only 239 were from local residents.[84] In addition, patent litigation is also very rare. Only a handful of patent cases has been litigated in Hong Kong since 1996.[85] "This demonstrated a sad reality in Hong Kong, that is, patent system has not been well developed largely due to the underuse and misconception of the system."[86] Misconceptions of the system include the situation that the short-term patent is used as a tactical measure, or "troll," to fend off any business competition. For example, in *SNE v. Hsin Chong* case, SNE registered the patent after the claimed method had already been disclosed to the public, merely for the purpose of preventing other parties from using its method after discovering that its contract with the defendant might be terminated.[87] The low patent filings and litigation may be also attributable to the lack of education about patent protection in Hong Kong. As *SNE v. Hsin* case demonstrated, the SNE patent was invalidated due to its own "prior art," that is, its disclosure of the patented method to other parties prior to the date of filing.[88]

---

[83] IBM China/Hong Kong Limited, "Smarter Hong Kong, Smarter Living, Consultancy Services for the Digital 21 Strategy Review for the Office of the Government Chief Information Officer, Strategy Report," September 2013, p. 8, www.digital21.gov.hk/eng/relate dDoc/download/IBM-ConsultancyStudyReport_eng.pdf.

[84] WIPO, "World Intellectual Property Indicators 2016."

[85] *SNE Engineering Co. Ltd.* v. *Hsin Chong Construction Company Ltd* [2014] 2 HKLRD 822; *Octopus Cards Ltd* v. *ODD HK Ltd* HCMP 104/2007 [CFI: validity of short term patents for electronic purse and chip protection case]; *Koninklijke Philips Electronics NV* v. *Orient Power Holdings Ltd* HCA 945/2005 [CFI: patents: CD and DVD machines: infringement: conspiracy: inducing breach of contract]; *Re Wing Yick Bamboo Scaffolders Ltd* [2004] 2 HKLRD 28 [*Tanashin Denki Co Ltd* v. *King Long Industrial Ltd* [1997] 4 HKC 217 [CFI: patents: infringement and validity: cassette tape recorder]; *Canon Kabushiki Kaisha* v. *Green Cartridge Co (Hong Kong) Ltd* [1996] 1 HKLR 69 [CA: patents: infringement and validity: toner cartridges: personal liability of director for company's tort].

[86] Yahong Li, "Hong Kong's Short Term Patent."

[87] As Judge Lok said, "In my judgment, the application was a tactical move by SNE to protect its interest under the Sub-Contracts after the circulation of the rumour about the possible termination of the Sub-Contracts." See *SNE Engineering Co. Ltd.* v. *Hsin Chong Construction Company Ltd.* [2014] 2 HKLRD 822, at para. 269. For the detailed discussion of the case, see Yahong Li, "Hong Kong's Short Term Patent."

[88] The court stated in its ruling: "SNE, and before its incorporation its partners, had done nothing to protect the secrecy of the invention. The facts suggest that they did not regard the method itself as confidential. They waited for a long time before the relationship between the parties turned sour, and only by then SNE considered to apply for the Patent in Hong Kong and not in Japan." *SNE Engineering Co. Ltd.* v. *Hsin Chong Construction Company Ltd.*

What has stifled innovation in Hong Kong despite of all its favorable conditions? In Chapter 6, Wan attributes it to government's "positive non-interventionism" policy, which prevents the government from subsidizing research in the private sector; Hong Kong's investment culture of "high return from a short-term investment with limited risk"; and the weak tie between research institutions and industries.[89] A commentator observed that the failure to attract intellectual talents to Hong Kong is another major factor, because "it takes more than infrastructure, data connections and a favorable business climate to attract a critical mass of entrepreneurial and intellectual talent", [90] and suggested the following strategies to solve the problem: fostering a vibrant venture capital community by using Hong Kong's role as a global financial center; encouraging multinational corporations to set up research centers in the city; supporting universities in their research with potential commercial applications; and improving SAR's primary and secondary education system.[91]

In addition to economic, social and educational factors, the patent system has also been considered as a factor blocking Hong Kong in its path of becoming an innovation hub. From Shay's comprehensive account of Hong Kong's patent system in Chapter 7 of this book, we can see that the SAR government considers the old re-registration system a "second-grade" patent system which "does not facilitate Hong Kong in promoting innovation or developing itself into a premier intellectual property-trading hub," and that adopting an original grant patent (OGP) system would change this situation.[92] In fact, the idea of establishing an OGP system in Hong Kong had been proposed 15 years ago by scholars and practitioners,[93] and the arguments for having it then is similar to those presented today, that is, to promote techno-logical innovation and turn Hong Kong into a "regional innovation and technology hub."[94] The rationale is that a local original grant patent system may boost confidence of inventor and investor in Hong Kong and attract them to file patents locally. Theoretically speaking, a full-fledged OGP system is more suitable for a region that has high technological capability and a strong demand for patent protection. The call made 15 years ago for an OGP system was based on the perspective that Hong Kong might acquire such a capability and become an innovation hub in Asia. However, after 15 years of develop-ment, this perspective has proven to be a mission impossible, and Hong Kong

[89] Ibid., p. 189.   [90] Jesse Friedlander, "Four Ways for Hong Kong to Become a Leader."
[91] Ibid.   [92] See Chapter 7 of this book (Section 7.3.1).
[93] See Yahong Li, "An Overview of Patent Protection," p. 45.
[94] Hong Kong Legislative Council, Panel on Commerce and Industry, "Updated Background Brief on Review of the Patent System in Hong Kong," April 21, 2015, p. 2, www.legco.gov.hk/yr14 -15/english/panels/ci/papers/ci20150421cb1-743-4-e.pdf.

has still yet to acquire such a capability because many technology and manufacturing companies have moved away from Hong Kong. Without a strong technological and manufacturing base, there would be no invention worthy of patent protection, how can the OGP system incentivize inventors to invent and apply patents in Hong Kong? Will the OGP system brings more problems than solutions to Hong Kong's patent system as it has to bear its own costs in patent examination related matters such as training patent examiners?

The last two chapters of this book, Chapters 8 and 9 may offer some answers to the above questions. Although the OGP system has already been adopted in June 2016 (effective date pending), the discussion of its pros and cons may still shed some light to the discourse of patent and innovation, and to the successful implementation of the new system. In Chapter 8, Mclean and Yue identified and discussed five advantages and 11 disadvantages for establishing an OGP system in Hong Kong. In summary, it is speculated that the OGP system would promote technological innovation, job opportunities, efficiency of patent prosecution, and cooperation with the mainland. On the other hand, the new system may fall short of the expectation of attracting R&D and patent filings, as there are many disincentivizing factors such as insufficient demand, priority concerns, lack of technical expertise and the quality of the patent granted and cost to the applicants and to the public.[95]

Chapter 9 of this book compares Hong Kong and Singapore in building their OGP systems (called "positive grant patent," system in Singapore).[96] Yu argues that, although Singapore's new system has strengthened its credential as an IP hub, created more job opportunities for IP professionals, and extended its impact to ASEAN countries, the success has not been translated into the increase in the patent numbers, particularly from local residents.[97] He argues that, by substantially outsourcing patent examination to the SIPO, Hong Kong may not be able "to reap the benefits from such local capability,"[98] and that "while Singapore's new patent search and examination (S&E) capability has won it some plaudits, it is too early to assess its full impact on the country's overall IP ecosystem in terms of new job creation, additional numbers of patents, more patent filings by local entities, or other indicators of increased innovative activity."[99]

[95] See Chapter 8 of this book.   [96] See Chapter 9 of this book, p. 232.   [97] Ibid., p. 240.
[98] Ibid.   [99] Ibid.

I.4 THE ROLE OF PATENTS IN INNOVATION WITHIN THE OCTS FRAMEWORK

I.4.1 *The History and Perspective of Patent Cooperation under the OCTS*

The legal systems of Mainland China and Hong Kong had been developing in parallel, without much connection and interaction until 1997, when China resumed its sovereignty over Hong Kong. After 1997, China and Hong Kong continued to maintain two separate legal systems under the OCTS framework.[100] While China's legal system has been influenced mainly by continental European civil law tradition with some socialist flavor, Hong Kong's legal system has maintained the British common law tradition.

However, it is particularly important to place Hong Kong within the context of China because, in addition to the fact the Hong Kong is a part of China, the two sides have been closely connected or integrated economically and technologically. Many innovation ideas conceived in Hong Kong's universities and research institutes are being developed and manufactured in China, and there are countless joint research projects being carried out across the border. Discussing the reform of Hong Kong's patent system without bringing it into a bigger picture of the Mainland is like studying the ecosystem of a tree without placing it in the forest.

In fact, the link between the two patent systems has been stronger than many people would have imagined. As mentioned, prior to 1997 and starting in 1986 when the Sino-British Joint Declaration was formulated, Hong Kong's patent system had already been brought into the political arrangement of OCTS in the sense that Hong Kong Patent Steering Committee had chosen the patent system that allows China's SIPO to examine Hong Kong's patent applications. In fact, in the past, among the three designated patent offices, the SIPO examined more than half of Hong Kong patents annually,[101] and patent professionals in Hong Kong and Mainland China have developed very strong

---

[100] Article 8 of the Basic Law provides, "The laws previously in force in Hong Kong, that is, the common law, rules of equity, ordinances, subordinate legislation and customary law shall be maintained, except for any that contravene this Law, and subject to any amendment by the legislature of the Hong Kong Special Administrative Region."

[101] According to Shay, "In 2016, out of the 14.092 applications for a standard patent filed in Hong Kong, 58.8 percent, 38.0 percent and 1.8 percent were based on patent applications filed with SIPO, EPO and UKIPO respectively. Among the 5,698 standard patents granted in Hong Kong in the same year, 68.1 percent, 30.2 percent and 1.7 percent were based on patents granted by SIPO, EPO and UKPO respectively. These percentages have remained relatively stable over the last five years." See Chapter 7 of this book, p. 203.

working relationships. For example, they share the IP databases,[102] and have regular training sessions for IP professionals based on the cooperative agreement entered between the SIPO and HKIPD.[103]

As to future collaboration of the two sides, in addition to SIPO's continuation of patent examination, though called "outsourcing" now under the new OGP system, and personnel training for HKIPD, parallel filing of invention patents and utility models in the Mainland and Hong Kong was also suggested.

I.4.2 *Patents and Innovation within the Context of OTCS*

The statistics of the World Intellectual Property Organization (WIPO) show that among the 10 patent offices receiving the most patent applications in 2015,[104] only two countries rank in the top 10 of the GII, US (4th) and Germany (10th); the other eight are either low or very low in the GII ranking.[105] It is clear that patents are more about "invention" rather than "innovation,"[106] because patents filed and granted for certain inventions only represent how many new ideas have been discovered and generated at the early stage of innovation, rather than how many of them have been developed into commercial products.

The academic circle has also been divided on the role of patents in innovation.[107] Some believe that patenting is a driver or an engine of innovation, as it provides incentive to invent, invest in, and develop new technologies.[108] Others believe that patents are largely irrelevant and are

---

[102]   HKIPD, "Intellectual Database for Guangdong, Hong Kong and Macau," www.ip-prd.net /main_e.htm
[103]   "Legislative Council Brief," p. 4.
[104]   The top 10 offices are China, the US, Japan, S. Korea, the EU, Germany, India, Russia, Canada, and Brazil. See WIPO, "World Intellectual Property Indicators 2016," www.wipo.int/edocs/pub docs/en/wipo_pub_941_2016.pdf
[105]   For example, China ranks 25th, Russia 43th, India 66th and Brazil 69th. See the GII 2016, Indicator.
[106]   BusinessDictionary.com defines invention as a "new scientific or technical idea, and the means of its embodiment or accomplishment. To be patentable, an invention must be novel, have utility, and be non-obvious. To be called an invention, an idea only needs to be proven as workable. But to be called an innovation, it must also be replicable at an economical cost, and must satisfy a specific need. That's why only a few inventions lead to innovations because not all of them are economically feasible." See "Invention" definition, www .businessdictionary.com/definition/invention.html.
[107]   For the detailed discussion on this issue, see Yahong Li, Imitation to Innovation in China, pp. 8–14.
[108]   John H. Barton and Ezekiel J. Emanuel, "The Patents-Based Pharmaceutical Development Process: Rationale, Problems, and Potential Reforms," 294 *JAMA* 2075 (2005); Dan L. Burk and Mark A. Lemley, "Policy Levers in Patent Law," 89 *Virginia Law Review*, 1575–1696, p. 1576

sometime even obstacles to innovation because of its monopolistic nature.[109] Between these two opposite views, some argue that the role of patents in innovation is industry-specific and varies by context. For example, while patent has been viewed as an insignificant incentive in innovation of some industries, such as software, it is considered indispensable in R&D in industries such as medical and IT hardware, and particularly biotechnology and pharmaceuticals.[110]

In the context of Mainland China and Hong Kong, as mentioned above, the rankings of patents and innovation for the two regions are completely opposite – with the mainland leading in patents but lagging in innovation, and Hong Kong leading the mainland in innovation but being dwarfed by the mainland in patents[111] – both of which show relatively weak link between patents and innovation. This result should serve as a reminder to both Hong Kong and Mainland China that "patents are important for innovation because they are crucial for further commercialization in some technology sectors, but they are not the sole indicator of innovation."[112] Therefore, over-emphasizing the role of patent system, either in promoting patent numbers, improving patent quality, or reforming patent system without taking into account of a holistic reform in political, social, economical, technological and educational systems will not lead to true innovation. It is also unrealistic to hope that a nominal change of a patent system without underlying technological base, innovation demand and professional resources to support the new system will turn a city into an innovation hub. As Cornish and Llewelyn observed, "it is very difficult to measure or assess the effect (if any) that a patent system is producing," although they recognize that "there is no

      (2003); See also "American Innovation at Risk: The Case for Patent Reform," available at http://judiciary.house.gov/hearings/February2007/jaffe07215.PDF.
[109] Klaus Boehm and Aubrey Silberston, *The British Patent System*, p. 37 (Cambridge University Press, 1967); Eric Schiff, *Industrialization without National Patents: The Netherlands, 1869–1912; Switzerland, 1850–1907*, p. 124 (Princeton University Press, 1971); Dugie Standeford, "Intellectual Property Regime Stifles Science and Innovation, Nobel Laureates Say," *Intellectual Property Watch Blog*, July 7, 2008, www.ip-watch.org/weblog/2008/07/07/intellectual-property-regime-stifles-science-and-innovation-nobel-laureates-say.
[110] Burk and Lemeley, "Policy Levers in Patent Law," p. 1575; Pamela Samuelson, "Why Software Startups Decide to Patent ... Or Not: Berkeley Patent Survey Finds First-Mover Advantage Trumps Patents for Some," *O'Reilly Radar*, July 21, 2010, http://radar.oreilly.com/2010/07/why-software-startups-decide-t.html; Stuart J. H. Graham et al., "High Technology Entrepreneurs and the Patent System: Results of the 2008 Berkeley Patent Survey," 24 *Berkeley Technology Law Journal*, 1255–1327, p. 1262 (2009); The Rt. Hon. Sir Robin Jacob, Patents and Pharmaceuticals: A Paper Given on 29th November at the Presentation of the Directorate-General of Competition's Preliminary Report of the Pharma-Sector Inquiry (Nov. 29, 2008), http://ec.europa.eu/competition/sectors/pharmaceuticals/inquiry/jacob.pdf.
[111] See Section I.3, p. 8.   [112] Yahong Li, "Intellectual Property and Innovation," p. 266.

clear evidence that corporations are not influenced in their research and development decisions by their chances of securing and taking advantage of patent protection."[113]

Through comparing Mainland China and Hong Kong, we can see more clearly that the former lacks what the latter has, that is, political and economic freedom as well as independent judiciary that guarantees effective enforcement of IP rights. To be a true innovative country, Mainland China must start to reform its political and economic systems, although this is too broad an issue to be explored in this book. Mainland China's weakness in IP commercialization indicates the need to strengthen the confidence of venture capitalists in a long-term investment in an uncertain political and economic environment. On the other hand, Hong Kong, despite the favorable political and economic environment, has been doing badly in technological innovation, as is indicated by the extremely low patent filings from local residents. What Hong Kong lacks is exactly what Mainland China has: that is, a robust technological capacity and a comprehensive government innovation strategy with significant funding support. However, it is not feasible for Hong Kong to compete with Mainland China or any other technologically advanced nations in technological innovation and it is also not advisable to do so, because of its "high return on a short-term investment with limited risk" investment culture, its path-dependence on finance, service and real estate sectors, and its lack of a technologic and manufacturing base, which cannot be changed overnight.

Hong Kong's best route for future development might be finding its own niche and trying to be more integrated into the mainland's framework of patents and innovation, rather than moving away from it. In fact, it is mutually beneficial for both Hong Kong and Mainland China to be more integrated economically and technologically because their respective strengths and weaknesses could be complimentary. For example, although both sides have a large pool of high-tech talent and impressive research institutions, neither has been able to translate these advantages into commercial success due to the lack of funding – from private venture capitalists in the mainland, and from government in Hong Kong – as well as other factors such as the lack of sophisticated financial system and professional trading services in the mainland, and the lack of manufacturing basis in Hong Kong. When two sides collaborate, one could provide the other with what is needed most. In reality, all kinds of collaborations between the two sides have already been

---

[113] William Cornish and David Llewlyn, *Intellectual Property: Patents, Copyrights, Trademarks and Allied Rights* 6th ed. (Sweet & Maxwell, 2007), p. 135.

happening.[114] Who reviews or grants Hong Kong patents should be the least concern at the moment, particularly when the old system had been working efficiently, there is no urgent need and necessary resources to install a new system, and it is more beneficial for Hong Kong to be integrated into China's technological development in the grand scheme of the Belt and Road Initiative.[115]

The political design of OCTs, after 20 years of practice, should draw Hong Kong and its mainland closer and make the two sides more integrated without tarnishing their own distinctiveness. Specifically as to patent systems, there should be more collaboration with an aim to promote innovation on both sides, particularly when the world trend is toward more patent integration.[116] It is encouraging to see that the HKSAR government has made IP service and trading as its strategic focus, has kept the registration system in parallel with the OGP system, and has established close collaboration with the SIPO on patent-related matters in spite of the adoption of the OGP system.

---

[114]   For example, Hong Kong researchers can apply for the funding support from the mainland's National Nature Science Foundation for collaborative research; see www.nsfc.gov.cn/nsfc /cen/xmzn/2017xmzn/10/index.html. Hong Kong is building R&D centers, research bases, and hospitals in Mainland China to use the local incentive schemes to facilitate the Hong Kong research projects.

[115]   It is also called "The Silk Road Economic Belt and the 21st-century Maritime Silk Road."

[116]   For example, the establishment of the European Unified Patent Court.

PART I

THE ROLE OF PATENTS IN CHINA'S INDUSTRIAL INNOVATION

1

Utility Model Patent Regimes and Innovation in China and Beyond*

Dan Prud'homme

1.1 INTRODUCTION

Although the modern utility model patent regime is often traced back to the German utility model patent regime that was introduced in 1891, the earliest antecedent in fact appears to be the United Kingdom's Utility Designs Act of 1843.[1] Utility model patents (or "utility models" for short) are typically considered to be a form of "second-tier" patent protection – meaning they are similar to what is considered a "normal" patent (i.e. the invention patent) but offer somewhat different protection and have lower requirements for granting.[2] Building on this definition, utility model/equivalent regimes are defined herein as those that provide a stand-alone patent-type of right that has a shorter allowable duration of protection and typically lower requirements for granting than an invention patent.[3] There appear to be more than 100 countries/territories that currently provide utility model/equivalent regimes.[4]

---

* Some sections of this paper are adapted from D. Prud'homme, "Creating a 'Model' Utility Model Patent Regime: A Comparative Analysis of the Utility Model Patent Regimes in Europe and China," IP Key Project Working Paper Series (2014), www.ipkey.org/zh/resources/ip-info rmation-centre/10-law-doc-category/3276-2014-dec-24-03-38-31.

[1] M.D. Janis, "Second Tier Patent Protection," *Harvard International Law Journal*, 40 (1999), 151–219.

[2] Ibid.

[3] Utility models/equivalent regimes as defined herein can have various names: utility models, utility certificates, patents for utility solutions, petty patents, petite/small patents, short-term patents, consensual patents, limited patents, simple patents, innovation patents, utility innovations, and inventor's certificates. They do not include patents of addition/certificates of addition, as these are not stand-alone patents like utility models/equivalents, but instead must emanate from a parent patent. They do not include designs, copyrights, or other intellectual property rights, which are generally distinct from what are considered a patent-type of right in most countries.

[4] Figure based on the author's review of all laws governing utility model/equivalent regimes around the world. Sources differ as to how many countries have a utility model patent regime

Currently, China utilizes its utility model patent regime far more than any
other country. Among the 10 patent offices receiving the most utility model
filings (who account for about 98 percent of all utility model applications
throughout the world), almost 90 percent of these are filed in China.[5]
Germany is the second most frequent destination for utility model filings,
and other destinations in the European Union (EU) are also among the top 10
destinations.[6]

Inter-country comparative analyses of how utility model regimes work and
perhaps should be reformed are currently of interest to a range of states,
including those in Europe and China, as they reassess governance of their
own utility model regimes. In 2015, the European Commission concluded a
study conducted by external consultants on the economic impacts of different
utility model regimes, which was meant to determine if Europe should
develop a uniform utility model patent regime.[7] The Chinese government,
which has experienced pressure in recent years to curtail a seeming rise in low-
quality utility models, has also become increasingly interested in comparative
analyses of the workings of utility model regimes around the world.[8]

While there is literature comparing the workings of utility model regimes in
various countries around the world,[9] there appears to be sparse literature

or an equivalent; at least one of the reasons for this difference in estimates appears to be in the
terminology used to name the regimes.

[5] WIPO, "WIPO IP Facts and Figures" (2013), www.wipo.int/edocs/pubdocs/en/statistics/943
/wipo_pub_943_2013.pdf.

[6] Ibid.

[7] A. Radauer, C. Rosemberg, O. Cassagneau-Francis, H. Goddar, C.R. Haarmann, "Study on
the Economic Impact of the Utility Model Legislation in Selected Member States." Report for
European Commission (2015), retrieved on June 12, 2015, http://bookshop.europa.eu/en/study
-on-the-economic-impact-of-the-utility-model-legislation-in-selected-member-states-pbE
T0415184/.

[8] Proceedings (unpublished) of the 2012 European Chamber-SIPO Working Group on Patent
Quality; Proceedings (unpublished) of the EU-China IPR Working Group, Beijing, China,
2014; IP Key Project 2014 Yearly Action Plan.

[9] For example, see U. Suthersanen, "Utility Models and Innovation in Developing Countries,"
UNCTAD Project on IPRs and Sustainable Development, Issue paper No.13, United Nations
Conference on Trade and Development (2006), retrieved on February 10, 2014, www.unctad
.org/en/docs/iteipc20066_en.pdf; Henning Grosse Ruse-Khan (with A.H. Mukhtar as the
national expert), "Utility Model Protection in Pakistan: An Option for Incentivizing
Incremental Innovation," Report commissioned by WIPO under the TRTA-2 Program
(2012), retrieved on November 13, 2014, www.ip.mpg.de/files/pdf2/WIPO_Study_on_Utility
_Model_Protection_in_Pakistan.pdf; T. Moga, "China's Utility Model Patent Regime:
Innovation Driver or deterrçent," US Chamber of Commerce Publications (2012); DIPP,
"Discussion Paper on Utility Models," Department of Industrial Policy & Promotion,
Government of India (2011), retrieved on July 16, 2014, http://dipp.nic.in/english/Discuss_pa
per/Utility_Models_13May2011.pdf; M. Llewelyn, "Proposals for the Introduction of a

providing a detailed and up-to-date comparison of the history of development of the utility model regimes in China and EU member states and conceptually analyzing how these regimes impact innovation. As mentioned, these are currently the most popular economies for utility models, and the governments of these states are eager to learn from comparative analyses as they reassess their own governance of utility model regimes. Motivated by a desire to shed light on this area, this chapter asks the following questions: How do the legal instruments in the utility model regimes in China and EU member states compare and contrast? What is the rationale for instituting or reforming these particular instruments? And what do the aforementioned analyses indicate about the ability of utility model regimes to encourage innovation?

This chapter seeks to contribute to the literature in several ways. First, it provides an up-to-date (as of 2015) historical comparison of development of the utility model regimes in China and the EU, currently the most popular economies for utility models. Second, it analyzes how specific legal instruments in utility model regimes may impact innovation based upon a conceptual framework drawing together theories often not sufficiently connected in existing literature. Third, it applies this framework at a more granular level of detail than what is available in existing work. Fourth, the chapter advances the literature by reaching the conclusion that although the precise balance among the principles of appropriability, accessibility, and patent quality in utility model regimes can differ among countries according to their individual technological and economic conditions, some balance must always be achieved or else the utility model regime will inhibit innovation.

The remainder of this chapter is structured as follows: Section 1.2 develops a conceptual framework explaining the relationship between legal instruments in utility model regimes and technological development, including innovation; Section 1.3 sets forth the methodology for analyzing the research questions; Section 1.4 presents and discusses the implications of the results; and Section 1.5 concludes.

Community Utility Model Regime: A UK Perspective," *Web Journal of Current Legal Issues* (1995); The Commission of the European Communities, "Green Paper: The Protection of Utility Models in the Single Market," presented by the Commission in Brussels July 19, 1995, retrieved on July 2, 2014, http://europa.eu/documents/comm/green_papers/pdf/utility_mode l_gp_COM_95_370.pdf; U. Suthersanen, "Incremental Inventions in Europe: A Legal and Economic Appraisal of Second Tier Patents," *Journal of Business Law* (2001), 319–343. Australian Council on Intellectual Property, "Review of the Innovation Patent Regime," retrieved on July 15, 2014, available at www.acip.gov.au/reviews/all-reviews/review-innovation -patent-regime/; JPO, "Comparison of the Utility Model Patent Regimes of Japan, South Korea, and PR China" (2012), retrieved on January 15, 2013, available at www.jpo.go.jp/cgi /link.cgi?url=/torikumi/kokusai/kokusai3/nicyukan_jitsuyou.htm.

1.2 CONCEPTUAL FRAMEWORK

The following framework draws on available literature to illustrate that a utility model patent regime's ability to stimulate innovation is contingent upon the approaches it adopts to enable appropriability, provide accessibility, and ensure patent quality. Although some literature uses alternative names for some of these principles, the terms formulated herein appear to be equally if not more appropriate.[10]

1.2.1 *Accessibility and Appropriability in Utility Model Regimes Can Enable Innovation*

1.2.1.1 Patent Protection as a Means of Appropriability

Fritz Machlup provides some of the first modern theoretical arguments for patent protection.[11] The first is the "natural-law" thesis that an individual has a natural property right over his/her own idea. The second is the "reward-by-monopoly" thesis that justice requires an individual to receive a reward for his/her inventive service. The third is the "monopoly-profit incentive" thesis that without monopoly profits guaranteed by the patent regime, inventors and capitalists would not make efforts and risk their money to invent. And the fourth is the "exchange-for-secrets" thesis that without the reward of patent protection, inventors and innovation entrepreneurs would keep their inventions secret.[12]

The monopoly-profit incentive thesis and the exchange-for-secrets thesis are most often discussed by modern economists as they most directly relate to

---

[10] Many works employ the concept of the "strength" of the patent regime when talking about the appropriability the regime affords. For example, see J. Ginarte, W.G. Park, Determinants of Patent Rights: A Cross-National Study, *Research Policy* 26 (1997), 283–301; H. Odagiri, A. Goto, A. Sunami and R. Nelson, "Introduction," in H. Odagiri, A. Goto, A. Sunami and R. Nelson (eds.), *Intellectual Property Rights, Development, and Catch-Up* (Oxford: Oxford University Press, 2010), 1–28. Alternatively, van Pottelsberghe de la Potterie calls the appropriability that patent regimes afford the "applicant-friendliness" of the patent system. See B. van Pottelsberghe de la Potterie, "The Quality Factor in Patent Systems," *Industrial and Corporate Change* 20 (2011), 1755–1793. The concept of "accessibility" used in this chapter can alternatively be conceptualized as the "strictness" of the utility model regime. See D. Prud'homme, "Utility Model Patent Regime 'strength' and Technological Development: Experiences of China and other East Asian Latecomers," *China Economic Review* 42 (2017), 50–73.

[11] F. Machlup, "An Economic Review of the Patent Regime," Study on the Subcommittee on Patents, Trademarks, and Copyrights of the Committee on the Judiciary, US Senate, 85th Congress. Washington DC, Government Printing Office (1958), https://mises.org/sites/default /files/An%20Economic%20Review%20of%20the%20Patent%20Regime_Vol_3_3.pdf.

[12] Ibid.

innovation and economic development.[13] Kenneth Arrow develops the concept of an "information paradox," which shares some broadly similar elements with Machlup's exchanges-for-secrets thesis. Arrow finds that purchasers of knowledge/technology cannot assess the value of information until it has been disclosed, but the buyer of such knowledge has no reason to compensate the seller *ex post*.[14] This paradox can be addressed through intellectual property (IP) rights such as patents that remove the disincentive to disclose information, including by disclosing it to the public.[15]

Other scholars parse Machlup's monopoly-profit incentive thesis, positing that there is an "invention motivation" therein driving inventors to invent, as well as an "induce commercialization" motivation particular to entrepreneurs and firms that drive them to spend to commercialize inventions.[16] Both of these theories are particularly relevant to innovation, given, as noted by Joseph Schumpeter, that only inventions that are exploited contribute to economic growth.[17] Specifically, Schumpeterian economics suggest that only exploited inventions constitute innovations, and innovation is one of the main methods to boost competitiveness and economic growth.[18]

Drawing on these concepts, economists have formulated the idea of "appropriability," which is often defined as the ability to protect knowledge from imitation via some form of monopoly, which allows capturing economic returns from such knowledge. And economists have identified that one of the main means of appropriating returns from technological knowledge is via the short-term monopoly protection provided by IP rights. A number of seminal works have been written on the concept of appropriability, including those from Joseph Schumpeter and Kenneth Arrow (both mentioned

---

[13]　H. Odagiri, A. Goto, A. Sunami, and R. Nelson, *Intellectual Property Rights, Development, and Catch-Up*.

[14]　"[T]here is a fundamental paradox in the determination of demand for information; its value for the purchaser is not known until he knows the information, but then he has in effect acquired it without cost." K. Arrow, "Economic Welfare and the Allocation of Resources for Invention," in R. Nelson (ed.), *The Rate and Direction of Inventive Activity, Economic and Social factors* (Princeton, NJ: National Bureau of Economic Research, Princeton university press, 1962), 609–626.

[15]　J. Gans and S. Stern, "Is There a Market for Ideas?," *Industrial and Corporate Change* 19 (2010), 805–837.

[16]　R. Mazzoleni and R. Nelson, "The Benefits and Costs of Strong Patent Protection: A Contribution to the Current Debate," *Research Policy* 27 (1998), 273–284.

[17]　"As long as they are not carried out into practice, inventions are economically irrelevant. And to carry any improvement into effect is a task entirely different from the inventing of it, and a task, moreover, requiring entirely different kinds of aptitudes. Although entrepreneurs may of course be inventors just as they may be capitalists, they are inventors not by nature of their function but by coincidence and vice versa." J. Schumpeter, *The Theory of Economic Development* (Cambridge, MA: Harvard University Press, 1934), 89.

[18]　J. Schumpeter, *Capitalism, Socialism, and Democracy* (New York: Harper & Brothers, 1942).

previously), as well as David Teece.[19] Arrow's 1962 work, previously mentioned, identifies that social returns to innovation in the form of knowledge diffusion can be substantial; however, firms cannot appropriate all returns from their R&D investment, forming a type of "market failure."[20] Modern appropriability-based arguments for patent protection find it is necessary to alleviate the market failures identified by Arrow, as well as address the dilemma identified by Machlup's monopoly-profit thesis and related theses – in effect providing the incentive for firms to invest in R&D, invent new technologies, and ultimately exploit these technologies, i.e. innovate in the Schumpeterian sense.

All of this being said, patent protection is not the only method of appropriating economic returns as a means to profit from innovation. In fact, there are multiple methods of technological appropriability available to economic agents outside of IP protection: lead-time advantage, secrecy, moving rapidly along the learning curve, complementary sales and service capabilities, and complementary manufacturing facilities.[21] Labor legislation, contracts, and human resource management practices also provide means to appropriate economic returns.[22] Firms may be able to appropriate economic returns from innovations through complementary assets regardless of the level of IP protection they have over intangibles, for example if they have superior distribution channels or manufacturing capacity.[23] As this chapter focuses on patent regimes, and utility model patent regimes in particular, it does not dwell further on these alternative methods of appropriability; however, it is important to recognize that, although often overlooked, these mechanisms provide useful appropriability.

1.2.1.2 Accessibility and Appropriability Provided by Utility Model Regimes

Utility model regimes are intended to provide an easier, cheaper, and faster method to obtain patent protection than the "normal" invention patent regime. These concepts are referred to hereafter as contributing to utility

[19]   S. Winter, "The Logic of Appropriability: From Schumpeter to Arrow to Teece," *Research Policy* 35 (2006), 1100–1106.
[20]   Arrow, "Economic Welfare."
[21]   W.M. Cohen, R.R. Nelson and J.P. Walsh, "Protecting Their Intellectual Assets: Appropriability Conditions and Why US Manufacturing Firms Patent (or Not)," NBER Working Paper No. 7552 (2000), www.nber.org/papers/w7552.
[22]   P. Hurmelinna and K. Puumalainen, "Nature and Dynamics of Appropriability: Strategies for Appropriating Returns on Innovation," *R&D Management* 37 (2007), 95–112.
[23]   D. Teece, "Profiting from Technological Innovation: Implications for Integration, Collaboration, Licensing and Public Policy," *Research Policy* 15 (1986), 285–305.

model regimes' "accessibility." Utility models are generally easier, cheaper, and faster to obtain than invention patents because they (a) are typically not required to undergo the same "substantiveness" (thoroughness/strictness) of examination before granting and/or (b) only have to meet a lower level of novelty or "inventiveness" (also called "inventive step"). This accessibility is particularly advantageous for individual inventors and small and medium-sized enterprises (SMEs) who do not have as much money to spend on patenting as their larger counterparts.[24] And, given the granting process for utility models is typically much faster than the invention patent granting process, it can especially enable innovation (e.g. by allowing companies to quickly commercialize protected technologies) when the life-cycle of a product is quite short, for example as it is for basic electronics.[25] The speed with which utility models can be obtained may also be beneficial for some start-ups, as they can use them as a signal to attract investors.[26]

The lower requirements for obtaining a utility model patent compared to an invention patent makes the utility model regime especially accessible for firms with lower levels of technological capabilities, particularly those in developing countries. In countries with lower inventive step requirements for utility models than for invention patents, the regime is particularly useful for entities skilled at making small/minor improvements on existing inventions because the utility model regime allows them to protect/appropriate these inventions.[27] Similarly, Uma Suthersanen finds that many inventions from SMEs in developing countries have a lower standard of inventiveness and thus are prime candidates for free-riding by competitors, thus the ability to protect/appropriate such inventions can help prevent such behavior and mitigate the effects of market failure by better stimulating innovation.[28]

---

[24]   C. Juma, *The Gene Hunters: Biotechnology and the Scramble for Seeds* (Princeton: Princeton University Press, 1989); Janis, "Second Tier Patent Protection."

[25]   Suthersanen, "Utility Models and Innovation." For recent empirical analyses on this topic see J. Heikkila and A. Lorenz "Need for Speed? Exploring the Relative Importance of Patents and Utility Models among German Firms," *Economics of Innovation and New Technology* 15 (2017), 1–26; S. Cao, Z. Lei, B. Wright, "Speed of Patent Protection, Rate of Technical Knowledge Obsolescence and Optimal Patent Strategy: Evidence from Innovations Patents in the US, China and Several Other Countries," *IPSDM Conference Paper*, retrieved on May 10, 2017, www.ipsdm2016.com/wp-content/uploads/2016/12/Cao-Lei-and-Wright.pdf.

[26]   H. P. Brack, "Utility Models and Their Comparison with Patents and Implications for the US Intellectual Property Law Regime," *Boston College Intellectual Property & Technology Forum* (2009), 1–15.

[27]   Juma, *The Gene Hunters.*   [28]   Suthersanen "Utility Models and Innovation."

The utility model regime can also provide a number of other benefits for domestic firms that cross-cut the principles of accessibility and appropriability. The lower costs and requirements associated with utility models, and the appropriability they provide, allow small-scale domestic innovators to stay in business in an environment where new technologies, foreign or otherwise, may threaten their competitiveness.[29] The regimes also enable catch-up by local/indigenous firms to foreign firms by enabling imitation and absorption of foreign technologies by local firms.[30]

Another line of argumentation in favor of utility model regimes lies in the flexibility they provide to countries otherwise restricted by commitments in the World Trade Organization's (WTO) Trade-Related Aspects of Intellectual Property Rights (TRIPs) Agreement. There is a lack of specific provisions in TRIPs governing the makeup of utility model regimes, although the agreement generally does allow countries to adopt second-tier patent regimes.[31] And some allege that developing countries gain little by adhering to the relatively strict standards in TRIPs for invention patent regimes,[32] in part because the standards therein are too high to optimally allow learning from the basic level of capabilities at which such countries start. As such, developing countries can at least rely on their utility model regime to protect their indigenous inventions which otherwise do not meet the strict invention patent requirements of TRIPs.[33] This prescription reflects that utility model regimes provide indigenous inventors a more accessible way than invention patents to appropriate economic returns.

1.2.1.3 Utility Model Regimes Can Stimulate Technological Learning and Innovation

Theoretical as well as empirical research illustrates how utility model patent regimes can enable technological learning and innovation, particularly in developing economies. And even though all of these works do not dwell on the theoretical concepts of appropriability and accessibility, these concepts are broadly reflected in the analyses. Work by the World Bank uses case studies from Brazil and the Philippines to show how the utility model regimes in those

---

[29]   Juma, *The Gene Hunters*.   [30]   Suthersanenn, "Utility Models and Innovation."

[31]   Janis, "Second Tier Patent Protection"; Grosse Ruse-Khan, "The international legal framework for the protection of utility models," Max Planck Institute for Intellectual Property & Competition Law Research Paper No. 12–10.

[32]   S. Oddi, "TRIPS – Natural Rights and a 'Polite Form of Economic Imperialism'," *Vanderbilt Journal of Transnational Law* 29 (1996), 415–470.

[33]   Janis, "Second Tier Patent Protection."

countries stimulated technological development.[34] Evenson and Westphal find that the utility model regimes in South Korea facilitated technological development.[35] Maskus and McDaniel, using econometric approaches, show that the utility model regime in Japan enabled increases in total factor productivity (TFP) and stimulated technological catch-up.[36] K. S. Kardam provides empirical evidence showing that utility model regimes enable improved technological diffusion and learning that leads to incremental innovation (which is distinct from "breakthrough innovation").[37] Nagesh Kumar, looking at the utility model regime in Japan, South Korea, and Taiwan, suggests that utility model regimes enable technological learning that leads to incremental innovation and ultimately higher levels of innovation.[38]

There are few, yet some, cross-country econometric studies analyzing how utility models are used in developing vs. developed countries. Research from Yee Kyoung Kim, Keun Lee, Walter Park, and Kineung Choo finds that utility model regimes in developing countries can facilitate technological learning, which in turn leads to incremental innovation and ultimately higher levels of innovation and other forms of competitiveness.[39] These authors succinctly

[34] World Bank, *Global Economic Prospects and Developing Countries* (New York: Oxford University Press, 2002).

[35] R. Evenson and L. Westphal, "Technological Change and Technology Strategy," in J. Behrman and T. N. Srinivasan (eds.), *Handbook of Development Economics*, 3A (Amsterdam: North-Holland, 1995), 2209–2299.

[36] K. Maskus and C. McDaniel, "Impacts of the Japanese Patent Regime on Productivity Growth," *Japan and the World Economy* 11 (1999), 557–574.

[37] K. S. Kardam, "Utility Model – A tool for Economic and Technological Development: A Case Study of Japan," World Intellectual Property Organization and Japanese Patent Office (2007), retrieved on June 25, 2014, available at www.training-jpo.go.jp/en/uploads/text_vtr/ws_pdf/ka rdam.pdf. "Breakthrough innovation" (which may also be called "radical" or "discontinuous" innovation) is the creation of brand-new/cutting-edge innovations; breakthrough innovations often have the potential to create completely new markets and/or displace existing innovations. "Incremental innovation" is the exploitation of existing innovations in a way that improves upon them, but less dramatically than via breakthrough innovation; incremental innovation typically involves less risk and takes less time than breakthrough innovation, resulting in solutions considered less cutting-edge than those from breakthrough innovation. See *Managing creativity and innovation: Practical strategies to encourage creativity* (Boston, MA: Harvard Business School Publishing, 2003).

[38] N. Kumar, "Intellectual Property Rights, Technology and Economic Development: Experiences of Asian Countries," *Economic and Political Weekly* 38 (2003), 209–226.

[39] K. Lee, Y. K. Kim, and W. G. Park, "Appropriate Intellectual Property Protection and Economic Growth in Countries at Different Levels of Development," Working Paper, The American University, College of Arts and Sciences, 2006, retrieved on August 1, 2014, available at www .american.edu/cas/faculty/wgpark/upload/Intellectual-Property-Rights.pdf. Y. K. Kim, K. K. Lee, W.G. Park, and K. Choo, "Appropriate Intellectual Property Protection and Economic Growth in Countries at Different Levels Of Development," *Research Policy* 41 (2012), 358–375.

describe how the process works: where domestic firms lag in technological capabilities, the utility model regime enables protection of minor/incremental innovations that can be learning tools for developing more inventive technologies.[40] Then, after acquiring higher technological capabilities, firms rely more on invention patents and less on utility models.[41] Hamdan-Livramento and Raffo also provide an empirical analysis showing that there are differences in the propensity to use utility models in developing vs. developed economies.[42] These works reflect the importance of utility model patents as an accessible instrument of appropriability, especially in developing economies.

Empirical work on the contribution of utility model regimes to technological advancement, including via innovation, in developed countries is scarce. One of the few studies in this area draws on survey data from Australian firms and suggests that developed countries that are net importers of new technology, such as Australia, could benefit from a utility model regime that aids the absorption and/or adaptation of such technologies by local firms.[43]

Several studies focus on the usefulness of the utility model regime in Mainland China in particular to stimulate competitiveness and incremental innovation. Some economists find that growth in utility models increased labor productivity in China.[44] Zhao and Liu find that utility models in China had a significant impact on TFP from 1988 to 1998, and from 1999 to 2009 both invention patents and utility models had significant impacts on TFP (although invention patents had stronger impacts than utility models).[45] Yahong Li

[40]   Ibid.   [41]   Ibid.

[42]   I. Hamdan-Livranmentio and J. Raffo, "What Is an Incremental but Non-patentable Invention?," OECD Working Paper (2016), retrieved on January 10, 2017, www.oecd.org/sti /157%20-%20OECD%20Hamdan%20Raffo%202016%205092016.pdf.

[43]   Although the author notes that the limited empirical survey results from the study do not provide strong enough evidence either way as to if such a regime provides net benefits to the Australian economy. J. Zeitsch, "The Economic Value of the Australian Innovation Patent," Report prepared for IP Australia Discovery House, Australia (2013), retrieved on May 19, 2014, www .acip.gov.au/pdfs/Economic_Value_of_the_Innovation_Patent_-_Final_Report_-_Verve_Eco nomics_-_24_Mar_2013.pdf.

[44]   W. Li, "Analysis of Impact of Different Types of Patents on Technological Advancement in China," *African Journal of Business Management* 6 (2012), 3623–3629. Also see H. Liu, "Patent Regime and Economic Development: Theory & Reality, Analysis on the Dynamic Utility of China's Patent Regime," *China Software Science* 10 (2002), 26–30. G. Sui, G. Shen, J. Song, "The industrialization of China's High-Tech Industry Based on the Region Regional Differences of Patent Level," *Management World* 8 (2005), 87–93 (in Chinese). Z. Huang, P. Yu, "The Effects of Technical Innovation to Economic Growth of Our Country in Recent Years: An Empirical Study Based on Panel Data Models," *Science and Technology Management Research* 8 (2007), 74–77 (in Chinese).

[45]   Y. Zhao and S. Liu, Effect of China's Domestic Patents on Total Factor Productivity: 1988– 2009, Working Paper, School of Statistics, Renmin University of China, 2011, retrieved on

describes how individual inventors and SMEs in particular, although also large companies to some extent, in China have benefited from learning opportunities afforded by using utility models, which can enable innovation.[46] These works broadly reflect the importance of utility model patents as an accessible instrument of appropriability.

A new paper of mine sheds light on how calibrating both the accessibility and appropriability of utility model regimes in China and several other latecomer economies over time impacts technological development.[47] By creating and econometrically analyzing the first known indexes of utility model regime strength, I find that several East Asian economies have pursued a dynamic catch-up strategy of transitioning from imitative to more sophisticated technological development by increasing both the strictness (restrictions on accessibility) and appropriability-strength of their utility model regimes in conjunction with increasing knowledge accumulation and, to some extent, technological capabilities.[48]

1.2.2 *Imbalanced Accessibility, Appropriability, and Patent Quality in Utility Model Regimes Discourages Innovation*

Some scholars have provided theoretical arguments against the usefulness of utility models on the basis that they allow abuse of appropriability. Herein, J. H. Reichman suggests that second-tier patent regimes are difficult to justify using classical IP theory, and the justification for such regimes has not been articulated properly.[49] Additionally, Mark Janis evokes a "tragedy of the anti-commons" argument against utility model regimes, which draws on Hardin's "tragedy of the commons" theory.[50] The tragedy of the anti-commons holds that rational individuals acting separately may consume less than the social optimum of a scarce resource in cases where too many individuals have the rights to exclude others from consuming that

---

March 1, 2014 from http://ftp.zew.de/pub/zew-docs/veranstaltungen/innovationpatenting2011/papers/Liu.pdf.

[46] Y. Li, "Utility Models in China," in C. Heath and A. Kamperman Sanders (eds.), *Industrial Property in the Bio-Medical Age: Challenges for Asia. Kluwer Law International* (Netherlands: Hague, 2003), 257–268.

[47] Prud'homme, "Utility Model Patent Regime 'Strength'."   [48] Ibid.

[49] J. H. Reichman. "Industrial Designs and Utility Models under the European Communities' Proposed Initiatives: A Critical Appraisal," in Hansen (ed.), *International Intellectual Property Law and Policy* (Vol. 2) Juris Pub. (Canada: Sweet & Maxwell, 1998), chap. 48.

[50] The tragedy of the commons occurs when rational individuals with the privilege to consumer a scarce resource, may, when acting separately, over-consume that resource. See G. Hardin, "The Tragedy of the Commons," *Science* 162 (1968), 1243–1248.

resource.[51] Janis applies this concept to utility model regimes by arguing that the low patentability requirements in utility model regimes create significant transaction costs that hinder the market's ability to mitigate anti-commons behavior.[52] This line of argumentation generally finds that utility model regimes can enable over-appropriation/misappropriation of economic rents, which can in turn hamper innovation.

Indeed, the appropriability power provided by patent regimes, utility model regimes included, is not always used in a way that encourages innovation. Although intended by their founders to foster innovation, patent regimes are in fact often not used strictly to protect innovations – rather they are used for other reasons. Utility models can be utilized in the same "strategic" ways in which invention patents are used, including, for example, "patent bullying," as shields/offensive patenting, "blocking" and "preemptive" patenting, and "as foils."[53] These forms of patenting appear to enable appropriation that is either rent-seeking in a way not conducive to innovation or is explicitly meant to discourage others from innovating in certain technological areas.

Other conceptualizations of strategic use of patent-based appropriability illustrate how utility models may hamper innovation. Given single patents in many technological fields can be easily invented around,[54] firms can increase the breadth of protection by filing multiple patents, in effect creating a "patent fence."[55] Filing multiple patents on closely related technologies in order to hedge risk associated with invalidation or otherwise ineffective patents, or for other strategic reasons, creates a "patent thicket" that can hamper competition and innovation.[56] Patents filed as part of a portfolio of complementary patents

---

[51] M. Heller, "The Tragedy of the Anti-Commons: Property in the Transition from Marx to Markets," *Harvard Law Review* 11 (1998), 621–688.

[52] Janis "Second Tier Patent Protection."

[53] These studies set forth the following reasons for patenting: (1) maintaining supra-competitive prices, (2) generating licensing revenues, (3) developing an arsenal for cross-licensing, (4) securing investment and financing, (5) patents as shields/offensive patenting, (6) patent bullying, (7) "blocking" and "preemptive" patenting, (8) patents as foils, (9) patents as substitutes for non-disclosure agreements, and (10) "image is everything" patenting. See S. Graham and T. Sichelman, "Why Do Start-Ups Patent?," *Berkley Technology Law Journal* 23 (2008), 1063–1097. T. Sichelman and S. Graham, "Patenting by Entrepreneurs: An Empirical Study," *Michigan Telecommunications Telecommunication Law Review* 17 (2010), 111–142.

[54] Cohen, Nelson and Walsh, "Protecting Their Intellectual Assets: Appropriability Conditions and Why US Manufacturing Firms Patent (or Not)," NBER Working Paper No. 7552 (2000), www.nber.org/papers/w7552.

[55] M. Reitzig, "The Private Values of 'Thickets' and 'Fences': Towards an Updated Picture of the Use of Patents Across Industries," *Economics of Innovation and New Technology* 13 (2004), 457–477.

[56] C. Shapiro, "Navigating the Patent Thicket: Cross Licenses, Patent Pools, and Standard Setting," in A. Jaffe, J. Lerner and S. Stern (eds.), *Innovation Policy and the Economy*.

used to decrease the efficiency of rival firms' production can have negative impacts on innovation and welfare.[57] Similarly, patenting can raise costs of innovation by competitors, thereby reducing incentives to innovate and thus create negative impacts on economic welfare.[58] Such strategic patenting seems to have developed since the mid-1990s,[59] and the information and communications (ICT) industry in particular has seen a steep upward trajectory of such patenting.[60] These trends appear to at least broadly be as applicable to utility models as invention patents.

Additionally, some evidence shows that the accessibility afforded by utility model regimes can be abused in a way that may hamper innovation, or at a minimum it might not be used in a way that encourages innovation. For example, some suggest that utility model regimes may be used against their original intention, whereby instead of being used by SMEs, large market players may use the regime as a method to circumvent the more stringent invention patent granting process.[61] Although the exact extent to which this behavior impacts innovation depends on a variety of factors, it inferably may hamper innovation if it results in knowledge being diffused into society that is less useful than the knowledge otherwise diffused by knowledge-intensive and well-moneyed firms if they were more restricted from using the utility model patent regime. By way of another example, a study commissioned by IP Australia employing several indicators of innovation and competitiveness finds that the Australian equivalent of a utility model patent (called an "innovation patent"), despite being more accessible in some sense than an invention patent, is not providing an incentive for Australian SMEs to innovate.[62]

(Cambridge, MA: National Bureau of Economic Research, 2001), 119–150. M. Lemley, and C. Shapiro, "Probabilistic Patents," *Journal of Economic Perspectives* 19 (2005) 75–98.

[57] D. Haroff, B. Hall and G. Graeventiz, et al., "The Strategic Use of Patents and Its Implications for Enterprise and Competition Policies," Final Report for European Commission (2007), 1–307, retrieved on October 30, 2013, www.en.innotec.bwl.unimuenchen.de/research/proj/laufendeprojekte/patents/stratpat2007.pdf.

[58] D. Carlton and R. Gertner, "Intellectual Property, Antitrust, and Strategic Behavior," NBER Working Paper 8976m (2002), retrieved on April 11, 2014, www.nber.org/papers/w8976.

[59] B.H. Hall and R. Ziedonis, "The Patent Paradox Revisited: An Empirical Study of Patenting in the US Semiconductor Industry, 1975-1995," *RAND Journal of Economics* 32 (2001), 101–128.

[60] B.H. Hall, "The Use and Value of Patent Rights," Research Paper for UK Economic Value of Intellectual Property Forum, Strategic Advisory Board for Intellectual Property Policy, London, UK (2009).

[61] Suthersanen "Utility Models and Innovation."

[62] M. Johnson, A. Bialowas, P. Nicholson, B. Mitra-Kahn, B. Man, S. Bakhtiari, "The Economic Impact of Innovation Patents," IP Australia Economic Research Paper 05, Report commissioned by IP Australia (2015), retrieved on June 12, 2015, www.ipaustralia.gov.au/uploaded-files/reports/Economic_impact_of_innovation_patents_-_Report.pdf.

Recent studies have also shown that utility model regimes face a disproportionate risk of being the source of "low-quality" patents.[63] Many utility model regimes do not require a substantive examination to be conducted before utility models are granted to ensure that they actually fully meet the statutory requirements for patentability.[64] This regime per se does not create patent quality problems for all countries with such regimes.[65] However, given that invention patents often face a relatively higher threshold for patentability and a relatively more rigorous process (a substantive examination) to ensure they meet this threshold, there is a higher chance that, on average, granted invention patents are of higher quality, and perhaps value, than granted utility model patents in many countries.[66] These concepts are also more generally reflected in the literature, which finds that invention patent regimes with fewer safeguards to ensure granted patents meet a certain threshold of quality are more likely to enable lower quality patenting.[67] In effect, these concepts illustrate that utility model regimes can be "too" accessible (i.e. not strict enough), to the detriment of patent quality.

Proliferation of low-quality patents, including low-quality utility models, can hamper innovation. An economy rife with low-quality patents is dangerously self-reinforcing, whereby in such an environment rational firms seek

---

[63] There are a number of ways to define "low-quality" patents. For the purposes of this chapter, the definition of quality and low-quality patents I have used previously is applied, i.e. "quality" patents meet the statutory requirements for patentability and contribute to economic, social, or environmental progress; and "low-quality"/value patents do meet these criteria. See D. Prud'homme, *Dulling the Cutting Edge: How Patent-Related Policies and Practices Hamper Innovation in China* (Beijing: European Chamber, 2012).

[64] Although not having a substantive examination is typically thought of as a core component of the utility model regime, quite a few economies/regions, like the Andean Community, Argentina, Brazil, Bulgaria, Chile, Guatemala, Indonesia, Malaysia, Mexico, Philippines, Poland, Portugal, South Korea, Thailand, Vietnam, among others, in fact require substantive examinations before grating utility models.

[65] For example, Australia, the Czech Republic, Finland, Ireland, Italy, Japan, Russia, and Turkey do not have substantive examinations for utility models and have a lower inventiveness threshold for utility models than invention patents. See DIPP, "Discussion Paper on Utility Models." Discussions the author held with the Japanese patent office at a seminar in Beijing in December 2013, and consultations by the author with the Czech, Finnish, and Italian patent offices in May 2014 indicate that the aforementioned components of these four countries' utility model regimes were not believed to create significant patent quality problems. See D. Prud'homme, "Rethinking What International Patenting Really Says about Chinese Innovation," *Journal of Intellectual Property Law & Practice* 9 (2014), 986–992.

[66] Prud'homme, *Dulling the Cutting Edge.*

[67] B. van Pottelsberghe de la Potterie, "The Quality Factor in Patent Systems," *Industrial and Corporate Change* 20 (2011), 1755–1793. M. de Saint-Georges and B. van Pottelsberghe de la Potterie, "A Quality Index for Patent Systems," *Research Policy* 42 (2013), 704–719.

more low-quality patents rather than higher-quality patents.[68] And poor patent quality generates uncertainty, which leads to lower incentives to innovate, which stifles technological development, entrepreneurship, employment, and ultimately growth and consumer welfare.[69] As such, given the risk that utility models in many countries will be of lower quality on average than invention patents, their unchecked proliferation may hamper innovation. Further, as described in Section 1.4, perverse government incentives for filing utility models may compound this risk, creating a particularly acute patent-quality problem that hampers innovation.

1.2.3 *Avoiding the Balancing Act: Innovation without Utility Model Patent Regimes*

Despite the evidence suggesting that utility model regimes that properly balance appropriability, accessibility, and patent quality can enable innovation, it is important to note that there is also evidence that utility model regimes are not necessary to enable innovation. Even among groups of countries with important, albeit broad, similarities – for example high-income countries in the EU – there are clear differences in the usefulness of utility model regimes. For example, Sweden does not have a utility model regime and has a notably stronger national innovation output than Italy and Spain, two countries who have maintained utility model regimes for a notable period of time.[70] Also, the US does not have a utility model regime (according to the second-tier patent regime definition of the concept), yet it is more innovative than a number of nations in the EU with utility model regimes.[71]

Additionally, there are examples of countries that adopted utility model regimes well after they became strong innovators and joined the ranks of developed countries.[72] For example, Finland did not adopt a utility model regime till 1993, and Austria did not adopt a utility model regime till 1994.

---

[68] R.P. Wagner, "Understanding Patent-Quality Mechanisms," *University of Pennsylvania Law Review* 157 (2009), 2135–2173.

[69] D. Guellec and B. van Pottelsberghe de la Lotterie, *The Economics of the European Patent Regime: IP Policy for Innovation and Competition* (New York: Oxford University Press, 2007); B.H. Hall, S. Graham and D. Harhoff, "Prospects for Improving U.S. Patent Quality via Post-Grant Opposition," NBER Working Papers No. 9731 (Cambridge, MA: National Bureau of Economic Research, 2003), retrieved on October 15, 2014, available at www.nber.org/papers/w9731.

[70] U. Suthersanen and G. Dutfield, "Utility Models and Other Alternatives to Patents," in U. Suthersanen, G. Dutfield, and K.B. Chow (eds.), *Innovation without Patents: Harnessing the Creative Spirit in a Diverse World* (UK: Edward Eldgar, 2007), 18–63.

[71] Ibid.   [72] Ibid.

Both countries were already high-income countries at that point and relatively sophisticated innovators.

As such, while the literature might support the idea that utility model regimes can enable innovation, it appears that such regimes per se are not necessary or sufficient to ensure high innovation performance. This realization reminds us that important factors not necessarily directly related to IP regimes contribute to innovation performance, including human capital; R&D; science and technology (S&T) institutions like universities and public research institutes, and their linkages with firms; among a variety of other elements in a country's national innovation system (NIS).[73]

1.3 FORMULATING A COMPARATIVE STUDY OF UTILITY MODEL REGIMES

As mentioned in the introduction, this chapter attempts to answer the following research questions: How do the legal instruments in the utility model regimes in China and EU member states compare and contrast? What is the rationale for instituting or reforming these particular instruments? And what do the aforementioned analyses indicate about the ability of utility model regimes to encourage innovation? This chapter tackles these questions through comparative analysis of the utility model patent regimes of China and several countries in the EU, which collectively include the foremost utilizers of utility models globally.

There are several reasons why certain EU member states that currently have or had utility model/equivalent regimes – namely Austria, Belgium, the Czech Republic, Finland, France, Germany, Italy, and the Netherlands – are analyzed in this chapter. First, there do not appear to be any existing analyses comparing the utility model regimes of all these countries to the Chinese regime. Second, they are all well-developed countries, and thus may have useful experiences that China can learn from as it seeks to transition from being a middle-income to high-income economy. Third, the EU countries analyzed collectively have diverse industrial structures and varying innovation capabilities, which may be useful for China to consider given its own diverse economy. Fourth, based upon preliminary analysis, it appeared that these countries collectively have relatively diverse legal frameworks for their utility

---

[73]   C. Freeman, *Technology Policy and Economic Performance: Lessons from Japan* (London: Pinter Publishers, 1987). B. A. Lundvall, *National Systems of Innovation: Towards a Theory of Innovation and Interactive Learning* (London: Pinter Press, 1992). R. Nelson and N. Rosenberg, "Technical Innovation and National Regimes," in R. Nelson (ed.), *National Innovation Regimes: A Comparative Analysis* (UK: Oxford University Press, 1993), 3–22.

model regimes. And fifth, because (and likely as a result of the aforementioned reasons) such countries were specifically requested by China's State Intellectual Property Office (SIPO) to be analyzed as part of a related research project conducted by the author in 2014 under the "IP Key" Project.[74] As Belgium and the Netherlands have recently abolished their utility model regimes, they are treated separately in the comparative analysis.

The results and discussion section of this chapter draws heavily on a comparative analysis the author conducted within the framework of the aforementioned IP Key-SIPO activity.[75] That activity consisted of a question-naire exchange on the workings of certain aspects of China's utility model regime, and those of certain EU member states. It also included a roundtable on the workings of the utility model regimes in China and Austria, the Czech Republic, Finland, France, Germany, and Italy – held from May 21–22, 2014, at SIPO's headquarters in Beijing, China – which included the following patent office representatives: Dr. Johannes Werner, Austrian Patent Office (APO); 15 representatives from SIPO; Šimon Bednář, Industrial Property Office of the Czech Republic (IPO CZ); Hanna Aho, Finnish Patent and Registration Office (PRH); Jean-Baptiste Barbier, French National Industrial Property Institute (French IP Office) (INPI); Dr. Johannes Holzer, German Patent and Trade Mark Office (DPMA); and Giovanni de Sanctis, Italian Patent and Trademark Office (UIBM).[76] In addition to information from the aforementioned exchanges, this chapter draws upon original legal and policy research, a literature review, and follow-up consultations with experts from the aforementioned patent offices as well as the Dutch patent office and Ministry of Economy and Belgian Ministry of Economy.

The analysis for the present chapter selects several examples, rather than attempting an exhaustive analysis, to illustrate how countries choice of legal instruments in utility model regimes reflects similar or different approaches to stimulate innovation. An analysis is first provided comparing all countries'

---

[74]   The "IP Key" project is implemented by the European Union Intellectual Property Office (EUIPO) and supported by the European Patent Office (EPO). It serves as the vehicle to carry out the New EU-China IPR Cooperation Agreement between the European Union and Government of the People's Republic of China (see www.ipkey.org).

[75]   Some parts of this chapter, including all consultations with patent office representatives, are adapted from this previously undertaken research. See D. Prud'homme, "Creating a 'model' Utility Model Patent Regime." For a shorter summary of the main findings in that paper, see D. Prud'homme, "Constructing Utility Model Patent Systems: Lessons from Europe and China," *European Intellectual Property Review* 38 (2016), 437–444.

[76]   Although not attending the seminar, Loredana Guglielmetti from UIBM and Emilie Gallois from INPI provided highly useful answers in writing to questions related to the research conducted in ibid.

legal instruments, and then, per each legal instrument, examples from China
and at least one other country are discussed in more detail. While there are
numerous individual legal instruments that make up a utility model regime –
and of course the regime as a whole has more of an impact on innovation than
any single instrument – the analysis only focuses on those instruments that
appear to have the most direct and noteworthy individual impacts on innovation. This assessment was made after a review of the literature already discussed in this chapter and via consideration of other directly relevant
literature.[77] The legal instruments' impacts on innovation are analyzed
through the lens of the conceptual framework developed in Section 1.3:
namely the importance of balancing appropriability, accessibility, and patent
quality in order to stimulate innovation, and the potentially negative impacts
on innovation by less-than-optimally balancing these principles.

1.4 IMPACT OF LEGAL INSTRUMENTS IN UTILITY MODEL REGIMES ON INNOVATION

1.4.1 *Official Costs and Monetary Incentives for Filing*

As mentioned in the conceptual framework, the relatively lower cost of utility
model patent protection relative to invention patent protection is a core
element making it more accessible to SMEs and individual inventors.
Figure 1.1 presents the official costs for invention patents vs. utility models
(for the maximum duration of the rights) in China and the EU countries
studied. It illustrates that the differences in total official fees for filing, granting, and maintaining an invention patent for its maximum duration versus
those for filing, granting, and maintaining a utility model for its maximum
duration are greatest in Finland, the Czech Republic, Italy, Germany, Austria,
China, and France, respectively.

   Figure 1.2 presents the official costs for utility models (for the maximum
duration of the rights) in China and the EU countries studied. The Czech
Republic has the cheapest total official fees for filing, granting, and maintaining
a utility model for the maximum duration of the right, at EUR 468. Austria has
the most expensive fees at EUR 2,323. The other countries fall in between this
range, with the fees for Italy being EUR 550, Finland being EUR 650, France
being EUR 844, Germany being EUR 1,160, and China being EUR 1,430.

77 In particular, see D. Prud'homme, "'Soft Spots' in China's Utility Model Patent Regime:
     Perceptions, Assessment, and Reform," *European Intellectual Property Review* 37 (2015),
     305–310.

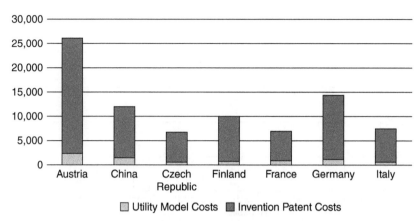

FIGURE 1.1 **Official Costs for Invention Patents vs. Utility Models per Country (for Full Life of Rights)**
Sources: Raw data from patent office representatives; author's calculations.[78]

Various countries provide reductions in official costs in order to improve accessibility of the utility model patent regime to specific types of entities, often SMEs and individual inventors.[79] The Czech patent office charges a reduced fee of 50 percent of the application fee (down to EUR 18 from EUR 36) for a utility model patent when an individual inventor (rather than a business or other entity) is the applicant.[80] The French office provides a 50 percent reduction off the official costs associated with the main procedure for filing and granting a utility certificate, as well as reduced maintenance fees to individuals, SMEs with less than 1,000 employees whose capital is not more than 25 percent owned by an entity not meeting certain conditions, and to

---

[78] Fees herein only include "basic" and mandatory official fees for filing and granting the invention patent (i.e. filing fees, maintenance fees for the full possible life of the right, any stamp tax/printing fees that are mandatory to grant the right, and mandatory substantive examination costs). ("Basic" fees do not include those for particularly extensive/lengthy applications – e.g. those with a large number of claims and many pages of drawings – for which additional costs are charged at some offices. They do not include "external" fees, for example fees for late payment of annuity fees. They do not include attorney/agent fees.) Fees converted to EUR based upon exchange rate as of September 2014; all conversions were rounded.

[79] Also, it is worth noting that several of the countries provide reduced application fees for filing electronically, although this appears first and foremost to foster processing efficiency at the patent office rather than necessarily to stimulate innovation. Specifically, Finland, France, Germany, and Italy provide reduced application fees for utility models filed electronically as opposed to by paper. China, the Czech Republic, and Austria do not provide reduced fees for utility model applications filed electronically.

[80] Written correspondence from Šimon Bednář, IPO CZ, May 2014.

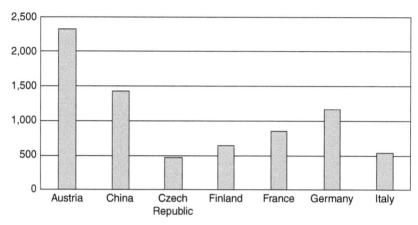

FIGURE 1.2 **Official Costs for Utility Models per Country**
(for Full Life of Rights)
Sources: Raw data from patent office representatives; author's calculations.[81]

non-profit organizations (NPOs) in the sector of education and research.[82] The Austrian[83] and Finnish[84] patent offices do not provide any such fee reductions. DPMA does not provide fee deductions for individual inventors or small businesses per se, but does exempt certain entities, like the Federal Republic of Germany itself, certain public law entities, municipal governments and municipal associations under certain conditions, and WIPO institutions, from paying official utility model fees.[85]

Italy provides several forms of monetary support for filing utility model patents to improve their accessibility. Universities and research institutes, the Ministry of Defence, and Ministry of Agriculture are not charged any official

[81] See previous footnote regarding parameters of fees analyzed.

[82] Written correspondence from Emilie Gallois, INPI, September 19, 2014. Fees for e-applications are reduced to EUR 13 from EUR 26, fees for paper applications are reduced to EUR 18 from EUR 36; fees for grant are reduced to EUR 43 from EUR 86; and fees for maintenance fees are reduced to EUR 18 from EUR 36 per year from the first to fifth year, and to EUR 54 from EUR 72 for the sixth year. SMEs and NPOs must make a request for fee reductions within the period of payment of the filing fee, certifying that they meet the criteria for entities qualifying for the fee reductions.

[83] Written correspondence from Dr. Johannes Werner, APO, September 15, 2014.

[84] Written correspondence from Hanna Aho, PRH, September 17, 2014.

[85] According to Section 4(1) of the Regulation of the Administrative Costs of the German Patent and Trade Mark Office. Applications meeting these requirements are seldom filed. The reductions do not include applications from private entities like companies whose shareholder is the Federal Republic of Germany or a German Federal State. (Source: Written correspondence from Dr. Johannes Holzer, DPMA, October 31, 2014.)

fees for filing utility models or invention patents in Italy.[86] Outside of these exemptions, UIBM itself does not provide incentives specifically designated for utility models; however, given that in Italy "simultaneous"/alternative applications are allowed for invention patents and utility models, and given one can be abandoned for the other, it is possible that an invention patent application could be filed and qualify for an incentive intended for invention patents although ultimately the right will take the form of a utility model which in effect enjoys the incentive.[87] In addition, outside of the central patent office and central-level Ministry of Economic Development, local chambers of commerce and provincial governments in Italy provide subsidies to entities for filing fees, patent attorney costs, among other costs associated with filing invention patents and utility models.[88]

China has provided significant government-led incentives for utility model patents to improve their accessibility. Individual inventors in China can submit a request to reduce their annual utility model maintenance fees by 25 percent and companies can submit a request to reduce annual utility model maintenance fees by 15 percent.[89] The central-level Ministry of Finance (MoF) and sub-central level MoFs in China have at one time, or still, provide subsidies for patent application costs, and other costs associated with Patent Cooperation Treaty (PCT) filings and other methods of filing abroad, as well as maintaining these patents abroad. These subsidies can apply to invention patents and utility models. And various provincial and local governments have provided subsidies specifically for costs associated with filing utility models (and other types of patents) in China. As of 2013, all 31 provinces in China had a patent subsidy program, and many of them provide funding well exceeding the actual costs incurred to obtain patents.[90]

---

[86] Consultations with Giovanni de Sanctis, UIBM, May 22, 2014 roundtable; written correspondence from Loredana Guglielmetti, UIBM, September 17, 2014

[87] Consultations with Giovanni de Sanctis, UIBM, May 22, 2014 roundtable. Note: In order to qualify for this scheme, the application must be thoroughly assessed according to a number of criteria. For more on monetary support/incentives for patents in Italy via the UIBM see www .uibm.gov.it/index.php/brevetti/archivio-articoli-brevetti/2007656-incentives-to-companies (retrieved on July 25, 2014)

[88] L. Xu and F. Munari, "The Impact of Public Support for SMEs' Patenting Activity: Empirical Evidence from Italy," in D. Prud'homme and H. Song (eds.), *Economic Impacts of Intellectual Property-Conditioned Government Incentives* (Singapore: Springer, 2016), 101–132.

[89] Written correspondence from Xie Qingyi, SIPO, May 2014.

[90] H. Song, Z. Li and D. Xu, "Study on Policies to Stimulate Patenting in China: What Led to the Upsurge of China's Domestic Patent Applications?," in Prud'homme and Song (eds.), *Economic Impacts*, 179–204.

1.4.1.1 Balancing Accessibility and Patent Quality: The Czech Republic, Italy, and China

The low official costs for utility models, and state support for these costs, in the Czech Republic and Italy do not appear to significantly damage patent quality in those countries. The Czech Republic's particularly low official costs (along with the quick grant time of about four months) – the lowest of the countries studied (see Figure 1.2) – and perhaps the reduced fees for utility models filed by individual inventors, are said to likely be key factors encouraging more utility models to be filed than invention patents in the Czech Republic each year.[91] Yet IPO CZ has not noticed negative impacts on patent quality or the Czech Republic's innovation trajectory resulting from such incentives.[92] Xu and Munari, who econometrically explore the patent subsidy programs in Milan province of Italy (which include subsidies for utility models), find that these programs do not significantly stimulate low-quality patents, although also do not stimulate quality patents.[93] As such, based upon currently available evidence, these cost-related utility model regime instruments do not per se appear to hamper innovation in these countries.

In contrast, in China, subsidies and other state-provided incentives have likely stimulated the explosion of patent filings and in the process stimulated some low-quality filings. Although not utility model-specific, recent research indicates that China's patent subsidies have encouraged behavior that maximizes patent quantity at the cost of quality, namely: repeated patent applications; splitting inventions into smaller inventions just to boost the number of applications; filings for products that are already published or otherwise disclosed (in some cases for a significant amount of time) and thus are not patentable; and filing applications only to get an application number in order to claim subsidies but not even paying official patent fees.[94] Some research suggests that patent subsidies have encouraged invention patents with a particularly narrow claim breadth and/or fewer forward citations, both

---

[91] Consultations with Šimon Bednář, IPO CZ, May 22, 2014 roundtable.   [92] Ibid.
[93] Xu and Munari, "The Impact of Public Support for SMEs' Patenting Activity."
[94] L. Gao, M. Li, and Y. Cheng, "Report on the quality of patents for invention in China," unpublished report commissioned under the "IPR2" Project (2011) (Unpublished manuscript). Also see Prud'homme, *Dulling the Cutting Edge*. Other scholars also find that Chinese patent subsidies have driven patent applications in China and encouraged firms to break-up patents in an attempt to capture a greater amount of patent subsidies. See Z. Lei, Z. Sun and B. Wright, "Are Chinese Patent Applications Politically Driven? Evidence from China's Domestic Patent Applications," OECD (2013), retrieved on May 5, 2014, www.oecd .org/site/stipatents/4-3-Lei-Sun-Wright.pdf.

indicators of low-quality patents.[95] Some find that provincial subsidy policies issued from 2010 onwards encouraged invention patenting in China at a much faster pace than the subsidies from 2001 to 2009, while at the same time they also created a decline in patent quality.[96] And some discuss how some patentees in China could claim subsidies from the government far exceeding the total costs of obtaining even low-quality patents via exploiting the lack of coordination between local and provincial/municipal governments.[97]

Regarding utility models in particular, the combination of the higher accessibility of utility model patents relative to invention patents and over-simplistically crafted government incentives for patenting has created a notable threat to patent quality in China in recent years, which in turn has likely somewhat hampered innovation. In China, no substantive examination is conducted before utility models are granted to ensure that they actually fully meet the statutory requirements for patentability (although a preliminary examination is conducted on formalities and "obvious" defects in utility model applications, as discussed in Section 1.4.6 hereto). And China's Patent Law stipulates a lower inventiveness threshold for utility models than for invention patents (as discussed in Section 1.4.5 hereto). This regime, which is shared by a number of other countries, per se does not create patent quality problems for all such countries.[98] However, given that invention patents in China face a relatively higher threshold for patentability and a relatively more rigorous process (a substantive examination) to ensure they meet this threshold, there is a higher chance that, on average, granted invention patents are of higher quality (and perhaps value) than granted utility model patents.[99] When IP-conditioned government incentives with weak patent-quality safeguards are introduced into this regime, it can encourage more filings of low-quality utility models than would be the case without the incentives, which in turn hampers innovation.[100]

---

[95] On claim breadth, see J. Dang and K. Motohashi, "Patent Statistics: A Good Indicator for Innovation in China? Patent Subsidy Program Impacts on Patent Quality," *China Economic Review* 35 (2015), 137–155. On forward citation rates, see Boeing and E. Mueller, "Measuring Patent Quality in International Comparison – Index Development and Application to China," Centre for European Economic Research Discussion Paper No. 15–051 (2013), retrieved on August 10, 2015, http://ftp.zew.de/pub/zew-docs/dp/dp16048.pdf.

[96] Song, Li and Xu, "Study on Policies to Stimulate Patenting in China."

[97] D. Prud'homme, "IP-conditioned Government Incentives in China and the EU: A Comparative Analysis of Strategies and Impacts on Patent Quality," in Prud'homme and Song (eds.), *Economic Impacts*, 13–74.

[98] Prud'homme, "Rethinking."   [99] Prud'homme, *Dulling the Cutting Edge*.

[100] Prud'homme, *Dulling the Cutting Edge*; D. Prud'homme, "China's Shifting Patenting Landscape and State-Led Patenting Strategy," *Journal of Intellectual Property Law & Practice* 10 (2015), 619–625; D. Prud'homme and H. Song, "Introduction," in Prud'homme and Song (eds.), *Economic Impacts*, 1–12; Prud'homme, "IP Conditioned Government Incentives."

This combination of factors can, rather paradoxically, stimulate proliferation of granted low-quality utility models that technically, according to the law, should not be granted. An interesting econometric analysis by Cheryl Xiaoning Long and Jun Wang empirically illustrates these dynamics by looking at renewal rates for utility models and other patents in China.[101]

In an attempt to better stimulate innovation, China has recently realized the need to better balance accessibility and patent quality in policy and legal approaches to utility model patents. SIPO has publicly said that although the quantity of utility model patents in China has exploded in recent years their quality deserves improvement, and initiatives have been undertaken to help ensure such quality.[102] SIPO promulgated the "Several Opinions of the State Intellectual Property Office on Further Improving Quality of Patent Applications" on December 18, 2013, which aims to overhaul the regime of IP subsidies and other incentives/state support for IP employed in China, including for utility models.[103] The document recommends a number of important initiatives directly related to utility models, for example that search reports should be provided along with applications for utility model subsidies; that funding should only be given to authorized utility models; that the level of funding a subsidy recipient can obtain is not higher than the sum of all official charges and patent agency service fees that the recipient pays; that patent targets and performance evaluation regimes better reflect patent quality; and that bad faith disincentives should be strengthened.[104]

By way of another example, SIPO has begun to view the higher ratio of utility model to invention patent filings in China as an indicator of a less-than-optimal innovation trajectory, and thus recently has targeted a ratio of more invention patents to utility models.[105] This policy shift inferably is in response

[101]   C. Long and J. Wang, "Evaluating Patent Promotion Policies in China: Consequences on Patent Quantity and Quality," in Prud'homme and Song (eds.), *Economic Impacts.*
[102]   SIPO, Patent Applications Surge in China but Quality Remains Low (2013), retrieved on May 19, 2014, http://english.sipo.gov.cn/news/official/201305/t20130523_800009.html. SIPO (2013), Development of China's Utility Model Regime, retrieved on May 6, 2014, http://english.sipo.gov.cn/news/official/201301/t20130105_782325.html.
[103]   Opinions (in Chinese), www.sipo.gov.cn/yw/2013/201312/t20131225_891833.html; Interpretation of Opinions (in Chinese), www.sipo.gov.cn/zcfg/zcjd/201401/t20140121_899716.html.
[104]   Ibid.; Prud'homme, "IP-Conditioned Government Incentives" and "Soft Spots."
[105]   "China Sees Larger Proportion of Invention Patent Applications," *Xinhua*, April 22, 2014. Retrieved on August 12, 2014, http://news.xinhuanet.com/english/china/2014–04/22/c_133281 638.htm; "China Eyes Quality Patent Amid Application Surge," *Xinhua*, April 24, 2014. Retrieved on August 12, 2014, www.chinaipr.gov.cn/newsarticle/news/government/201404/18 10614_1.html. G. Fu, "Patent Quality Control Mechanisms at SIPO," presentation at IP Key-SIPO Experience-Sharing Roundtable on Utility Model Regimes in Europe and China, State Intellectual Property Office of China, Beijing, China, May 22, 2014.

to the risks previously discussed regarding utility models being heavily utilized in recent years given they are easy instruments for meeting patent targets and claiming government incentives.[106] All of these initiatives reflect a rebalancing act in China's utility model regime to prioritize patent quality more than accessibility, in order to create an environment more conducive to innovation.

The analysis in this section indicates that nations need to carefully calculate their official costs for utility models and cautiously design IP-conditioned state incentives related to utility models. There appears to be some flexibility to do this on a country by country basis. However, at the same time, regardless of country-specific circumstances, a balance between the principles of accessibility and patent quality is needed when formulating these instruments to avoid discouraging innovation.

1.4.2 *Duration of Right, Time to Grant*

As mentioned previously, utility models typically have a shorter maximum duration of protection than invention patents. Austria, China, the Czech Republic, Finland, Germany, and Italy provide up to 10 years of protection for their utility models from the date of filing. France only provides up to six years of protection for its utility certificates from the date of filing. Fees must be paid at different periods within this time period in order to maintain the validity of the utility models/utility certificates. By way of comparison, the duration of protection for an invention patent in all the seven countries studied is 20 years from the filing date.[107]

The time to grant utility models varies among countries studied, from a few months to just under two years. Finland and Germany appear to have the shortest average time for granting a utility model: about three months (or few

---

[106] Additionally, although not immediately apparent that SIPO's new targets are in response to the findings, it is worth noting that some scholars suggest that the catch-up of filings of invention patents with utility model/petite patents in an economy is one main indicator of technological catch-up. This shift in the ratio of invention patents to utility models took place in Japan, Korea, and Taiwan on their way to catch up with technology leaders in the West. See L. Lee and Y.K. Kim, *"IPR and Technological Catch-Up in Korea,"* in H. Odagiri, A. Goto, A. Sunami and R. Nelson (eds.), *Intellectual Property Rights, Development, and Catch-Up*, 133–162.

[107] Consultations with respective patent offices, May 2014. Though China and the six countries from the EU studied set a maximum duration for utility model at 10 years or less, it is worth noting that some other countries in the world, for example, Portugal (an EU country), allow longer durations of protection for utility models (e.g. 15 years) (see Suthersanen and Dutfield, "Utility Models and Other Alternatives").

days, when expedited) from the filing date. Italy has the longest average time for granting a utility model: 23 months from the filing date.[108]

1.4.2.1 Balancing Accessibility and Appropriability: France and China

Given the more accessible nature of utility models, namely in terms of the lower/less strict granting requirements, policymakers have decided it is more suitable to provide less appropriability for utility models in the form of a shorter maximum duration of protection than for invention patents. However, some countries face challenges ensuring that this duration of protection is set at an equilibrium between appropriability and accessibility in a way optimally encouraging innovation.

For example, the short maximum duration of protection for utility certificates in France is said to be one of several important factors reflecting a less-than-optimal balance between the regime's appropriability and accessibility. The fact that utility certificates in France can only be maintained for a maximum of six years makes them unattractive tools for most firms to appropriate returns from their innovations.[109] (This is compounded by the uncertainty inherent in the French utility certificate – owed to the fact that no written opinion on full patentability of the right is provided by INPI, and thus its full patentability can only be determined in a court proceeding (see Section 1.4.6). It is also compounded by the fact that utility certificates and invention patents in France have the same inventive step threshold (see Section 1.4.5). Further, it takes, according to INPI, approximately 21 long months to grant a utility certificate in France. These factors collectively make France's utility certificate a weak means of appropriability and a not particularly accessible IP right.[110]) In contrast, the duration of protection afforded by France's invention patent is said to provide patentees a much stronger assurance that they will not be infringing on others' technology.[111] As such, the short maximum duration of the utility certificate in France, taken along with other aspects of the regime, does not appear to optimally balance the principles of appropriability and accessibility to encourage innovation.

In contrast, the current Chinese regime, which provides protection for 10 years, has not been seriously challenged as reflecting a less-than-optimal balance between appropriability and accessibility. And, as mentioned,

---

[108] See Prud'homme, "Creating a 'Model' Utility Model System," for more details on the average time to grant utility models, as well as the timing under which utility model applications are published (which, depending on the country, can differ from the granting date).
[109] Ibid.   [110] Consultations with Jean-Baptiste Barbier, INPI, May 21–22, 2014, roundtable.
[111] Ibid.

Austria, the Czech Republic, Finland, Germany, and Italy also provide up to 10 years of protection for their utility models. As such, it appears that affording utility models up to 10 years of protection may reflect a reasonable balance between appropriability and accessibility. This balance may enable innovation better than a shorter duration of protection, although the full implications of this balancing act must be assessed alongside other legal instruments in each country's utility model patent regime. At the same time, regardless of country-specific circumstances, it is clear that some form of balancing act is required for any country in order to stimulate innovation.

The shorter time to grant utility models when compared to invention patents is another classic component making utility model patents more accessible than invention patents and in the process providing them quicker appropriability. This is meant to reflect the often less-substantive nature of the examination process for utility models when compared to invention patents. As explained in the conceptual framework, and as confirmed by discussions with SIPO and the patent offices of the seven EU countries analyzed in this section, this added appropriability provides utility model rights holders quickly enforceable protection. This is particularly important for technologies with relatively short life-cycles, can enable raising start-up capital, and provides other benefits.

1.4.3 *Patentable Subject Matter*

The scope of subject matter protected by a patent regime is a fundamental determinant of the appropriability it offers. In general, the utility model patent regimes of the countries studied appear far more restrictive in their scope of patentable subject matter for utility models than invention patents. Similar to the approach to duration of protection, given the more accessible nature of utility models in terms of the lower granting requirements than invention patents, some policymakers have decided it is more suitable to institute a more restricted scope of appropriability for utility models than for invention patents in the form of a narrower scope of patentable subject matter. However, as explained further below, not all policymakers have followed this approach.

Table 1.1 provides a comparison of a number of important areas of patentable subject matter for utility models across the countries studied in this chapter. It shows that Austria and France have a wider scope of patentable subject matter for utility models than the other countries analyzed. In some areas, like microbiological products, Finland and the Czech Republic also have comparatively wide scopes of protection. In contrast, Italy and China have the most restricted scopes of patentable subject matter for utility models.

TABLE 1.1 *Utility Model Subject Matter in Seven Countries Surveyed (Non-exhaustive Comparison)*

Subject matter for utility models	Country excludes (Section/Article)*	Country allows (Section/Article)*
Processes (in general)	China (PL2); Czech Republic (3); Finland (1); Germany (2); Italy (IC82)	Austria (4); France
Inventions inconsistent with the public interest, order, policy, and/or morality	Austria (2); China (PL5); Czech Republic (3); Finland (1); France (L611-17); Germany (2); Italy (IC50)	
Schemes, rules and methods for mental/intellectual activities	Austria (1); China (PL25); Czech Republic (2); Finland (1); France (L611-10); Germany (1); Italy (IC45)	
Schemes, rules and methods for playing games	Austria (1); China (PL2±, PE2.1.4.2); Czech Republic (3); Finland (1); France (L611-10); Germany (1); Italy (IC45)	
Substances obtained by means of nuclear transformation	China (PL25)	Austria; Czech Republic; Finland (1); France (L611-19)±; Germany; Italy (IC)±
Scientific theories	Austria (1); China (PL25)±; Czech Republic (2); Finland (1); France (L611-10); Germany (1); Italy (IC45)	
Scientific discoveries	Austria (1); China (PL25); Czech Republic (2); Finland (1); France (L611-10); Germany (1); Italy (IC45)	
Mathematical methods	Austria (1); China (PL25)±; Czech Republic (2); Finland (1); France (L611-10); Germany (1); Italy (IC45)	

Aesthetic creations	Austria (1); China (PL3, 25)±; Czech Republic (2); Finland (1); France (L6n-10); Germany (1); Italy (IC82)±
Schemes, rules, and methods for doing business	Austria (1); China (PL2±, PL25±); Czech Republic (3, PL3)±; Finland (1); France (L6n-10); Germany (1); Italy (IC82, 45)±
Presentations of information	Austria (1); China (PL2±, PE2.1.4.2); Czech Republic (2); Finland (1); France (L6n-10); Germany (1); Italy (IC45)
Schemes, rules, and methods for programs for computers	Austria (1); China (PL2±, PE1.2.6.1); Czech Republic (2); Finland (1); France (L6n-10)†; Germany (1); Italy (IC82, 45)±
Program logic on which programs for data processing regimes are based (the verbalized algorithm of a software)	China (PL2, PE 1.2.6.1)±; Czech Republic (2)±; Finland (1); France††; Germany (1); Italy (IC82)±
Certain methods for treatment of the human body by surgery or therapy (as distinct from products, including substances and compositions, for use in any of these methods)	Austria (2); China (PL25)±; Czech Republic (PL3); Finland (PL1); France (L6n-16); Germany (PL2); Italy (IC45)
Certain methods for treatment of animals by surgery or therapy (as distinct from products, including substances and compositions, for use in any of these methods)	China (PL25)±; Czech Republic (PL3); Finland (PL1); France (L6n-16); Germany (PL2); Italy (IC45)

Austria (1)

Austria±

TABLE 1.1 *(continued)*

Subject matter for utility models	Country excludes (Section/Article)*	Country allows (Section/Article)*
Diagnostic methods practiced on humans (as distinct from products, including substances and compositions, for use in any of these methods)	Austria (2); China (PL25)±; Czech Republic (PL3); Finland (PL1); France (L611-16); Germany (PL2); Italy (IC45)	
Diagnostic methods practiced on animals (as distinct from products, including substances and compositions, for use in any of these methods)	China (PL25)±; Czech Republic (PL3); Finland (PL1); France (L611-16); Germany (PL2); Italy (IC45)	Austria±
Microbiological processes	Austria; China (PL2)±; Czech Republic (3); Finland (1)±; Germany (2, PL2)±; Italy (IC82)	France (L611-19)
Microbiological products	Austria; China (PL2)±; Germany (1)±; Italy (IC82)	Czech Republic; Finland (PL1)±; France (L611-19)
Compositions containing microorganisms; nucleic acids	China (PL2)±; Italy (IC82)±	Austria; Czech Republic; Finland; France; Germany
"Essentially" biological processes for the production of plants and animals	Austria (2); China (PL2±, PE2.1.4.4); Czech Republic (3,PL4); Finland (1); France (L611-19); Germany (1, PL2); Italy (IC45, 81)	
Certain plant varieties	Austria (2); China (PL2±, PL25); Czech Republic (3); Finland (1); France (L611-19); Germany (2); Italy (IC5 etc.)	But different rules allow protection of some plant varieties
Animal varieties	Austria (2); China (PL25); Czech Republic (3); Finland (1); France (L611-19); Germany (2); Italy (IC45)	

Microstructure of a substance (e.g. crystalline structure of substance, nano-structure) that is part of a technical solution	China (PL2±, PE1.2.6.2); Italy	Austria; Czech Republic; Germany; Finland; France
Design of an apartment, campus planning or the residential district planning, and the design of an overpass	Austria; China (PL2, PE); Czech Republic (2)±; Finland; France; Germany (1); Italy (IC45)±	
Certain substances like liquids and compositions and components of substances under certain conditions	China (PL2)±; Italy	Austria; Czech Republic; Finland; France (IC); Germany;
Certain sets of equipment or complex regimes with multiple devices	–	Austria; China (PL)±; Czech Republic; Finland; France; Germany; Italy

Source: Author's review of the utility model, patent and industrial property codes of each country, and consultations with each patent office.[a]

[a] Note 1: *Numbers pertain to the according article from the according countries' relevant legislation, whereby utility model laws have no alphabetical abbreviation, patent law is abbreviated as "PL," wider industrial property codes are abbreviated with "IC," and patent examination guidelines are abbreviated with "PE" (whereby the numerical citation therein is in the form of part, chapter, section [e.g. PE2.1.4.2 indicates Part 2, Chapter 1, Section 4.2]). Entries without an article referenced are taken from the author's correspondence between April and September 2014 with the relevant patent office. Note 2: "±" indicates that although relevant law does not explicitly state that the subject matter as worded is excluded or allowed, it appears reasonable to assume from the wording in the cited article that the matter should be classified as it is in Table 1.1. Note 3: † In France, "computer-implemented inventions" are patentable by utility certificates if they are new, inventive and are industrially applicable. Note 4: †† The patentability by utility certificates in France of program logic on which programs for data processing regimes are based depends on the claims, whereby although technical methods are patentable, intellectual methods, even if implemented in a computer, are not patentable (Source: written correspondence from Emilie Gallois, INPI, September 19, 2014).

59

China restricts utility model protection to technical solutions relating to the shape, structure, or combination thereof, of a product.[112] Italy restricts utility model patents to solutions apt to provide particular efficacy or convenience of application or use for machines, or parts thereof, instruments, tools or functional objects in general.[113] Austria, the Czech Republic, Finland, France, and Germany do not have such broad overall limitations on utility models.

1.4.3.1 Balancing Appropriability and Accessibility: Austria, Finland, and China

Austria allows a relatively wide scope of patentable subject matter for its utility models, and thus a relatively wide scope of appropriability, in an attempt to foster innovation in emerging technologies. Austria uniquely (among the countries studied, at least) allows program logic on which data processing systems are based to be patented by utility models. One of the reasons for this approach appears to be that the drafters of the Austrian Utility Model Law (which is the youngest out of the countries studied, introduced in 1994) were particularly in tune with the evolving nature of computer program and Internet-related technological trajectories.[114] Additionally, the rationale behind this allowance is to provide a cheap and fast IP protection tool with a shorter duration of protection than for invention patents given the lifecycle of computer program inventions can be relatively short.[115]

This approach to patentable subject matter in Austria is one attempt to enable innovation that might not be spurred in the absence of such appropriability conditions. However, the actual impact of such allowance on innovation appears to be under-researched. It is possible that strategic usage of invention patents in the ICT industry, which can hamper innovation in the ways described in the conceptual framework hereto,[116] may be exacerbated if too wide of a scope of patentable subject matter for utility models is allowed. Such issues deserve further research.

By way of another example, Austria uniquely (among the countries studied, at least) allows utility model protection of diagnostic methods practiced on animals, and methods of treating animals by surgery or therapy. This

---

[112] Article 2, Patent Law of China (2008).
[113] Article 82, Italian Code of Industrial Property (2012).
[114] The next youngest utility model regimes are the Finnish regime, introduced in 1993, and the Czech regime, introduced in 1992.
[115] Written correspondence from Dr. Johannes Werner, APO, June 13, 2014.
[116] For example, see Hall and Ziedonis, "The Patent Paradox Revisited," and Hall, "The Use and Value of Patent Rights."

allowance, which TRIPs disallows for invention patents, is nonetheless in compliance with TRIPs given the agreement does not set forth specific rules governing utility models.[117] The patentability of such matter reflects relatively liberal economic and social values in Austria. It also reflects an approach to patentable subject matter that may enable innovation perhaps not spurred in the absence of such appropriability conditions, although the full impact of such allowance on innovation deserves further research.

By way of another example from the EU, Finland substantially expanded the appropriability afforded by its utility model regime when it reformed the scope of subject matter patentable by utility models two years after its utility model law was enacted. In 1995, Finland changed the requirement that its utility models could only protect "concrete objects," to subsequently allow chemical compounds, medicines, and foodstuffs to also be protected by utility models.[118] These reforms reflect an approach to patentable subject matter that may enable innovation that might not be spurred in the absence of such appropriability conditions, although the full impact of such allowance on innovation deserves further research.

There have been discussions in China recently at SIPO about if the scope of patentable subject matter for utility models should be expanded, providing Chinese utility models a wider scope of appropriability. As mentioned, among the countries studied, China has one of the most restricted scopes of patentable subject matter. Drawing from the abovementioned research, it appears that any widening of the scope of patentable subject matter protectable by utility models should carefully balance the principles of appropriability and accessibility to best enable innovation; however, robust guidance as to how exactly achieve this balance is lacking.

As mentioned at the outset of this section, given the more accessible nature of utility models, namely in terms of the lower granting requirements, some policymakers have decided it is more suitable to provide a more restrictive scope of appropriability for utility models. However, at the same time, as mentioned in the above case of Austria, there are also arguments for allowing a wide scope of patentable subject matter to foster technological development. This latter rationale might be particularly relevant to China's initiatives to encourage development of newly state-designated "strategic emerging industries."[119] More generally, these dynamics indicate that countries should

---

[117] See Grosse Ruse-Khan "The international legal framework for the protection of utility models" and Janis "Second Tier Patent Protection," and the conceptual framework section of this chapter, for related commentaries.

[118] Written correspondence from Hanna Aho, PRH, September 17, 2014.

[119] These are issues that China's patent and innovation policymakers could explore in more detail in the future. Note: Strategic emerging industries, for example including the "new

design their patentable subject matter requirements for utility models according to their own socio-economic and technological conditions. Yet, regardless of country-specific circumstances, a balance between the principles of appropriability and accessibility is needed when designing these requirements in order to foster innovation.

1.4.4 *Novelty*

All of the countries studied except Germany require an absolute novelty standard for utility models. Germany has a relative novelty standard for utility models, which means publications from all over the world comprise the state of the art as does usage (available to the public) in Germany (meaning usage outside of Germany alone does not destroy the novelty of the utility model).[120] In contrast, Austria,[121] China,[122] the Czech Republic,[123] Finland,[124] France,[125] and Italy[126] have an absolute novelty requirement for their utility models (and for invention patents).[127] None of the countries studied have merely a "local"

generation IT" industry, have been designated by China's central government as of 2010. For a discussion of intellectual property-related challenges (although not focusing on utility models or patentable subject matter in particular) in China's strategic emerging industries, see H. Song, J. Wan and Z. Reng, "Woguo zhanlue xing xinxing chanye neihan tezheng, chanye xuanze yu fazhan zhengce yanjiu (Characteristics of China's strategic emerging industries, industry selection, and development policy research) (in Mandarin Chinese)," *Science & Technology for Development* 5 (2010), 1–14. See also D. Prud'homme, "Dynamics of China's Provincial-Level Specialization in Strategic Emerging Industries," *Research Policy* 45 (2016), 1586–1603; D. Prud'homme, "Forecasting Threats and Opportunities for Foreign Innovators in China's Strategic Emerging Industries: A Policy-Based Analysis," *Thunderbird International Business Review* 58 (2016), 103–115

[120] DPMA – Utility Models FAQ, retrieved on August 25, 2014, http://dpma.de/english/utility _models/faq/index.html. However, absolute novelty is required for invention patents in Germany.

[121] Section/Article 3, Austrian Utility Model Law (2009); Sonn & Partner, Intellectual Property Questions & Answers, retrieved on August 17, 2014, www.sonn.at/patentanwalt.php ?l=e&m=info&t=frage_antwort_03.

[122] Article 22, Patent Law of China (2008). Prior to the 2008 revision to the Patent Law, which came into effect on October 1, 2009, prior use of prior knowledge outside of China did not constitute novelty-destroying prior art for utility models (or for invention patents).

[123] Section/Article 4, Czech Republic Utility Model Law (2006). J. Engelova Pavkova, "Possibilities for Protection of Technical Solutions in the Czech Republic," Roundtable on Providing Access to Grey Literature, Czech Republic (2013), 1–8.

[124] Finnish Patent Consulting FPC, Essential IPR concepts and term definitions, retrieved on August 26, 2014, www.sci.fi/~reki/en/IPR_terms_glossary.htm.

[125] Article L611-11, Intellectual Property Code of France (2014).

[126] Societa Italiana Brevetti, "Intellectual Property Consultants, Utility models," retrieved on August 25, 2014, www.sib.it/en/areas-of-practice/inventions/utility-models.html.

[127] Consultations with patent office representatives, May 2014.

novelty standard, meaning the state of the art is only formed from publications or use within the country.

1.4.4.1 Balancing Accessibility, Patent Quality, and Appropriability: Germany and China

The contrasting choices of novelty standards for utility models in China and Germany reflect different approaches to balancing accessibility, patent quality, and appropriability. China moved to the absolute novelty standard as a result of the 2008 revision to its Patent Law (which came into effect on October 1, 2009). There appear to be a number of reasons for this revision, including foreign pressure but also an endogenous-led desire to better foster patent quality and innovation. It is reasonable to assume that this strengthening of the novelty standard was calibrated based upon an estimate of the equilibrium at which the prior novelty standard resulted in more negative impacts on patent quality and linked innovation than was counterbalanced by its positive impacts on accessibility and appropriability useful for Chinese firms' catching-up process. This balancing act is generally in line with the literature suggesting that countries tend to strengthen their patent regimes as they develop technologically and economically from low-income to middle- and high-income statuses.[128] In contrast, in Germany, which is a technological forerunner country, some still view the relative novelty standard for utility models as "compensation" for the shorter protection time/less appropriability afforded by the utility model compared to the invention patent.[129]

In effect, the global novelty standard reflects a balancing of accessibility, patent quality, and appropriability in which less accessibility and less appropriability inferably better stimulates patent quality than the greater accessibility and appropriability offered by the relative (or local novelty) standards. Specifically, the absolute novelty standard provides a higher threshold for appropriating knowledge, which is useful in an increasingly interconnected

---

[128] Ginarte and Park, "Determinants of Patent Rights." P. Yu, "Intellectual Property, Economic Development, and the China Puzzle," in D. Gervais (ed.), *Intellectual Property, Trade and Development: Strategies to Optimize Economic Development in a TRIPs Plus Area* (Oxford: Oxford University Press, 2007), 173–220; B. Hall, "Does Patent Protection Help or Hinder Technology Transfer?," in S. Ahn, B.H. Hall and K. Lee (eds.), *Intellectual Property for Economic Development* (Northhampton, MA: Edward Elgar and Korean Development Institute, 2014), 11–32; Odagiri et al. "Introduction"; W. Park and D. Lippoldt (2008), "Technology Transfer and the Economic Implications of the Strengthening of Intellectual Property Rights in Developing Countries," OECD Trade Policy Working Papers No. 62; D. Prud'homme, "Utility Model Patent Regime 'Strength'."

[129] Written correspondence from Dr. Johannes Holzer, DPMA, September 10, 2014.

world where information and knowledge is increasingly accessible across international borders, and electronic translation tools have enabled easier diffusion of public patent information. As such, a global novelty standard for utility models appears to be more conducive to innovation in many middle- and high-income countries – although there may be economic arguments for maintaining a relative novelty standard for a certain period of time as a country technologically catches up. And, as in the case of Germany, some may otherwise argue for a relative novelty standard in order to counterbalance a lack of appropriability provided by other legal instruments in the utility model regime. While these issues should be assessed on a country-by-country basis, it remains clear that, regardless of the country, crafting a utility model regime that optimally encourages innovation requires a careful balancing of the principles of appropriability, accessibility, and patent quality.

1.4.5 *Inventive Step*

China, the Czech Republic, Finland, and Italy have lower inventive step requirements in statute for utility model patents than invention patents. In China, invention patents should possess "prominent substantive features" and represent "notable progress," but utility models only need to possess "substantive features" and represent "progress."[130] In the Czech Republic, the solutions patentable as utility models must "exceed the framework of mere professional skill" but those patentable as invention patents must be "not obvious to a person skilled in the art."[131] In Finland, solutions must be "new in relation to what was known before the filing date" and must "differ essentially" for the prior art to be protected by an invention patent, but only need to "differ distinctly" from the prior art to be protected by a utility model.[132] In Italy, although there is no specific statutory definition of inventive step for utility models, given the restrictive definitions in statute on what subject matter they can protect, utility models in Italy have a notably different inventiveness requirement than for invention patents.[133] (This being said, solutions in both

---

[130]   Article 22 of the Patent Law of China (2008).
[131]   Czech Republic's Utility Model Law (2006), Section/Article 1; Section/Article 6 of the Czech Republic's Patent Act (2007).
[132]   Section/Article 2 of the Finnish Utility Model Act (2013); Section/Article 2 in the Finnish Patents Act (2013).
[133]   Article 82.1 of Italian Industrial Property Code (2012) sets forth the inventive step threshold for utility models, and the inventive step requirement in Article 48 of Italian Code of Industrial Property (2012) applies both to utility model and invention patents.

invention patents and utility models in Italy must meet the requirement that they are "not obviously included in the prior art for an expert in the field".)[134]

Germany and Austria follow similar statutory approaches regarding inventive step. Although the German Utility Model Law (2013) stipulates utility models must have inventive step, it does not provide a definition for inventiveness. In the German Patent Law (2013), inventiveness for patents is determined as being "not obvious to a person skilled in the art from the state of the art."[135] Similarly, the Austrian Utility Model Law (2009) does not clearly distinguish a different inventive step requirement for utility models vis-à-vis invention patents, although requires inventive step. And the Austrian Patent Act (1994) defines the inventive step requirement for invention patents in the same way as Germany's Patent Law (2013) – namely as being for inventions that are "not obvious to the person skilled in the art from the state of the art."[136]

The situation in Germany is distinct from the other countries studied in that a court decision changed the way inventive step was assessed for invention patents vs. utility models. In 2006, the German Supreme Court decided that the inventive step of a utility model should be equivalent to the inventive step of invention patents.[137] Previously, the Supreme Court of the German Reich (from 1908 onwards) and the Federal Supreme Court in Germany (until 2006) required a lesser degree of inventive step for utility models than invention patents.[138]

In contrast to Germany, in 2006, for the first time since the promulgation of the Austrian Utility Model Law in 1994, the Austrian Supreme Court formally decided that the inventive step requirement for utility models was lower than for invention patents. Specifically, it decided that the inventiveness for utility models need not be measured as non-obvious to the person skilled in the art given non-obviousness is only a requirement in the Austrian Patent Law. Instead, it was ruled that inventive step for utility models only needs to meet the threshold that the solution in question is not merely the result of routine work.[139]

---

[134]   Ibid.
[135]   Section/Article 4 of the German Patent Law (2013). The only mentions of the term "inventive" in the German Utility Model Law (2013), are in Section/Article 1.1 and Section/Article 8.1.
[136]   Section/Article 1(1) of Austrian Patent Act (2009); Section/Article 1(1) of Austrian Utility Model Law (2009).
[137]   Decision of the Demonstrationsschrank, German Federal Supreme Court, X ZB 27/05, June 10, 2006.
[138]   Written correspondence from Dr. Johannes Holzer, DPMA, June 2014.
[139]   Decision of the Austrian Supreme Court, No. 4 Ob 3/06d, July 12, 2006.

France differs from the countries studied in its statutory treatment of inventive step for utility certificates. The inventive step requirement for utility certificates and invention patents in France is the same, namely patentable solutions should be "not obvious to a person skilled in the art."[140]

It is important to note that although the statutes and case law in a number of countries studied may stipulate that utility models have a lower inventive step threshold than invention patents, in practice some countries still treat the requirements as essentially the same. For example, in Austria and the Czech Republic, the inventive step for both types of patents is assessed as basically the same by the respective patent offices.[141] One reason for this approach appears to be the difficulty in developing a robust procedure to differentiate the inventive step for utility models compared to invention patents.[142]

1.4.5.1 Balancing Accessibility, Appropriability, and Patent Quality: Germany and China

The 2006 German Supreme Court decision regarding the inventive step of utility models has at least somewhat contributed to the phenomenon that filing of utility models by German entities is decreasing at a time where utility models are being strategically used by entities from other countries to compete against German firms.[143] From one perspective, this may be somewhat problematic because it constitutes a restriction on accessibility and appropriability beyond what was once available for German firms.

However, from another perspective, given the nature of strategic patenting as mentioned in the conceptual framework, the change in the inventive step requirement for utility models in Germany does not necessarily represent a restriction on accessibility and appropriability that will negatively impact innovation. This is because the more stringent inventive step requirement could serve as a safeguard to ensure higher patent quality and, in doing so, filter out patents that may act as a drag on innovation.

---

[140] Article L611-14 of the Intellectual Property Code of France (2014). Written correspondence with Jean-Baptiste Barbier, INPI, May 2014, confirmed that the inventive step requirement in France is the same for utility certificates and invention patents.

[141] Prud'homme, "Creating a 'Model' Utility Model Regime."

[142] Although some offices still use procedures for determining the inventive step of a utility model in an invalidation proceeding that they do not use in invalidation proceedings for invalidation proceedings. For example, some offices limit the number of pieces of prior art and technological fields when determining the inventive step of a utility model in an invalidation proceeding. See Prud'homme, "Creating a 'Model' Utility Model Regime."

[143] Consultations with Dr. Johannes Holzer, DPMA, and Elliot Papageorgiou, Chair of EU Chamber's IPR Working Group, May 21, 2014.

When deciding how to appropriately balance the inventive step requirement for utility models, one should also consider the arguments from the conceptual framework in favor of a comparatively lower/more accessible inventive step requirement. A lower inventive step requirement enables SMEs and individual inventors to appropriate returns for minor/incremental inventions, in effect allowing them to innovate in ways not possible in the absence of such protection. Arguments could be made that this type of accessibility is useful in both developed and developing economies; however, given utility models are typically preferred over invention patents by firms still seeking to catch up with forerunners, the need for this type of accessibility is likely more prevalent in latecomer firms in latecomer countries.[144]

Returning to our country comparison, China's status at as a developing country, both technologically and economically, warrants that it undertakes at least some different considerations than technologically advanced countries like Germany when calibrating its inventive step requirement for utility models. This idea is predicated on the concept that more accessibility in the form of a lower inventive step requirement for utility models vis-à-vis invention patents can be a useful tool to enable indigenous firms in latecomer countries to engage in technological learning in order to catch up with more technologically-sophisticated incumbent firms from forerunner countries.[145] And this can ultimately enable indigenous innovation in such latecomers.

However, another factor to be considered when calibrating the inventive step requirement for utility models in China in a way that best fosters innovation is the impact of the requirement on patent quality. Some businesses have recently argued that in order to improve the quality of its utility models, China should raise its inventive step requirement, just as Germany raised its requirement. While it is possible that this approach could improve patent quality in China, at the same time, for the reasons already mentioned, it could also limit important technological-development-stimulating effects owed to the greater accessibility and appropriability a lower inventive step requirement provides. In an attempt to find a balance between these issues, I have argued that China should not revise the inventive step requirement for utility models upwards in the near future; however, in place of this revision, other reforms should be made, for example reforming the country's perverse system of government incentives for patents (mentioned previously) and less-than-

---

[144]   See Kim et al., "Appropriate Intellectual Property Protection," and Lee and Kim, "IPR and Technological Catch-Up in Korea," regarding the preferences for invention patents over utility models at later stages of development.
[145]   D. Prud'homme, "Utility Model Patent Regime 'Strength'."

optimal Search Report regime (mentioned below), to improve the quality of utility models and thereby create a healthier innovation environment.[146]

The analysis in this section indicates that countries should design their inventive step requirements for utility models according to their own economic and technological conditions. Yet, regardless of country-specific circumstances, a balance among the principles of appropriability, accessibility, and patent quality is needed when designing these requirements in order to foster innovation.

1.4.6 Examination and Search Reports

None of the countries studied required a full substantive examination of utility models. However, all conduct a preliminary/formal (referred to interchangeably hereafter for simplicity) examination on the formalities within utility model applications. Some countries also assess certain substantive matters in their preliminary examination of utility models.

In China, the preliminary examination assesses both "obvious" substantive defects and formal requirements. In terms of substantive requirements, the examination considers if the application "obviously" is in non-conformity with the novelty, industrial applicability, and patentable subject matter requirements for utility models.[147] Building on the assessment of novelty in particular, China's September 16, 2013, revision to its Patent Examination Guidelines requires that SIPO examiners in the preliminary examination phase shall judge if utility model applications "obviously" lack novelty. This includes the requirement that the examiner shall determine, based on the reference documents obtained through search or information obtained through other channels, if "abnormal" utility model applications (such as applications that obviously copy prior art or are repeatedly filed with substantially identical content to another application) indeed "obviously" lack novelty.[148] Preliminary examinations for utility models in China also assess formality issues like the clarity and completeness, and enablement, of the description within the application; ensure the drawings on the shape and/or the structure of the product are clear and concise, follow the unity principle, and are supported in the description; and consider the issue of amendments and

---

[146] D. Prud'homme, "Soft Spots."
[147] Article 44 of Implementation Regulations of Patent Law of China (2010).
[148] Article 1 and Article 2 of SIPO's Decision on Amending the Patent Examination Guidelines (September 16, 2013). This builds on the requirement to assess obvious substantive defects regarding novelty stipulated in Article 44(2) of the Implementing Regulations of the Patent Law of China (2010) (referring to Article 22 of the Patent Law of China (2008)).

divisional applications (namely, to ensure that these do not cause the claims to cover something not disclosed in the original application).[149]

In Austria, the preliminary examination for utility models considers both substantive and formal requirements. While the APO technically does not examine novelty of a utility model in the preliminary examination phase, it has a unique regime among the countries studied of conducting a mandatory search report for all utility models. If there are no objections to the publication and registration of a utility model, APO then publishes its search report on the utility model,[150] although this search report is not actually incorporated into the examination process for the utility model (i.e. it is not actually substantively considered by APO when granting the utility model).[151] In the preliminary examination phase, the APO examines what it calls "irreparable deficiencies," namely disclosure, technical character, and patentable subject matter exceptions according to the law – though it does not examine industrial applicability.[152] The APO also assesses formalities like the form of the description, form of figures, form of claims (including their unity), and form of the abstract in the application.[153]

The preliminary examination for utility models in Finland requires an assessment of formalities as well as substantive aspects. In Finland, the preliminary examination for utility model applications includes an assessment on certain substantive issues, namely if the claims only cover subject matter patentable by utility models, the industrial applicability of the solution, and the issue of amendments. It also includes an assessment of formalities like the clarity and conciseness of claims, sufficiency of disclosure, and unity of claims.[154]

Like in China, the preliminary examination procedure for utility models in the Czech Republic assesses "obvious" substantive defects as well as a range of formalities. Specifically, IPO CZ's preliminary examination determines obvious non-conformity with subject matter patentable by utility models[155]

149　For one source giving an overview of the procedure, see "Utility Model in China." Presentation by SIPO at conference in Malaysia (September 2012), slide 20. Retrieved on June 16, 2014, www.wipo.int/edocs/mdocs/aspac/en/wipo_ip_kul_12/wipo_ip_kul_12 _ref_t3d.pdf.

150　Section/Article 19 of Austria Utility Model Law (2009).

151　Consultations with Dr. Johannes Werner, APO, May 21, 2014, roundtable. Theoretically, this could result in a situation where the office produces a Search Report that indicates a utility model is in fact not novel, although the utility model is still granted.

152　Presentation by Dr. Johannes Werner, APO, May 21, 2014, roundtable.　153　Ibid.

154　Written correspondence from Hanna Aho, PRH, September 17, 2014.

155　Section/Article 11 (1) of the Utility Model Law of the Czech Republic (2006) (referring to Sections/Articles 2 and 3).

and obvious non-conformity with requirements on industrial applicability of inventions in utility model applications.[156] It also assesses formalities like clarity of the claims, unity of the claims, and legal compliance of amendments and divisional applications.[157]

France and Italy require an assessment of formalities and the patentability of subject matter in the claims of utility certificates/models. In France, the formality examination conducted for utility certificate applications includes assessing the adequacy of support for the claims in the specification, clarity and unity of claims, and if the claimed invention constitutes patentable subject matter.[158] In Italy, the preliminary examination of utility models assesses the formalities of the clarity and conciseness of claims, among some other formal elements examined in other countries studied;[159] as well as the patentable nature of subject matter in the claims.[160]

The preliminary examination for utility models in Germany assesses formalities and one substantive issue. It assesses clarity and completeness of claims and the descriptions, and the usability of drawings for publication. The only substantive element examined in the preliminary examination phase is if the invention in a utility model application has a technical background.[161]

---

[156] Section/Article 11 (4) of the Utility Model Law of the Czech Republic (2006) (referring to Section/Article 5).
[157] Written correspondence from Šimon Bednář, IPO CZ, September 2, 2014.
[158] Cabinent Beau de Lomenie. The French Patent Regime, retrieved on October 4, 2014, www .bdl-ip.com/upload/Etudes/uk/bdl_the-french-patent-regime.pdf. Note: Substantive assessment of utility certificate patentability is left to the courts in invalidation cases.
[159] Written correspondence from Loredana Guglielmetti, UIBM, September 17, 2014.
[160] Article 170 of the Italian Industrial Property Code (2012) (referring to Articles 45, 50, and 82). Note: Substantive assessment of utility model patentability is left to the courts in invalidation cases.
[161] Article/Section 8 (1) of the German Utility Model Law (2013) finds that: "Where an application complies with the requirements of Section 4, the Patent Office shall order registration in the Utility Model Register. No examination of the subject matter of the application as to novelty, inventive step or industrial applicability shall be carried out. Section 49(2) of the Patent Law shall apply mutatis mutandis." Beyond this article, which, via referencing Article/Section 4, clearly allows examination of formalities in utility model applications, there are no provisions in the German Utility Model Law (2013) that provide exact guidance about the full extent of the Preliminary Examination allowable for utility models. A 1996 decision by the Federal Patent Court affirmed that novelty can only be assessed in the cancellation procedure and has to be examined by a person skilled in the art (see case 5 W (pat) 437/96 (sec. 38)). In 2009, the Federal Patent Court decided that those skilled in the art at the Utility Model Section of DPMA have the right to assess the existence of a technical rule in the application procedure for utility models (see case 35 (W) pat 46/09 (sec. 22)). The assessment on if an invention in a utility model application has a technical background can result in matter like (for example) working plans for a gardener being rejected (Source: Written correspondence from Dr. Johannes Holzer, DPMA, October 31, 2014). Note: a range of substantive elements in a utility model are examined if challenged in an invalidation/cancellation procedure at DPMA.

Although not a mandatory part of the pre-grant examination for utility models, some countries studied provide search reports ad hoc for a fee. Outside of mandatory search reports conducted for all utility models in Austria, the APO provides search reports to any entity upon request for a fee.[162] In France, a search report can be conducted at the written request of the applicant for a fee if he/she has transformed a patent application into a utility certificate application and a preliminary examination report has been conducted on the application but it has not yet been published.[163] DPMA offers search reports on granted utility models to any entity at request for a fee, and to the applicant for a utility model prior to the publication of the utility model at request for a fee; and these reports can be accessed by the public.[164] Finland has a broadly similar regime to DPMA.[165] IPO CZ does not offer search reports for utility models, although can provide a service to requestors that lists relevant prior art documents within a narrow technical scope (these findings are not made public).[166] In China, for a period of time prior to October 1, 2009, only basic search reports were available for granted utility models.[167] However, if a utility model has been granted after October 1, 2009, a

---

[162] Written correspondence from Dr. Johannes Werner, APO, September 15, 2014.

[163] Written correspondence from Emilie Gallois, INPI, September 19, 2014.

[164] A Search Report for a utility model can be requested in Germany for a fee, and in fact about 40–50 percent of applicants request this report. However, if the search report is negative (i.e. showing that the invention in the application is not novel), this does not necessarily prohibit the utility model from being granted. In Germany, applications for search reports, and the fact that a search report has been conducted, are made public. Although the search report itself is not published, after the utility model on which it was conducted is granted, any entity can access records relevant to the utility model, including the search report. (Source: written correspondence from Dr. Johannes Holzer, DPMA, September 10, 2014.)

[165] PRH's report does not include X, Y, and A category prior art references. The report does not actually make an assessment on the novelty of a utility model, rather is just a list of relevant documents and comments on their contents. These rules apply because the report is not intended to be a direct basis for invalidation. In Finland, if the utility model is registered, the report is also published in PRH's database along with the other application documents. (Source: Written correspondence from Hanna Aho, PRH, May 2014 and September 17, 2014.)

[166] IPO CZ does not offer search reports for utility models. However, IPO CZ does offer a type of search service for the public. This service does not produce a patent/utility model search report but rather provides a list of documents that are from the same field as the subject specified at the beginning of the search. These documents may be relevant to applicants seeking to draft their own claims. The specification of the subject to be investigated must be quite precise, much narrower than is usual in claims. Because there is no assessment of relevancy, no X, Y, or A category indications are given. The results are provided directly to the requestor, and are not published. (Source: written correspondence from Šimon Bednář, IPO CZ, October 13, 2014.)

[167] Article 57 of the revision to China's Patent Law made in the year 2000 provides that, in an infringement case, the people's court or the administrative authority for patent affairs (SIPO) "may" ask patentees to furnish a Search Report made by SIPO. And articles 55 and 56 of the 2002 Implementing Regulations of China's Patent Law allow a patentee to request a Search Report.

patent evaluation report can now be provided upon request.[168] There are restrictions in Chinese law on the circumstances in which such reports can be provided;[169] however, these might be loosened.[170] In Italy, UIBM does not provide search reports for utility models.[171]

1.4.6.1 Balancing Accessibility and Patent Quality: Austria, the Czech Republic, Finland, Germany, Italy, and China

Substantiveness/strictness in the examination process is a main way to prevent low-quality utility model applications from being granted. In order to mitigate fears of a rising stock of low-quality utility models, which could drag down innovation, Austria requires a full search report be conducted and provided alongside all utility model applications. The published search report serves as information for the public and can be a powerful tool for invalidating a utility model if the applicant does not adapt its claims in accordance with the novelty information present in the report.[172]

Other preliminary-examination–phase measures have been taken to ensure the quality of utility models, which may better enable utility model patents to contribute to innovation. In China, SIPO's 2013 revision of the Patent Examination Guidelines, mentioned previously, represents an initiative to further strengthen the substantiveness of the examination phase in order to prevent the granting of low-quality utility models. By way of juxtaposition, some patent offices in Europe that were studied noted that even if their examiners knew that the same solution for a utility model has been already described in the prior art, they are prohibited from conducting any novelty assessment during the preliminary examination phase – meaning that the examiners must still register the low-quality utility model.[173] This imbalance in a utility model regime can hamper innovation.

---

[168]   This arrangement was made in amendments to the Chinese Patent Law (2008), which came into effect on October 1, 2009. See C. Jingjing (2014). Dual Enforcement System. In S. Luginbuehl and P. Ganea (eds.), *Patent Law in Greater China* (UK, Cheltenham: Elgar Intellectual Property Law and Practice), 195–208.

[169]   Prud'homme "Soft Spots."

[170]   Provisions have been introduced in the latest (as of the writing of this chapter) draft of the Chinese Patent Law (released in 2015) regarding new circumstances in which SIPO might issue patent evaluation reports for utility models. See T. Zhang, D. Prud'homme, O. Lutze, "China's New Patent Commercialization Strategy," *Journal of Intellectual Law & Practice* (2017).

[171]   Written correspondence from Loredana Guglielmetti, UIBM, September 17, 2014.

[172]   Consultations with Dr. Johannes Werner, APO, May 21, 2014 roundtable.

[173]   May–September 2014 discussions with, and correspondence from, representatives of the IP offices in Europe studied for this chapter.

Another preliminary-examination–phase tool to ensure the quality of utility models is the requirement to assess their industrial applicability. As mentioned, Finland requires an assessment of industrial applicability of utility models in the preliminary examination stage, and China and the Czech Republic[174] require assessing if utility models "obviously" lack industrial applicability. These approaches act as safeguards to ensure better patent quality, which in turn create an environment more conducive to innovation.

Yet another preliminary-examination–phase tool to ensure quality of patents is to assess the patentability of subject matter in the utility model application. This is required in Austria, the Czech Republic, China, Finland, France, and Italy. In contrast, preliminary examinations of utility models in Germany only consider if the invention in the application has a technical background. The former approaches provide a stronger filter against low-quality utility models, while the latter more so emphasizes accessibility.

The level of substantiveness of pre-grant patent examinations determine the extent to which they serve as safeguards to ensure better patent quality, which can have direct impacts on innovation. At the same time, the more substantive of the examination approaches also limits the accessibility of utility model regimes vis-à-vis regimes without such safeguards. This is because such examinations require additional efforts from the patent office to administer, which in turn result in additional costs and, in some cases, longer waiting times that applicants experience until they have legal appropriability over their inventions. Considering these trade-offs, the optimal equilibrium between the principles of accessibility and patent quality in the context of utility model examination rules can only be fully determined on a country-by-country basis. For example, China – which has recently already modestly reformed its regime to better balance patent quality and accessibility in the interest of stimulating innovation – may benefit from an even less accessible/stricter pre-grant examination that includes mandatory consideration of search reports.[175] However, at the same time, regardless of country-specific circumstances, it is clear that a balance between the principles of accessibility and patent quality is fundamental to encouraging innovation.

---

[174] Note: this assessment is performed in the Czech Republic so as to avoid registration of utility models protecting a perpetual motion machine that are not otherwise excluded from patentable subject matter restrictions (Source: Written correspondence from Šimon Bednář, IPO CZ, September 2, 2014).

[175] Prud'homme, "Soft Spots"; Prud'homme, "Utility Model Patent Regime 'Strength'."

1.4.7 *Third-Party Observations*

France has a formal procedure for third-party observations for utility certificates.[176] At the date of publication of the application for the utility certificate (which is approximately eighteen months from the filing date), up until the time of payment of the fee for granting and printing of the specification of the certificate (which can be 21 months or longer), any party may submit observations to INPI on the patentability of the invention.[177]

Although there is no formal third-party observation mechanism established in the Italian Industrial Property Code (2012) for utility models, third parties in Italy may submit petitions/observations during the examination procedure, for example indicating the existence of relevant prior art.[178] These submissions are often made public before the utility model is granted, but are sometimes also made public after the utility model is granted. They do not, however, serve as a legal basis for UIBM to not grant a utility model (and in fact even if the submissions show the utility model lacks novelty, it will still be granted).[179]

The other countries studied have different regimes. In Austria, as mentioned, there is a search report mechanism provided for all utility models, and while there is no formal mechanism to collect third-party observations, if third parties provide APO with their observations they will be considered prior to the publication of the search report.[180] In the Czech Republic,[181] Finland,[182] and Germany[183] there is no formal third-party observations mechanism in the application procedure for utility models. In China, there is also no formal third-party observations mechanism in the application procedure for utility models because utility models are only published when they are granted.[184]

---

[176] See L. 612–13 Industrial Property Code of France (2014).

[177] Written correspondence from Jean-Baptiste Barbier, INPI, May 2014.

[178] Written correspondence from Loredana Guglielmetti, UIBM, September 17, 2014. The Italian Industrial Property Code (2012) only establishes specific rules for third-party observations before granting for trademarks and plant varieties (not for invention patents or for utility models).

[179] Written correspondence from Loredana Guglielmetti, UIBM, September 17, 2014.

[180] Written correspondence from Dr. Johannes Werner, APO, September 17, 2014.

[181] Written correspondence from Šimon Bednář, IPO CZ, September 2, 2014.

[182] Written correspondence from Hanna Aho, PRH, September 17, 2014.

[183] Written correspondence from Dr. Johannes Holzer, DPMA, September 10, 2014.

[184] Article 40 of the Patent Law of China (2008). However, under special circumstances, third parties may submit observations to SIPO. For example, if the international search report or international preliminary report on patentability of a utility model filed via the PCT enters into the national phase in China and lists documents which refer to the novelty of the application, or interested parties submit information referring to the utility model's application to SIPO (in the form of search reports, prior art or conflicting applications) – SIPO's "examiners would consider this relevant information during the examination procedure or the process of making an

1.4.7.1 Balancing Accessibility and Patent Quality: France, Italy, and China

Mechanisms allowing third parties to submit observations about the patent-ability of a utility model are intended to ensure patent quality. A formal third-party observation mechanism is used by INPI in France to gather and consider possible novelty-destroying prior art before utility certificates are granted.[185] In Italy, the allowance of third parties to submit observations regarding the existence of relevant prior art can be a useful quality oversight mechanism enabling third parties and the owner of the utility model to consider the observations and the possibility of invalidation proceedings.[186]

At the same time, the third-party observation mechanism approach to ensure patent quality makes the utility model patent regime somewhat less accessible. Maintaining a third-party observation mechanism requires efforts from the patent office to administer, which results in additional costs and in some cases, can prolong waiting times applicants experience until they have legal appropriability over their inventions.[187] Considering these trade-offs, the optimal equilibrium between the principles of patent quality and accessibility in the context of third party observations for utility models can only be fully determined on a country-by-country basis. However, at the same time, regardless of country-specific circumstances, it is clear that a balance between the principles of accessibility and patent quality is fundamental to ultimately encouraging innovation.

1.5 WHEN UTILITY MODEL REGIMES CAUSE MORE HARM TO INNOVATION THAN GOOD

Utility model regimes in some EU countries have created problems so significant that the regimes were ultimately abolished entirely. In 1995,

---

Evaluation Report of a utility model patent. The results handled by examiners would not be made public to third parties submitting information" (from written correspondence from Wang Jianjian, SIPO, on September 30, 2014). Note: the first version of China's patent law (promulgated in 1984) included a provision for pre-grant third party observations for utility models, although it was removed in the 1992 revision to the law. The mechanism was removed because an invalidation mechanism also existed in the law and it was thought that having both mechanisms constituted an unnecessarily strong and resources-intensive legal framework to administer (Prud'homme, "Utility Model Patent Regime 'Strength').

[185] Consultations with Jean-Baptiste Barbier, INPI, May 21, 2014 roundtable.
[186] Written correspondence from Loredana Guglielmetti, UIBM, September 29, 2014.
[187] Among some of the other patent offices surveyed, opinions differed as to whether the third-party observation mechanism would be useful to introduce to their regime. Some saw the value of the mechanism limiting low quality patents, but at the same time noted the need to ensure their utility model regime still enabled fast grants.

the Netherlands introduced a "short-term" patent, equivalent to a utility model as defined in this chapter, which had a maximum duration of protection of six years. The short-term patent did not require a prior art search before being granted.[188] An evaluation of the Dutch patent regime in 2006 confirmed suspicions that the short-term Dutch patent was only popular with the limited number of applicants of such type of patent and that, overall, the short-term patent regime was creating significant legal uncertainty because a substantive examination was not conducted as a precondition for granting the right.[189] And this could notably hamper patent quality and ultimately innovation. As such, the short-term patent was abolished on June 5, 2008.[190]

By way of comparison, as of 1995, a prior art search was conducted for the 20-year Dutch patent yet this type of patent was granted regardless of the outcome of the search.[191] The aforementioned 2006 investigation of the Dutch patent regime led to the requirement that a written opinion on aspects of patentability should be included with the search report for each 20-year patent application, and that search fees should be reduced for the 20-year patent.[192] After the 2006 changes to the Dutch patent regime, the total number of patent filings for 20-year patents were nearly equal to the sum of the filings for the short-term and 20-year patents before the changes.[193] In the words of D.J. de Groot, Director of the Dutch Patent Office:

> It is therefore safe to assume that the users of the six year patent [short-term patent] have changed over to the 20-year patent. It should however be kept in mind that at the same time the fee structure was also changed in favour of the applicants and furthermore the option to file in English was introduced, both of which have an upward effect on filing numbers.[194]

This finding is corroborated by recent econometric analysis from Jussi Heikkila.[195]

---

[188] Written correspondence from D.J. de Groot, Director of the Netherlands Patent Office, August 22, 2014.

[189] Written correspondence from A.A.M van der Meer, Dutch Ministry of Economic Affairs, on March 27, 2014 and August 21, 2014.

[190] Ibid. The last short-term patent in the Netherlands expired on June 3, 2014.

[191] Written correspondence from D.J. de Groot, Director of the Netherlands Patent Office, August 22, 2014.

[192] Ibid.   [193] Ibid.   [194] Ibid.

[195] J. Heikkila, "Does Utility Model Protection Substitute or Complement Patent Protection? (The Relationship between First and Second Tier Patent Protection: The Case of the Dutch Short-Term Patent System Abolition)". DRUID Academy conference paper (2015). http://druid8.sit.aau.dk/druid/acc_papers/ukfty228itioveim59c2027tcrvo.pdf.

A fate similar to that of the Dutch short-term patent befell the Belgian equivalent of the utility model patent. In 1987, Belgium introduced a "small/ petite patent," a type of patent equivalent to a utility model as defined in this chapter, which had a maximum duration of protection of six years.[196] Similar to the investigation of the Dutch short-term patent, an analysis of the Belgian petite patent regime concluded that the lack of a novelty search before granting the right created significant legal uncertainty. As a result, the Belgian petite patent regime was abolished in 2009. According to the Belgian Ministry of Economy, the abolition of the petite patent regime has had little influence on the number of filings or preference for invention patents in Belgium from 2009 till present.[197]

The cases of the Netherlands and Belgium illustrate that an imbalance of the principles of appropriability, accessibility, and patent quality in a utility model regime can inhibit innovation. The lack of a novelty assessment in the pre-grant phase for utility model equivalents in the Netherlands and Belgium made the IP right cheaper and quicker to obtain for applicants than their equivalent of an invention patent, and thus comparatively accessible. However, the lack of a novelty assessment also created significant uncertainty as to if the granted right in fact actually met the statutory requirements for patentability. And legally appropriating knowledge that has a notable risk of not even being patent-worthy created adverse economic consequences by potentially dragging down patent quality and consequentially hampering innovation. Rather than attempt a rebalancing of its legal instruments to better reflect the principles of appropriability, accessibility, and patent quality in order to better enable innovation, the Dutch and Belgian authorities opted to completely abolish their equivalent of utility model regimes.

It is possible that the Dutch and Belgian choice to flatly abolish their utility model regimes rather than reform them could be related to the fact that they are both developed countries. Accordingly, the literature appears to suggest that these countries might not need utility model regimes as much as lesser-developed economies in order to progress technologically. However, the legal and policymaking culture in both nations surely also played a role in this decision, in addition to potentially other factors. A further investigation into these dynamics is worthy of a separate research paper.

---

[196] DIPP, "Discussion Paper on Utility Models."
[197] Written correspondence from Geoffrey Bailleux, OPRI, Belgian Ministry of Economy, July 2, 2014. Note: Petite patents granted before January 8, 2009 are still maintained under the old legal regime in Belgium until they expire.

1.6 CONCLUSION

This chapter illustrates how constructing a utility model patent regime that encourages innovation requires carefully balancing the principles of appropriability, accessibility, and patent quality. Comparative analysis shows how the legal frameworks for utility models in Mainland China and several EU countries attempt to balance these principles and the lessons they learned during this process. It is concluded that although the precise balance among the principles of appropriability, accessibility, and patent quality can differ among countries according to their individual technological and economic conditions, some type of balance must always be achieved or else the utility model regime will inhibit innovation.

2

Greening Chinese Patent Law to Incentivize Green Technology Innovation in China

Li Gao

2.1 INTRODUCTION

As a country characterized by spectacular economic growth, a large population, relatively high levels of poverty and severe environmental degradation, the Chinese central leadership is keen to address environmental and developmental concerns concomitantly and strike a balance between environmental protection and economic development. One way that this can be achieved, in the author's view, is through the development of green technology ("green-tech"). By linking environmental benefits, economic growth and technological progress together, the development of green-tech is expected to safeguard the environment without necessarily hindering economic growth or technological progress, holding the key to the environmental sustainability.[1]

Given that the conflict between environment and economy is much more exacerbated in current China than in Western countries, the development of green-tech must be of greater importance to China.

A close look at the Chinese green-tech industry shows that China has made remarkable progress in the green-tech sector, especially in energy efficiency technology, CO_2 mitigation technology and renewable energy generation technology, but fails to achieve a balanced development, and its green-tech industry is faced with the "big but not strong" problem. Although China has surpassed "the U.S. and several western European countries to become the world's top manufacturer of both solar panels and wind turbines,"[2] it is lagging far behind them in other green-tech sectors. In addition, China's green-tech

[1] René Kemp, "Technology and the Transition to Environmental Sustainability: The Problem of Technological Regime Shifts" (1994) 26 *Futures* 1023–1046.

[2] Christina Larson, "America's Unfounded Fears of a Green Tech Race with China" *Yale Environment 360*, February 8, 2010, http://e360.yale.edu/feature/americas_unfounded_fears_of_a_green-tech_race_with_china/2238/.

achievements are more about manufacturing. In contrast with its fast-growing manufacturing sector, China is weak in green-tech innovation. This results in China's lack of some core technologies and bottlenecks in the sustainable development of its green-tech industry. Indeed, lacking key environmentally friendly technologies has become the biggest problem encountered by China in driving its green economy. Consequently, encouraging green-tech innovation proves to be China's top priority.

Instead of repeating the popular policy advice on green-tech innovation or encouraging the adoption of any of the existing tools or initiatives, this chapter attempts to approach the issue of green-tech innovation from a new perspective of law and institutional design, and seeks to stimulate green-technological change through the "greening" of the Chinese patent law. Specifically, the author argues that the current Chinese patent law per se should be refined to offer better incentives to green-technological change by preventing the patenting of very environmentally harmful inventions and giving environmentally beneficial inventions priority over others. By taking this approach, the green-tech innovation can be better promoted, which in turn would contribute to China's environmental improvement without coming at the expense of impeding economic and technical progress.

The remainder of this chapter consists of four sections. Section 2.2 justifies the need for tailoring the patent law to incentivize green-tech innovation. Section 2.3 analyzes the Chinese patent law's performance in promoting green-tech innovation and catering for environmental protection in detail and discusses the existing problems and deficiencies. Section 2.4 raises specific proposals for the further "greening" of the Chinese patent law with a view to providing stronger incentives for green-tech innovation. Section 2.5 concludes by advocating the adoption or consideration of the proposals by the Chinese lawmakers and policymakers.

2.2 JUSTIFICATIONS FOR TAILORING PATENT LAW TO GREEN-TECH INNOVATION

The current patent system is technology-neutral. It indiscriminately promotes all types of innovation. For instance, the current patent system has little interest in distinguishing between environmentally benign technology and environmental harmful technology, and has "little concern for environmental protection or degradation."[3] Incentives for "inventing and using

---

[3] Paul Gormley, "Comment: Compulsory Patent Licenses and Environmental Protection" (1993–1994) 7 *Tulane Environmental Law Journal* 131–164, p. 132.

environmentally beneficial technology have generally been no greater than those for environmentally harmful technology."[4] As a classical tool for promoting new and useful innovations, the patent law system can and should be tailored to better stimulate green-tech innovation.

First, the current patent system was designed more than 100 years ago to satisfy the simpler needs of an industry era in which most of if not all the "useful arts" were mechanical inventions, so it made sense to have an undifferentiated and one-size-fits-all patent system.[5] With the dramatic change of technology, the application of static patent rules to ever-changing technologies has presented structural problems for patent law, which requires "the development of technologically tailored patent rules," including patent rules tailored to incentivize green-tech innovation.[6]

Second, unlike the goal of the current patent law regime defined in exclusively economic terms, the goal of the early patent system was defined as promoting a full array of human values and broadly-defined social progress, and inventions that were injurious to "the well-being, good policy, or sound morals of society" were excluded from patentability because such inventions found no place in the early social conception of technology as a tool of social progress.[7] The patent system as an institution should rethink its value "as a means to the end of social good" and recognize "its role in the health, safety, and environmental problems of modern technology, or its potential role in creating solutions."[8] This calls for the exclusion of very environmentally harmful inventions from patent right and the formulation of patent rules tailored to serve higher environmental goals.

Third, technologies are not neutral tools "that can be used well or poorly, for good, evil or something in between."[9] Instead, it is the way in which technologies are designed and built that produces "a set of consequences logically and temporally *prior to any of its professed uses.*"[10] Rather than being directed by an innate logic, technologies are "the product of a web of social and political forces, embedded with the values and goals of those who produce and control them."[11] Thus, if technologies are not neutral, a system that incentivizes the innovation of them cannot and should not be

[4] Ibid., 195.
[5] Dan L. Burk and Mark A. Lemley, "Is Patent Law Technology-Specific?" (2002) 17 *Berkeley Technology Law Journal* 1155–1206.
[6] Ibid., 1185.   [7] Ibid., 788.   [8] Ibid., 820.
[9] Langdon Winner, *The Whale and the Reactor: A Search for Limits in an Age of High Technology* (Chicago: University of Chicago Press, 1986), pp. 44–45.
[10] Ibid., emphasis in original.
[11] Dana Remus Irwin, "Paradize Lost in the Patent Law? Changing Visions of Technology in the Subject Matter Inquiry" (2008) 60 *Florida Law Review* 775–823, p. 818.

neutral.[12] Given that different technologies have different impacts on the environment that are either beneficial, neutral or detrimental, the patent system should distinguish between environmentally friendly technologies and environmentally harmful technologies and treat them differently. Otherwise, it may cause a paradoxical situation – the products or processes incentivized and protected by patent law may be prohibited from entering the market by environmental law, causing a significant waste of social resources.

Fourth, patents are granted in order to promote innovation, and so patents should be granted in a way that best incentivizes such innovation. Given that innovation occurs differently from industry to industry, the patent system should be adapted to the specific incentive requirements of various industries.

Fifth, research shows that while patent law is "technology-neutral in theory, it is technology-specific in application."[13] Burk and Lemley use inventions in biotechnology and computer software industries as examples to demonstrate how a court has applied the theoretically unified rules "in a way that effectively creates different standards for different industries."[14] The research conducted by Lunney shows that the application of standards may not be consistent even within the same industry.[15] All these highlight the need for a technology-specific patent law system.

Finally, there exist precedents that new forms of industry-specific patent rights would be created when the patent system failed to provide the necessary development incentives such as the US Semiconductor Chip Protection Act of 1984 and the US Orphan Drug Act of 1983.[16] It is indeed not a radical suggestion to tailor the patent system to the needs of promoting green-tech innovation and deterring the development of environmentally harmful technology, i.e. the "greening" of the patent law.

2.3 THE CHINESE PATENT LAW'S CATERING FOR GREEN-TECH INNOVATION

The Chinese patent law has already catered for green-tech innovation, mainly through its provisions on aim of patent law, patentable subject matter, criteria

---

[12] Ibid., 818–819.   [13] Burk and Lemley, "Is Patent Law Technology-Specific?," 1156.
[14] Ibid., 1160.
[15] Glynn S. Lunney, Jr., "E-Obviousness" (2001) 7 *Michigan Telecommunications and Technology Law Review* 363–422.
[16] Natalie M. Derzko, "Using Intellectual Property Law and Regulatory Processes to Foster the Innovation and Diffusion of Environmental Technologies" (1996) 20 *The Harvard Environmental Law Review* 1–73, p. 7.

of patentability and patent prosecution process, but in an implicit way and to a rather limited extent.

2.3.1 *Aim of Patent Law*

2.3.1.1 Provision

Article 1 of the Patent Law of the People's Republic of China (PRC Patent Law) clearly sets out its goal by providing that "[t]his law is enacted for the purpose of protecting the legitimate rights and interests of patentees, encouraging inventions, giving an impetus to the application of inventions, improving the innovative capabilities, and promoting scientific and technological progress as well as the economic and social development."[17] The terms "progress" and "development" are prescribed in this Article. Thus, according to the letter of the PRC Patent Law, it is enacted not only to encourage innovation and advance technology, but also to promote progress and social development. Recognizing that a good environment is conducive to social good, such a relative broad aim of the PRC Patent Law, although implicitly, has catered for the preservation of the environment, thus increasing incentives for the innovation and development of environmentally friendly technology.

2.3.1.2 Problem and Deficiency

First, the terms "progress" and "social development" are not defined by any patent law or regulation, and it is not clear whether they cover higher social values and broader social welfare.

Second, the legal provisions for the aim of patent law have been rarely considered or even noticed by patent examiners and judges, letting alone having any effects on environmental protection. The author interviewed three examiners from the Patent Office of the State Intellectual Property Office of PRC (SIPO) in 2014. Among them, one was responsible for preliminary examination of a patent invention application, one for substantive examination and another one for re-examination. None of them recognized or even noticed the correlation between the "aim" of the PRC Patent Law and their examination of patent and thus routinely focused on the technical details of a certain application without thinking about whether it promotes social

---

[17] Article 1 of Patent Law of the People's Republic of China, No. 11 Order of the President of the People's Republic of China, 1984 (amended in 1992, 2000 and 2008), http://en.pkulaw.cn/dis play.aspx?cgid=111782&lib=law.

progress and development. As to environmental concerns, none of them recognized or even noticed that environmental interests could be something with which the patent law should align or at least not contradict. They never took environmental interests into consideration during their examination or re-examination of patent applications, and all inventions were treated equally, whether they were environmentally friendly or environmentally harmful. Similarly, an interview with the three intellectual property (IP) judges showed that the "aim" provision had no impact on their determination of patent cases, and they had never witnessed a case in which a judge relied on the "aim" provision to make a judgment in favor of or against a party for the purpose of preserving the environment.

2.3.2 *Patentable Subject Matter*

Basically, patents shall be "available for any inventions, whether products or processes, in all fields of technology."[18] Patent laws or patent practices in many jurisdictions, however, provide that certain subject matters are not patentable for the purpose of morality, *ordre public*, legality, public health and environmental protection.[19] The exclusion of environmentally harmful inventions from patentability helps to discourage potential inventors from inventing polluting products or processes, and helps increase incentives to invent "green."[20]

2.3.2.1 Provision

The PRC Patent Law limits its scope of patentable subject matter through the "morality and *ordre public*" provision and an explicit list of exclusions of patent rights. A close look at the list shows that it does not include environmentally harmful inventions.[21] As to the "morality and *ordre public*" provision, it provides that "[n]o patent shall be granted for an invention that contravenes any law or social moral or that is detrimental to public interests."[22] Clearly, the

---

[18] Article 27(1) of Agreement on Trade-Related Aspects of Intellectual Property Rights, Marrakesh, April 15, 1994, in force January 1, 1995, 1869 UNTS 299, 33 ILM 1197.

[19] Shawn Kolitch, "The Proper Scope of Patentability in International Law" (2007) 11 *Marquette Intellectual Property Law Review* 150–179, p. 166.

[20] Ibid., 62. *See also* W. Less and Travis Lybbert, "Do Patents Come too Easy?" (2004) 44 *IDEA* 381–407, p. 387.

[21] Article 25 of Patent Law of China. Article 25 provides for a list of exclusions of patent rights which includes, *inter alia*, scientific discoveries, rules and methods for mental activities, methods for the diagnosis or for the treatment of diseases, and animal and plant varieties.

[22] Ibid., Article 5.

Chinese "morality and *ordre public*" provision does not explicitly write down the serious prejudice to the environment as contrary to *ordre public* and does not expressly exclude very environmentally harmful inventions from patent rights. It should be noted, however, that the term "public interests" is defined by the 2010 Guidelines for Patent Examination (Examination Guidelines) as covering environmental interests. According to the Examination Guidelines, the expression of "detrimental to public interests" means that the exploitation or use of an invention "may cause detriment to the public or the society or may disrupt the normal order of the State and the society."[23] In particular, the Examination Guidelines list several typical examples that shall be regarded as being "detrimental to public interests." Among them, one example directly addresses the issue of environmentally harmful inventions and provides that patent right shall not be granted for an invention whose exploitation or use may "seriously pollute the environment, seriously waste energy or resources, disrupt the ecological balance, or impair the health of the public."[24] The Examination Guidelines make it clear that environmental interests fall under the category of public interests, and thus a very environmentally harmful invention shall be excluded from patent right because it is detrimental to public interests.

2.3.2.2 Problem and Deficiency

The biggest problem of the Chinese "morality and *ordre public*" provision is that it does not explicitly write down the serious prejudice to the environment as contrary to *ordre public* and does not expressly exclude very environmentally harmful inventions from patent rights. Although "public interests" can be interpreted as covering environmental interests, such an interpretation is not as effective as an explicit exclusion of environmentally harmful inventions in preserving the environment. In addition, the exclusion of environmentally harmful inventions from patentability by the Examination Guidelines is not effective enough due to its limited legal effect and scope of application. First, the Examination Guidelines were enacted by the SIPO and fall within the category of "rule" (*guizhang*). According to the Legislation Law, "rule" is at the lowest level of the hierarchy of legal norms and has the lowest legal authority. Thus, the legal effect of the Examination Guidelines is rather limited. For instance, the

---

[23] Article 3(1), Chapter I, Part II of Guidelines for Patent Examination, the State Intellectual Property Office of the People's Republic of China (SIPO), 2010, www.sipo.gov.cn/zlsqzn/scz/.
[24] Ibid.

Administrative Procedure Law of PRC provides that in handling administrative cases and examining the legality of specific administrative acts, the
court shall take laws and regulations as criteria while taking rules only as
references.[25] Thus, in examining the legality of decisions of the Patent
Reexamination Board including the rejection of an application and invalidation or maintenance of a patent, the court can only refer to the
Examination Guidelines rather than make a judgment based on it.
The Examination Guidelines are legally binding on patent examiners, but
not on courts. In this case, it is possible for a decision made by the Patent
Reexamination Board on the basis of the Examination Guidelines to be held
by the court as unlawful. Examples in judicial practice include the Shu
Xuezhang case[26] and Zeng Zhanchi[27] case in which the courts' decisions on
"double patenting prohibition" and "functional definition" are not consistent or even in conflict with the relevant provisions of the Examination
Guidelines. Second, the Examination Guidelines were enacted to provide
guidance to patent examiners and thus have a limited scope of application.
They serve as bases and standards that patent examiners must refer to and
follow in accepting, examining and granting patents.[28] Apart from patent
examiners, the Examination Guidelines are rarely referred to or considered
by others including patent enforcement agencies, inventors and the general
public and have no binding effects on them. In order to let all other people
including inventors have clear guidance as to whether environmentally
harmful inventions are patentable or not, the relevant provisions prescribed
in the Examination Guidelines must be explicitly included in the PRC
Patent Law or the Detailed Rules for the Implementation of the Patent
Law of the People's Republic of China (Implementation Rules of the PRC
Patent Law).

Another problem is the lack of standard or guidance for the use of the
"morality and *ordre public*" provision. Although the Examination
Guidelines identify the scope of protection by listing certain types of environmental damage, they do not clarify the degree of "seriousness" of environmental damage or meaning of "detriment to the environment," in particular
whether such a detriment means potential detriment or actual detriment or

[25]   Articles 52–3 of Administrative Procedure Law of P. R. China, Order No.16 of the President of
       the P.R. China, 1989, http://en.pkulaw.cn.eproxy1.lib.hku.hk/display.aspx?cgid=4274&lib=law.
[26]   *Jining Pressureless Boiler Factory* v. *Patent Re-examination Board of the State Intellectual
       Property Office and Shu Xuezhang (the third party)* (2008) XTZ No. 3, Supreme People's
       Court of PRC.
[27]   *Zhenyu Company* v. *Zeng Zhanchi* (2006) GMZZ No. 367, Higher People's Court of Beijing.
[28]   Guidelines for Patent Examination, Preamble.

both. In addition, the Chinese patent law does not contain any provisions that mandate, allow or even mention the adoption of the precautionary principle by patent authorities or courts in determining the patentability or invalidation of environmentally harmful inventions. Considering that the harms to the environment and human health are likely to be irreversible and/ or destructive, the precautionary principle should be incorporated into the Chinese patent law to cope with the potential environmental or health crisis in advance of scientific consensus so as to avoid the most costly and painful results.

Finally, the "morality and *ordre public*" provision is rarely used by the Chinese patent authorities or courts in determining the patentability of an environmentally harmful invention in practice. During the author's interview with three examiners, all of them recognized the existence of the "morality and *ordre public*" provision in the PRC Patent Law and understood that public interests included environmental interests. However, they have never rejected a patent application or invalidated a patent based on these provisions. According to the interviewees, there has not been any invention in China yet that was excluded from a patent right merely because of its serious prejudice to the environment. The interviewees gave several reasons. First, the PRC Patent Law does not require the applicant to describe his invention's possible environmental effects in the application documents and thus the applicant normally does not reveal whether his invention is detrimental to the environment; additionally, the examiners are not empowered to demand such a disclosure of environmental impacts. This makes it difficult for patent examiners to figure out an invention's real environmental effects, and they are habitually neglectful of environmental interests in the examination procedures. Second, examiners cannot hold an invention unpatentable unless they have strong reasons for doing so. In practice, examiners are inclined not to exclude an invention from patentability based on its environmental impacts due to the following considerations: most examiners are not environmental experts and thus lack expertise in assessing an invention's environmental effects; no clear standards or guidance are provided under the current patent law regime for examiners to determine whether an invention is "seriously" detrimental to the environment and thus disqualified from patentability; there exist no precedents for examiners to follow or refer to. The interviewed IP judges took a similar stance and stated that an invention was seldom invalidated or excluded from patent right because of its serious prejudice to the environment in judicial practice.

2.3.3 *Criteria of Patentability*

2.3.3.1 Provision

Article 22 of the PRC Patent Law provides for three criteria of patentability – novelty, inventiveness, and practical applicability. Among them, "inventiveness" means that as compared with the prior art, an invention has "prominent substantive features"[29] and "a notable progress";[30] "practical applicability" means that an invention "can be made or used and can produce effective results."[31] It is worth noting that the "notable progress" and "effective results" required by the criteria of "inventiveness" and "practical applicability" can be respectively interpreted as being conducive to green-tech innovation.

Specifically, the term "notable progress" is defined by China's Examination Guidelines as "advantageous technical effects as compared with the prior art."[32] It further interprets the term "advantageous effects" as including, *inter alia*, "saving of energy consumption" and "reparation or cure of environment pollution."[33] The Examination Guidelines also list several circumstances where an invention shall be regarded as producing advantageous technical effects if it, *inter alia*, better "saves energy" or "prevents or controls pollution" as compared with the existing technology.[34] According to this, the environmental impacts of an invention must be considered by patent examiners in assessing whether an invention has "inventiveness" and a "greener" invention shall usually be regarded as producing advantageous technical effects and therefore representing "a notable progress." Also worth mentioning is that the Implementation Rules of the PRC Patent Law requires an invention's advantageous effects by comparison with the technology currently available to be clearly indicated in the patent specification[35] and makes such advantageous effects, including advantageous environmental effects, important criteria "for determining whether an invention represents a notable progress."[36]

As to the term "effective results," the Examination Guidelines defines it as – the economic, technical, or social effects of an invention that "can be expected by a person skilled in the art" and "these effects shall be positive and advantageous." An invention shall be regarded by examiners as having no "practical applicability" and therefore denied patent protection if it lacks "effective results."

[29] Article 22(3) of Patent Law of China.   [30] Ibid.   [31] Ibid., Article 22(4).
[32] Article 2(3), Chapter 4, Part I of Guidelines for Patent Examination.
[33] Ibid., Article 2.2.4 (3), Chapter 2, Part II.   [34] Ibid., Article 3.2.2(1), Chapter 4, Part II.
[35] Article 17(3) of Detailed Rules for the Implementation of the Patent Law of the People's Republic of China, Order No. 569 of the State Council, 2001 (as amended in 2002 and 2010 respectively), http://en.pkulaw.cn.eproxy1.lib.hku.hk/display.aspx?cgid=126176&lib=law#.
[36] Ibid.

Although the PRC Patent Law does not explicitly write down the relationship between "effective results" and "environmental interests," the "effective results" are usually interpreted as covering the preservation of the environment and the prejudice to the environment is recognized as going against them. First, many scholars have interpreted "effective results" as including effective environmental effects.[37] Second, and more importantly, despite the absence of an explanation under the current Chinese patent law, the term "effective results" was clearly defined by the 1993 Examination Guidelines and 2001 Examination Guidelines as covering environmental concerns. The 1993 Examination Guidelines lists several typical examples of "effective results" which include, *inter alia*, energy saving and pollution prevention or control.[38] Moreover, it provides that an invention that seriously pollutes environment or highly consumes energy or natural resources is not producing "effective results" and therefore not having practical applicability.[39] Similarly, the 2001 Examination Guidelines also exclude very environmentally harmful inventions from patent protection by explicitly writing down such inventions as against "effective results" and thus not meeting the patentability criterion of practical applicability.[40] All these indicate that the meaning of "effective results" includes superior environmental effects and an invention's environmental effects must be considered by patent examiners in deciding its practical applicability.

2.3.3.2 Problem and Deficiency

Although the Chinese patent law has already catered for the environmental protection through the inclusion of environmental concerns into the existing criteria of patentability, its impact on green-tech innovation and environmental protection is rather limited, and an invention does not have to be "green" to qualify for patent protection.

---

[37] For example, Wu and Huang state that a highly energy-consuming or serious-pollution invention is not qualified for patent protection because it is not producing "effective results" and therefore not fulfilling the patentability criterion of "practical applicability." In addition, Xu and Tong regard environmental interests as a type of advantageous and positive effects that fall under the category of "effective results." See Boming Wu and Yifen Huang, *Patent Examination* (Beijing: Patent Literature Publishing House, 1994), pp. 287–288. See also Yawen Xu and Haichao Tong, "Obligation of Intellectual Property Law to Protect the Environment" (2012) 12 *Journal of China University of Geosciences* 40–44, pp. 42–43.

[38] Article 2(5), Chapter V, Part II of Guidelines for Patent Examination 1993, Order 4 of the Patent Office of PRC, 1993, www.sipo.gov.cn/zlsqzn/scz/.

[39] Ibid., Article 3(2), Chapter V, Part II.

[40] Article 3(2), Chapter V, Part II of Guidelines for Patent Examination 2001, SIPO, 2001, www.cdpsn.org.cn/policy/dt299l246.htm.

First, the existing patentability criteria's catering for environmental protection is merely interpreted rather than clearly defined. For instance, the term "effective results" is just interpreted as covering environmental effects. Under the current Chinese patent law regime, however, there is no definition or explanation as to whether the meaning of "effective results" includes positive environmental effects or not. The relevant Articles regarding the relationship between "effective results" and environmental effects in the 1993 Examination Guidelines and the 2001 Examination Guidelines were deleted during the later revision of the Examination Guidelines. The 2006 Examination Guidelines and the current 2010 Examination Guidelines do not address this issue any more.

Second, under the Chinese patent law regime, the positive environmental effect is not a criterion that an invention must fulfill in order to be patentable, but only a factor for consideration in assessing an invention's patentability. In other words, an invention does not necessarily have to be "green" in order to be patentable. For instance, a "greener" invention fulfills the requirements of "notable progress" and "effective results," and thus may be granted a patent if it is new and simultaneously meets the other requirements of "inventiveness" and "practical applicability." An environmentally harmful invention, however, may also qualify for patent protection if it can represent a "notable progress" and produce "effective results" in other respects, such as the improvement in quality, the increase of output and the representation of a new trend of technical development.[41] The positive environmental effect is merely one of the circumstances in which an invention can be regarded as meeting some of the requirements of patentability criteria, but it is not the only one or a necessary one. The Examination Guidelines further support this argument by providing that an invention still represents a "notable progress" if it, despite negative effect in a certain respect, "produces outstanding positive technical effects in other respects."[42] In addition, the deletion of relevant Articles that clearly write down the serious prejudice to the environment as contrary to the requirement of "practical application" by the 2006 Examination Guidelines and 2010 Examination Guidelines further make "environmental effect" a less important factor to be considered by examiners in assessing an invention's criteria of patentability.

Third, other than require a complete disclosure of an invention's environmental impacts, the Chinese patent law simply requires the disclosure of an invention's advantageous environmental impacts.

---

[41] Article 3(2), Chapter 4, Part II and Article 2(5), Chapter 5, Part II of Guidelines for Patent Examination.

[42] Ibid., Article 3(2), Chapter 4, Part II.

Fourth, the interview result shows that, in practice, an invention's environmental effects are rarely considered by examiners in determining whether it fulfills the three patentability criteria of "novelty," "inventiveness" and "practical application" due to the relevant vague legal provisions.

2.3.4 Patent Prosecution Process

To stimulate green-tech innovation, the Chinese patent law also gives special administrative advantages to "green" patent applicants, including faster examination of "green" inventions, reduction or postponement of the payment for patent fees and the payment of prizes to innovators who significantly contribute to green-tech advancement. By reducing the time and cost spent on acquiring a green-tech patent and, more importantly, by sending a signal that environmentally beneficial technologies are easier to protect than the harmful ones, these administrative advantages aim to attract more potential inventors to invent "green."

2.3.4.1 Faster Examination of "Green" Inventions

PROVISION. The 2012 Administrative Measures for the Priority Examination of Invention Patent Applications (Measures for Priority Examination) expressly list several types of patent applications that fall within the bounds of priority examination, including, *inter alia*, "applications for important patents involving technologies related to energy conservation, environmental protection" and "applications for important patents conducive to environment-friendly development, such as those related to low-carbon technologies and resource conservation."[43] Such patent applications shall be given priority examination and shall be "concluded within one year of the approval of the applicant's priority examination request."[44] The faster examination process for environmentally friendly inventions takes no more than one year and it is a great saving of time as compared with the normal process that usually takes an applicant around three to four years to obtain a patent.[45] One thing worthy of particular attention is that China gives preferential treatment to all "green" inventions equally, rather than identifying specific "green-tech" sector

---

[43] Articles 4(1) and 4(2) of Administrative Measures for the Priority Examination of Invention Patent Applications, Order No. 65 of the State Intellectual Property Office, 2012, http://en.pkulaw.cn.eproxy1.lib.hku.hk/display.aspx?cgid=177648&lib=law.

[44] Ibid., Article 2.

[45] He Jun, "From Green Technology to Green Patent – Whether a Special Patent System for Addressing Climate Change Is Needed" (2010) 20 *Intellectual Property* 37–41, p. 41.

priorities, so as to promote the innovation of various types of environmentally beneficial technologies. In addition to "green" inventions, some other types of inventions also fall within the bounds of priority examination, such as inventions involving technologies related to new generation information, biology, high-end equipment manufacturing and new materials, and inventions that are of significance to the national interest or public interest.[46]

PROBLEM AND DEFICIENCY. A possible side effect of the faster examination of priority inventions is that it may slow the examination speed of other non-priority inventions and cause a patent backlog in other technological sectors. Applicants in other technological areas may have to "wait longer for responses because, when accelerated patents jump up the waitlist, other patents, by default, are moved down the waitlist."[47] Possible ways to address this issue include hiring new examiners, training current examiners to raise their working efficiency, and setting a limit to the maximum number of applications subject to priority examination. According to the interviewed patent examiners, none of these measures had been taken by the SIPO to balance the workload and avoid an increase of patent backlog in other technology sectors. However, so far the examination speed of inventions in other fields has not been influenced. Two reasons are given by the interviewed patent examiners. First, given the program of faster examination is rather new in China, there are not many applications filed under this program. Second, although no examiners are hired specifically for the purpose of implementing the Measures for Priority Examination, China has established several Patent Examination Assistance Centers since 2011 to recruit new examiners and cope with the dramatic increase of patent applications in recent years. Therefore, at present, the problem of patent backlog is not serious in China. With the development of this program and an increase of applications for faster examination, the problem of a longer patent examination time for other non-priority inventions may occur which deserves further attention.

2.3.4.2 Reduction or Postponement of Patent Fees

PROVISION. The Chinese patent law does not contain any provisions in relation to a reduction or postponement of the patent fee for "green"

[46] Measures for Priority Examination, Article 4.
[47] Kate Nuehring, "Our Generation's Sputnik Moment: Comparing the United States' Green Technology Pilot Program to Green Patent Programs Abroad" (2011) 9 *Northwestern Journal of Technology and Intellectual Property* 609–628.

inventions, but provides for a general reduction or postponement of payment where an applicant or patentee has difficulty in paying patent prosecution fees.[48] In particular, the Measures for the Reduction or Postponement of the Payment of Patent Fees (Measures for Reduction or Postponement of Patent Fees) set down the conditions and requirements for the application for a reduction or postponement of patent fees in detail. For example, it provides for the scope of patent fees subject to a reduction or postponement, including the application fee (wherein the publishing and printing fee and the associate application fee shall not be reduced or postponed), annual fee (within three years as of the year when patent right is granted), and fees for the substantive examination and reexamination of an invention patent under application.[49] Furthermore, it stipulates for the specific percentage of payment for reduction or postponement on the basis of the various types of the patent fees and the various types of applicants or patentees.[50] All these provisions are applicable to "green" inventions. Where a "green" patent holder or applicant has difficulty in paying the patent fees, he may apply for a partial reduction or postponement of the application fee, annual fee or fees for the substantive examination or reexamination.

PROBLEM AND DEFICIENCY. Although the Chinese patent law provides for a general reduction or postponement of patent fees in some situations, it does not contain any provisions with respect to a special reduction or postponement of patent fees for "green" inventions. A close look at the patent fees of China shows that they are indeed not high, at least not high enough to be unaffordable for the general green-tech innovators. In addition, according to the interviewed patent examiners, payment reduction or postponement is quite common in practice, and most of such applications can be approved by the Chinese patent authorities. It seems that it does not matter very much whether

---

[48] Article 100 of Implementation Rules of the Patent Law of China. Article 100 provides that "[w]here an applicant or patentee has difficulty in paying the various fees provided in these Rules, he/it may, in accordance with relevant provisions, submit a request to the administrative department for patent under the State Council, requesting reduction or postponement of payment."

[49] Article 3 of Measures for the Reduction or Postponement of the Payment of Patent Fees, Order of the State Intellectual Property Office, No. 39, 2006, http://en.pkulaw.cn.eproxy1.lib .hku.hk/display.aspx?cgid=80820&lib=law. Actually, Article 3 also subjects the maintenance fee for invention patents under application to a reduction or postponement, but such a fee has already been canceled during the amendment of the Implementation Rules of the Patent Law of China in 2010. The mistake should be taken seriously and the Measures for the Payment of Patent Fees should be updated according to the newly amended Implementation Rules of the Patent Law of China.

[50] Ibid., Article 4.

China provides for a special reduction or postponement of the patent fees for "green" inventions besides the existing general provisions. In the author's view, however, reducing the cost spent on acquiring a "green" patent is not only for the purpose of subsidizing "green" innovators having difficulty in paying the patent application fees, but also and more importantly, for the purpose of sending a signal that "green" patents are easier to obtain than "non-green" ones and environmentally beneficial technologies are easier to protect than the harmful ones, thus attracting more potential inventors to invent "green." In view of this, it is important to include special provisions aimed primarily at reducing or postponing patent fees for "green" inventions into the Chinese patent law.

2.3.4.3 Payment of Prizes

PROVISION. The Chinese patent law also incentivizes green-tech innovation by awarding prizes to the innovators who significantly contribute to green-tech advancement. For instance, Measures of Guangzhou Municipality for the Administration of Patent Prize empowers the patent authorities to award a prize to the patentee whose patent proves to be important in preserving the environment and/or saving energy during the exploitation.[51] The Measures of Beijing Municipality for the Administration of Invention Patent Prize provides for certain types of invention patents qualified for monetary award, including, *inter alia*, the invention patents significantly contributing to energy saving and/or emission reduction.[52]

In addition to prizes, subsidies are given to patent applicants for the purpose of promoting technological innovation and development. The most common conditions that an application must fulfill in order to qualify for a subsidy include, *inter alia*, foreign patent applications, applications with bright market prospects and applications falling within the priority technical fields or industries. For instance, the Chinese Ministry of Finance issued Measures for the Administration of Special Funds for Subsidizing Foreign Patent Applications in 2012, which provide that special funds shall be set up for subsidizing domestic applicants in paying fees when applying for foreign

[51] Article 9(3) of Measures of Guangzhou Municipality for the Administration of Patent Prize, Order No. 37 of Guangzhou People's Municipal Government, 2010, www.gz.gov.cn/public files/business/htmlfiles/gzgov/s8263/201009/614659.html.
[52] Article 5(2) of Measures of Beijing Municipality for the Administration of Invention Patent Prize, [2007]33, General Office, Beijing People's Municipal Government, www.most.gov.cn /kjzc/kjzcdfgz/dfzcbj/200804/t20080403_60313.htm.

patents.[53] The Measures of Beijing Municipality for the Administration of Funds for Subsidizing Patent Applications provide that applicants whose inventions fall within this municipality's strategic emerging industries or priority technical field shall get prioritized access to subsidy.[54] Considering that China has made a policy priority of developing low-carbon and energy-saving technologies, the "green" patent applicants are normally qualified for such subsidies in practice. It is also noteworthy that most subsidies are awarded without imposing the requirement that the subsidy receivers must have difficulty in paying the patent fees, which makes the subsidy a special type of reward for innovative activities.

PROBLEM AND DEFICIENCY. The provisions pertaining to the award of prizes to "green" innovators merely exist in local regulations and rules. So far, no such provisions have been included in the PRC Patent Law or other national patent regulations or rules. Although national prizes have been created by the SIPO in practice, they are not specifically set up for "green" innovators. Since 1989, SIPO has held the Chinese Patentee Award every two years (before 2010) or annually (since 2010) to pay tribute to the patentees whose inventions play an important role in driving technological progress, promoting economic growth and shaping society. Thousands of patentees have been awarded prizes under this scheme, including those whose inventions are significantly conducive to green-tech progress and environmental enhancement. Likewise, there exist no special provisions aimed primarily at subsidizing "green" patent applicants, at least no such provisions at the national level.

2.4 THE GREENING OF PATENT LAW

As previously discussed, the Chinese patent law has already catered for green-tech innovation, but in an implicit way and to a rather limited extent. To address the deficiencies and make the Chinese patent law more environmentally friendly and conducive to the green-tech innovation, the author suggests the adoption of the following measures to further "green" the Chinese patent law.

---

[53] Article 3 of Notice of the Ministry of Finance on Issuing Measures for the Administration of Special Funds for Subsidizing Foreign Patent Applications, No. 147 [2012] of the Ministry of Finance, http://en.pkulaw.cn.eproxy1.lib.hku.hk/display.aspx?cgid=175211&lib=law.

[54] Article 10 of Measures of Beijing Municipality for the Administration of Funds for Subsidizing Patent Applications, [2014]178, Intellectual Property Bureau and Finance Department, Beijing People's Municipal Government, www.bjipo.gov.cn/zwxx/zwgg/201410/t20141020_32 950.html.

2.4.1 *The "Greening" of Aim of Patent Law*

Although Article 1 of the PRC Patent Law sets out its goal as "promoting scientific and technological progress as well as the economic and social development,[55] it does not make it clear whether the terms "progress" and "social development" cover higher social values and broader social welfare, and more specifically, whether they cover environmental interests. For legal certainty, the aim of patent law can be clarified by taking either of the options. First, Article 1 of the PRC Patent Law can be expressly written to state the pursuit of sustainable development as one goal of the patent law. The wording of this amended Article could be something like this: "This law is enacted for the purpose of . . . promoting scientific and technological progress as well as the economic and social development, in particular with a view to serving higher social values and promoting sustainable development." The second option is for Article 1 to remain unchanged, but define the "progress" and "social development" as covering higher social values and broader social good including the protection and enhancement of the environment in the Examination Guidelines or preferably in the Implementation Rules of the PRC Patent Law. To address the issues in the relevant provisions on the aim of patent law that have rarely been considered or even noticed by patent examiners and judges, measures must be taken to raise the awareness of patent authorities, courts and innovators that the "progress" and "development" can and should be interpreted as including higher social values and broader social welfare rather than only the technological progress and economic development, and that "the ultimate objective of patent laws, however, is to benefit society."[56] In practice, it is important for the patent office or court to set an example in denying or invalidating a patent because it is detrimental to the environment and thus contradicts the broadly defined aim of patent law. Until then, the aim of the Chinese patent law will remain effective only in theory.

2.4.2 *The "Greening" of Patentable Subject Matter*

A "morality and *ordre public*" provision[57] has been included in the PRC Patent Law, but it fails to write down the serious prejudice to the environment as

[55] Article 1 of Patent Law of China.
[56] Cole. M. Fauver, "Comment: Compulsory Patent Licensing in the United States: An Idea Whose Time Has Come" (1998) 8 *Northwestern Journal of International Law & Business* 666–685, p. 666.
[57] Article 5 of Patent Law of China. Article 5 provides that "[n]o patent shall be granted for an invention that contravenes any law or social moral or that is detrimental to public interests."

contrary to public interests and therefore fails to expressly exclude environmentally harmful inventions from patent rights. Although the term "public interests" can be interpreted as covering environmental interests, such an interpretation is not as effective as an express exclusion of "non-green" inventions from patentability by law. For legal certainty, either of the following approaches can be taken. First, also ideally, the "morality and *ordre public*" provision can be amended to clearly write down the serious prejudice to the environment as against public interests so as to expressly exclude from patentability inventions likely to cause a serious detriment to the environment. Second, the "morality and *ordre public*" provision remains unchanged; instead, a new Article can be added to the Implementation Rules of the PRC Patent Law to expressly define public interests as covering environmental interests. There exist possibilities that the environmentally harmful inventions deprived of patent rights fall into the public domain and damage the environment to a greater extent. This, however, may occur simply in the short term. In the long run, the exclusion of environmentally harmful inventions from patentability will improve "environmental consciousness" of potential innovators and redirect future technological development in a more environmentally favorable way. More importantly, given the withdrawal of eventual profit, the level of money and funding flowing into the innovation and development of environmentally harmful technologies will substantially dwindle, thus addressing the technology-related environmental damage at its source.

In addition, to facilitate the use of "morality and *ordre public*" provision, clear standards must be established ideally by the PRC Patent Law or by the Implementation Rules of the PRC Patent Law. The author proposes to use environmental standards as yardsticks to assess the degree of "seriousness." In other words, whether an invention meets environmental standards should become a major consideration when deciding whether an invention's detriment to the environment is serious. No patent shall be granted for any invention that fails to satisfy the national environmental standards such as the national discharge standards of pollutants and the national energy conservation standards. As to those inventions whose exploitation or use may involve environmental standards stricter than the national ones, for example stricter local environmental standards and environmental standards for nature reserves, they must simultaneously meet the stricter environmental standards. Given that the formulation of environmental standards has taken various considerations into account including the environmental carrying capacity, environmental self-repair capacity, social-economic conditions and technical capability, it would be a practical and effective means to use environmental standards to assess the degree of "seriousness." Moreover, for legal certainty, it is important for the PRC Patent Law or the Implementation Rules of the PRC Patent Law to explicitly write down whether the detriment to the environment means potential detriment or actual detriment or both. In the author's view, in order to mitigate the possible environmental harms caused by new technologies to the most degree, the detriment should include both actual and potential detriment. Specifically, no patent shall be granted for any invention that is known, or strongly suspected, to cause a serious detriment to the environment.[58]

Finally, the precautionary principle should be incorporated into the Chinese patent law – ideally the PRC Patent Law or the Implementation Rules of the PRC Patent Law – to address the environmentally risky inventions. Actually, the exclusion of very environmentally harmful inventions from patentability itself is a practical and effective means of incorporating a form of the precautionary principle into the Chinese patent law. In this way, the Chinese patent law will provide no patent incentive to develop technologies known, or strongly suspected, to produce harmful environmental impacts.[59] As highlighted by Kolitch, all environmentally harmful inventions must be excluded from patentability not only "during the era of scientific certainty with respect to the invention's impacts,"[60] but also during times of scientific uncertainty, "if scientific evidence suggest a strong possibility of potential harm, and a risk assessment indicates that this possibility outweighs the putative economic benefits of providing a patent incentive to develop the technology."[61] Aside from the explicit exclusion of inventions deemed seriously detrimental to the environment from patentability by law, the patent authorities and courts must take a precautionary approach to determining the patentability of environmentally harmful inventions under the morality and *ordre public* provisions. In addition, given shifting the burden of proof is one of the three archetypal versions of the precautionary principle, it is important to include in the Chinese patent law that the burden of proof shall be shifted to the party "that will benefit from the activity and that is most likely to have the information"[62] when an activity poses threats of harm to the environment.

[58] Shawn Kolitch, "The Environmental and Public Health Impacts of U.S. Patent Law: Making the Case for Incorporating a Precautionary Principle" (2006) 36 *Environmental Law* 221–256, p. 222.
[59] Ibid.   [60] Ibid., 254.   [61] Ibid., 256.
[62] Peter L. deFur, "The Precautionary Principle: Application to Policies Regarding Endocrine-Disrupting Chemicals," in Carol Raffensperger and Joel Tickner (eds.), *Protecting Public Health and the Environment: Implementing the Precautionary Principle* (Washington, DC: Island Press, 1999), 327–348, pp. 345–346.

Specifically, in case of determination of an invention's potential detriment to the environment, it should not be the patent authority, but the inventor who should take the burden to prove that his invention is not environmentally harmful and meets the environmental standards. Similarly, in opposition proceedings before patent authorities or courts to determine whether to invalidate an environmentally risky invention or not, the patent authorities or courts should require the patentee to provide evidence that the invention is environmentally safe rather than to require the opponent to establish that the invention is not safe. Given that the Chinese law has explicitly mandated the reversal of the burden of the proof in deciding environmental tort cases,[63] it is practically possible and necessary to incorporate this approach into the Chinese patent law to determine the patentability of environmentally harmful inventions under the morality and *ordre public* provisions.

2.4.3 *The "Greening" of Criteria of Patentability*

First of all, for legal certainty and legal effect, ideally the PRC Patent Law or the Implementation Rules of the PRC Patent Law should make it clear that the term "notable progress" required by the criterion of "inventiveness" includes a notable progress in the environmental performance and the term "effective results" required by the criterion of "practical applicability" includes advantageous environmental effects. In this way, an invention shall be regarded as satisfying the requirements of "notable progress" and "effective results" respectively if its environmental performance is superior to that of the prior art and if it has advantageous environmental effects. Such an extension of the meaning of the existing patentability criteria to include environmental concerns can help to prevent an invention's environmental harms and improve its environmental performance to some extent.

---

[63] For instance, Article 66 of the Tort Law of the People's Republic of China provides that "[w]here any dispute arises over an environmental pollution, the polluter shall assume the burden to prove that it should not be liable or its liability could be mitigated under certain circumstances as provided for by law or to prove that there is no causation between its conduct and the harm." See Article 66 of Tort Law of the People's Republic of China, Decree No. 21 of the President of PRC, 2009, http://en.pkulaw.cn.eproxy1.lib.hku.hk/display.aspx?cgi d=125300&lib=law. Similarly, Article 4 (3) of Some Provisions of the Supreme People's Court on Evidence in Civil Procedures provides for the reversal of the burden of proof in environmental tort cases by stating that "[i]n a compensation lawsuit for damages caused by environmental pollution, the infringing party shall be responsible for producing evidence to prove the existence of exemptions of liabilities as provided in laws or that there is no causal relationship between the his act and the harmful consequences." See Some Provisions of the Supreme People's Court on Evidence in Civil Procedures, Document No. [2001]33, Supreme People's Court, http://en.pkulaw.cn.eproxy1.lib.hku.hk/display.aspx?cgid=38083&lib=law.

Second, it is important for the PRC Patent Law or the Implementation Rules of the PRC Patent Law to make the disclosure of information pertaining to an invention's environmental impacts as "the *quid pro quo* for the patent grant."[64] Specifically, besides the disclosure of technical information, a patent applicant must clearly and completely write down the potential environmental impacts of the claimed invention in the patent specification, including both the advantageous impacts and negative impacts.[65] Patent authorities can reject a patent application on the ground that an invention's environmental impacts are not disclosed or not appropriately disclosed in conformity with the statutory requirements.[66] The environmental information that is required to be disclosed may include: an invention's basic environmental information such as the materials, types and amounts of pollutants emitted, and types and amounts of energy consumed; the potential environmental impacts should the invention be exploited; the alternative methods of preventing or mitigating the environmental harm; and, if any, the advantageous environmental performance as compared with the prior art. After being examined, the certified environmental information of the issued patent becomes part of a constantly updated valuable databank "which will greatly reduce the difficulty of environmental impact assessment" and improve the "greenness" of innovation.[67] Considering that patent specifications are open to all, besides inventors, patent examiners and potential innovators, there is indeed a wider range of possible user groups of the disclosed environmental information such as researchers, consumers and environmental NGOs, which will raise the environmental consciousness of the public, "lead to changes in behavior and decision-making,"[68] and promote the dissemination of the green-tech information.

Finally, should the proposed examination of an invention's environmental impacts become statutory requirement, it would require a new patent examination department/section of "Environmental Impact" or, at least,

---

[64] Carolyn Abbot and David Booton, "Using Patent Law's Teaching Function to Introduce an Environmental Ethic into the Process of Technical Innovation" (2009) 21 *The Georgetown International Environmental Law Review* 219–255, p. 232.

[65] Ibid.

[66] As the current practice, patent authorities will require the patent applicant who fails to disclose or appropriately disclose the claimed invention's environmental impacts to state his/its opinions or rectify his/its application at the stage of the preliminary examination. The application shall be rejected only when the patent authorities still consider the environmental specification not in conformity with the statutory requirements after the applicant has stated opinions or made rectifications.

[67] Mu-Yen Hsu, "Green Patent: Promoting Innovation for Environment by the Patent System," in *Proceeding of Portland International Center for Management of Engineering and Technology* (Oregon: PICMET, 2007), 2491–2497, p. 2494.

[68] Abbot and Booton, "Patent Law's Teaching Function," 245.

environmental experts as examiners to fulfill the job. In light of this, the author suggests that the Patent Office of SIPO consider training and/or hiring new examiners with specialized environmental expertise to prepare for the future needs. Another benefit of doing this is that it would help current Chinese patent law be implemented in a way more favorable to the green-tech innovation and environmental advancement. Actually, several aspects of the current Chinese patent law have already catered for environmental protection in principle, but the environmental impacts of an invention are routinely ignored by patent examiners in practice partly due to their lack of environmental awareness and environmental knowledge. Training and/or hiring new examiners with professional environmental knowledge may make up for this deficiency.

2.4.4 *The "Greening" of Patent Prosecution*

The Chinese patent prosecution process can be further "greened" through the adoption of the following measures.

First, the Patent Office of SIPO must pay close attention to the implementation of Measures for Priority Examination, especially to whether the faster examination of priority inventions (including environmentally beneficial inventions) would slow the examination speed of other non-priority inventions. Should this take place or be likely to take place, the Patent Office of SIPO must take measures to balance the workload and garner necessary resources, including hiring new examiners, training the current examiners to raise their working efficiency, limiting the number of applications that can be fast-tracked, and reducing the types of inventions qualified for a faster examination.

Second, with the development of China's priority examination program and the increase of "green" patent applications and certified "green" patents, SIPO should take advantage of the environmental information to establish a "green" patent database that allows users to exclusively search for "green" patent applications and "green" patents under this program. Given that all patent applications have been uploaded to SIPO's Patent Search and Service System (PSSS), it is feasible for SIPO to create such a new feature under the PSSS to allow the exclusive search for patent applications and issued patents for "green" inventions. Such a "green" patent database would enable society to have easier access to green-tech information "without having to wade through all the applications and patents" at the PSSS of SIPO.[69]

---

[69] Nuehring, "Our Generation's Sputnik Moment," 627.

Third, special provisions aimed primarily at reducing or postponing patent fees for "green" inventions can be incorporated into the Implementation rules of the PRC Patent Law and fleshed out by the Measures for Reduction or Postponement of Patent Fees to allow a further reduction or postponement of patent fees for "green" inventors based on their application. As to the exact percentage or types of patent fees that can be reduced or postponed, this is not very important because the Chinese patent fees are actually not high, and the proposal for reducing or postponing patent fees for "green" inventions is not merely for the purpose of subsidizing "green" innovators having difficulty in paying the patent fees but, more importantly, for the purpose of attracting potential inventors to invent "green." For the same reason, special provisions aimed primarily at awarding prizes or subsidies to innovators having significantly contributed to green-tech innovation and dissemination should be included in the Chinese patent law both at the national level or local level.

Fourth, given that the "greening" of the Chinese patent law will inevitably necessitate increased participation of environmental experts in various stages of the patent prosecution process, a cooperation mechanism between the SIPO and the Ministry of Environmental Protection of PRC (MEP) can be established to provide patent examiners with much-needed expertise on environmental knowledge and science.

Finally, Article 2 of the Implementation Rules of the PRC Patent Law provides that all formalities "shall be fulfilled in a written form or another form provided by the administrative department for patents under the State Council."[70] The PRC Patent Law also specifies the use of a written form by a patent applicant for claiming the right to priority,[71] waiving his or its patent,[72] and assigning "the right to apply for a patent or a patent right."[73] The written form is the main form for fulfilling the formalities required by the Chinese patent law. Given the dramatic increase of the patent applications in recent years, paper filing has caused a waste of large amounts of paper, which is in itself environmentally harmful. To address this issue, the electronic filing of patent applications and documents should be encouraged and relevant conditions be created to realize a change of patent prosecution from a paper-intensive process to a paperless process. The United States Patent and Trademark Office's (USPTO) experience in promoting an electronic patent application can be used for reference. The USPTO developed an electronic filing system (EFS-Web) that allows a simple, safe and secure filing of patent applications and documents, and gives an applicant "all of the same benefits as

[70]   Article 2 of Implementation Rules of the Patent Law of China.
[71]   Article 30(10) of Patent Law of China.   [72]   Ibid., Section 2(44).   [73]   Ibid., Article 10(10).

paper filings, including an electronic receipt that acknowledges [his] submission date."[74] Moreover, the USPTO requires an additional USD 400 non-electronic filing fee (USD 200 if the applicant qualifies as a small entity or a micro entity) for each utility application filed in paper,[75] which provides applicants with incentives to submit electronic patent applications and documents.

2.4.5 The "Greening" of Mind

Most Chinese laws are progressive in principle, "but at the stage of implementation,"[76] the "power" of law "weakens considerably."[77] Therefore, besides the "greening" of the Chinese patent law, it is also important to "green" the minds of the people who interpret or implement the law. In order to engage all sectors of the society in a concerted effort to innovate "green," produce "green" and consume "green," the minds of innovators, consumers, entrepreneurs and even the public should be "greened." Good practices in this regard must be publicized and encouraged. One example of such a good practice is the case of *Wuhan Jingyuan Environmental Engineering Co., Ltd. v. Japanese Fuji of the Water Co., Ltd. and Huayang Electric Industry Co., Ltd* (Jingyuan case). In this case, the court decided "not to apply permanent injunction out of consideration of the factor of environmental interests."[78] This is a landmark case in China because for the first time, the court made environmental interest trump monopoly right by not enjoining the infringer from using a patented technology. In deciding the Jingyuan case, the Fujian Higher People's Court concluded that given "installation of flue-gas desulfurization devices in a thermal plant conformed to the essential national environment protection policy and the industrial policy, was conducive to building up an environmentally friendly society and produced good social benefits,"[79] that the "power supply had direct impact on the local

---

74 USPTO, "About EFS-Web," www.uspto.gov/patents/process/file/efs/.
75 USPTO, "United States Patent and Trademark Office Fee Schedule," www.uspto.gov/web/offices/ac/qs/ope/fee031913.htm.
76 Hannes Veinla, "Scope and Substance of the Integration Principle in EC Law and Its Application in Estonia" (2008) XV *Juridical International* 4–13, p. 9.
77 Ibid.
78 Meng Pu, Wu Yuhe, Xiong Yanfeng, Li Jiang, Cheng Miao, Li Rongxin and Liu Feifei, "Latest Developments in Application of Permanent Injunction as Remedy against Patent Infringement" (2010) 2 *China Patents and Trademarks* 3–16, p. 15.
79 Ibid., pp. 13–14. See also *Wuhan Jingyuan Environmental Engineering Co., Ltd. v. Japanese Fuji of the Water Co., Ltd. and Huayang Electric Industry Co., Ltd.*, Judgment of Fujian Higher People's Court, No. (2001) Minzhichuzi 4, May 12, 2008.

economy and life of the local people,"[80] and "ceasing use of the devices would have adverse effects on the local economy and life of the local people."[81] Clearly, environmental interests were considered by courts in deciding the Jingyuan case. Hopefully, this landmark case would set an example to judges, patent examiners and attorneys and encourage them to take environmental interests into consideration. Another example is the Eco-Patent Commons, "launched by IBM, Nokia, Pitney Bowes and Sony in partnership with the WBCSD" in January 2008.[82] The Eco-Patent Commons is a pool of "green" patents pledged by patent owners for free use by anyone without royalty. It was designed to facilitate the dissemination of existing patented green-tech and "encourage collaboration for new innovation through an online collection of environmentally beneficial patents."[83] Although there has not been any Chinese business dedicating its patented invention to the public domain so far, the Eco-Patent Commons provides useful ideas for China to consider in developing its own ways to "green" the Chinese patent law and the mind of the people that can only be achieved "step by step" rather than a "great leap forward."

2.5 CONCLUSION

China is the most populous nation, the largest developing country with relatively high levels of poverty, the fastest-growing economy and one of the world's most polluted countries. Its sustainable development and environmental improvement depends very much on the innovation of green-tech, and the successful development of green-tech depends very much on a properly designed patent law system that incentivizes green-tech innovation to the greatest extent, i.e. the "greening" of the Chinese patent law.

At the current stage, it is not yet to be known whether or when or to what extent the measures proposed in this chapter shall be adopted or considered. One of the biggest obstacles to the adoption of the proposals is the absence of precedents for China to follow. Given the idea of "greening" patent law to stimulate green-tech innovation is rather recent, the US, the EU and even the whole international community haven't yet taken any effective measures in this regard. This may discourage China's adoption of the proposals since the Chinese patent law is more inclined to mirror the US or European patent law

---

[80] Pu et al., "Latest Developments," p. 14.   [81] Ibid., p. 14.
[82] WBCSD, "Eco-Patent Commons," www.wbcsd.org/work-program/capacity-building/eco
      -patent-commons.aspx.
[83] Eco-Patent Commons, "The Eco-Patent Commons," http://ecopatentcommons.org/.

or follow their practices on important issues.[84] Nevertheless, if China chooses to fulfill its commitment to sustainable development, to embark on a path to industrialization featuring high technology, good economic returns, and low resource-consumption and environmental pollution, to meet its ambitious targets for energy conservation and emissions reduction, and to become a world leader in green-tech field, it must make every effort to promote the innovation of technologies that benefit the environment. One way that this can be encouraged is by taking any of these proposals. Considering green-tech's particular significance to China's environmental improvement and the fierce global race for green growth, every day the patent law is hindered from serving environmental goals is another day we harm our planet and another day lost in stimulating green-tech innovation.[85]

It is worthy of mentioning that the proposals per se "should be seen as a prolegomenon to discussion, rather than providing any positive conclusions."[86] The key elements influencing the adoption of any of these proposals must be thoroughly examined, which deserves further theoretical and empirical research. Due to the lack of ripe experience and successful precedents for China to follow, gradual changes to the relevant aspects of the Chinese law are preferred to radical reforms. Attempts to adopt any of the proposals may initially take the form of a pilot program or be confined to a smaller area if needed. Indeed, some of the proposals might not be able to be approached in a short-term perspective and can only be regarded as China's long-term goals.

---

[84] Yahong Li, *Imitation to Innovation in China: The Role of Patents in Biotechnology and Pharmaceutical Industries* (Cheltenham: Edward Elgar Publishing Limited, 2010), p. 98.

[85] USPTO, "Green Patent Report Summary," April 26, 2012, www.uspto.gov/patents/init_events /green_report_summary20120426.pdf. Michael Bowman, "The USPTO Green Tech Program: Guidepost for the Future," February 4, 2013, www.ipwatchdog.com/2013/02/04/the -uspto-green-tech-program-guidepost-for-the-future/id=34450/.

[86] Brad Sherman and Nicola Atkinson, "Intellectual Property and Environmental Protection" (1991) 13 *European Intellectual Property Review* 165–170, p. 170.

3

Traditional Chinese Medicines and Patent Law
Incompatibilities and Remedies

Yifu Chen

3.1 INTRODUCTION

Traditional Chinese Medicine (TCM), a parallel of the concept of Western medicine, is a medical style based on a unique Chinese medical theory characterized by concepts like *Qi (气)*, *Yin & Yang (阴/阳)*, Five Elements, and *Bian Zheng Lun Zhi (辨证论治)*,[1] and by a medicinal therapy derived from animal, mineral and plant sources.[2] As a medical system, TCM is evolving and capable of innovation.

Patenting of TCM inventions has shown a significant growth over the past two decades. Ever since the revision in 1993 of the Patent Law of the People's Republic of China (PRC), when the drug patent system was opened to the public, applications for and approval of TCM patents have been on the rise. According to a research report of China IP Studies, the number of TCM patents application exceeded 1,000 in 1993, and 3,000 in 2001.[3] In 2008, 7,374 TCM patents were granted.[4] The number of TCM patents granted in 2011 exceeded 8,000. However, in countries and regions beyond the PRC, TCM patents are also on the rise. According to research on the data of the Derwent Innovations Index (DII), by 2008, there were 3,369 herbal medicine patents/patent applications in total in the US, 9,709 in Japan, and 26,927 in the PRC.[5] Compared with the large number of TCM patents/patent applications inside China, patent applications for herbal medicines outside China are relatively

[1] Zhanwen Liu, "The Philosophical Aspects of Chinese Medicine from a Chinese Medicine Academician," in Kelvin Chan and Henry Lee (eds.), *The Way Forward for Chinese Medicine* (Taylor & Francis, 2002), pp. 23–50.
[2] Kelvin Chan, "The Historical Evolution of Chinese Medicine and Orthodox Medicine in China," in Chan and Lee (eds.), *The Way Forward for Chinese Medicine*, pp. 1–22.
[3] China IP Studies Association, *Patent Technologies in Various Industries: Present and Development Trend Report 2007–2008* (Beijing Science Press, 2008), p. 10.
[4] Ibid.   [5] Ibid.

scarce. Taking the US as an example, according to inquiry results on the patent database of the United States Patent and Trademark Office (USPTO), TCM formulae applications there numbered only 21 in 2011.[6] Explanations have been offered from a variety of perspectives. An important one is the incompatibility of patent systems and TCM inventions. TCM medical culture is more recognized in China and in Asia, and to a large extent, medical differences influence the judgment of novelty, practicality and inventiveness in patent examination. In addition, it is also implied that the TCM market exists mainly in countries and regions strongly influenced by Chinese culture. Of the patents approved in China, only 0.72 percent were from overseas applicants, and only 195 out of 333 service-invention patents considered to have relatively high technical content were from overseas applicants.[7]

The current patent system has been developed and designed to mainly suit chemical pharmaceuticals, which inevitably gives rise to compatibility problems with TCM as a distinct medical practice to Western pharmaceuticals. This chapter argues that the conflict between patent law and TCM has been caused by the way that the patent applications for TCM are examined, that is, the examinations are conducted based on the terms of reference designed for chemical pharmaceuticals, not for TCM. To solve this conflict, this chapter proposes that it can be remedied with an industry-specific amendment of patent policy that can accommodate the inventions and innovations of the TCM industry.

3.2 BASIC CHARACTERISTICS AND THEORIES OF TCM

Controversy persists in academic circles about the appropriate extension of the concept of "traditional Chinese medicine." TCM is often conceptualized in the narrow sense of "the traditional medicine of the Han Chinese," and thus refers only to the medical practices developed by the Han Chinese.[8] In its broader sense, the concept of TCM incorporates the medical practices of the Han Chinese and other Chinese nationalities.[9] Both the traditional medicine of the Han Chinese and that of minor Chinese nationalities treat the human

---

[6] Patent search at USPTO online database: the search key words were "Chinese medicine," and the area searched was the granted patent-report abstracts section.

[7] China IP Studies Association, *Patent Technologies in Various Industries*, p. 12.

[8] Xiaoting Song, *Legal Protection of the Intellectual Property of Traditional Chinese Medicine* (Intellectual Property Publishing House, 2008), p. 5.

[9] Tonghua Liu and Shiying Xiao, *The 12th Special Topic of Outline of the National Intellectual Property Strategy, Protection and Use of Intellectual Property of Traditional Chinese Medicine: Analysis of the Traditional Chinese Drug Market Both at Home and Abroad*, 2nd edition (The Press of Traditional Chinese medicine Science and Technology, 2005), p. 3.

body as a whole, and share many other medicinal characteristics. Their common theoretical basis and medicinal compositions give rise to the same issues of patentability. In practice, due to the exchange and integration of medical practices, it is sometimes impossible to differentiate the practices of the traditional medicine of the Han Chinese and that of Chinese minorities. For the purpose of discussing the relationships of TCM and international patent law, this chapter adopts the definition of TCM in its broader sense. Some special characteristics of the traditional medicine of the Chinese minorities will also be discussed with regard to patentability.

TCM has existed and evolved in China and other regions of the world over several thousand years, but the term "Traditional Chinese Medicine" emerged as a concept less than a century ago. The usage of "TCM" first appeared in an English magazine to differentiate the medical practices of the Chinese from those of "Western medicine." TCM and Western medicine are profoundly different in both theory and practice. For example, TCM treats the human body as an integrated whole, and the medicines applied are mostly TCM medicines with complicated chemical ingredients, while Western medicine emphasizes the study of the structures and functions of the various organs of the human body, and treats patients with medicines of clearly defined chemical structure.

From the perspective of medical practice, TCM refers to disease prevention, diagnosis, and treatment, as well as to rehabilitation in accordance with TCM theory.[10] TCM theory and TCM medication are the inseparable components of the TCM concept. The theoretical basis of TCM forms its own unique system. In TCM theory, the basic and most important concepts are the treatment of the human body as a whole, and syndrome identification and treatment differentiation.[11] TCM drugs are mainly the TCM material resources (prepared crude drugs) and TCM *yinpian* (饮片) (raw materials). These are generally regarded as the pillars of the TCM industry.[12] TCM drugs are applied under the guidance of TCM theory. The modern TCM industry has refined the processes of the production of traditional Chinese drugs, thereby bringing TCM extracts into being. TCM theory and TCM drugs are interrelated concepts, with TCM theory being the theoretical guide, and TCM drugs its material expression.

[10]   Deguang Wan, *Research of Quality for Traditional Chinese Medicine-Theory, Methodology and Practice* (Shanghai Science & Art Press, 2008), p. 3.
[11]   Expert Committee for Professional Technical Qualification Tests, The State Administration Bureau for Traditional Chinese Medicine (eds.),*Traditional Chinese Medicine (Junior)* (The China Press of Traditional Chinese Medicine, 2010), p. 105.
[12]   Wan, *Research of Quality for Traditional Chinese Medicine-Theory*, p. 3.

3.3 INCOMPATIBILITIES BETWEEN TCM AND PATENT LAW

3.3.1 *Overview of the Issues of Incompatibility*

The compatibilities between TCM and patent law can be observed from various aspects of patent law, for instance, patentable subject matter, scope of patent right, and the three criteria of patentability.

The patent practices of countries usually define the patentable subject matter by excluding the items that shall not fall into the scope of subject matter. As is the universal practice, scientific discoveries, including naturally occurring substances, are excluded from patentability. The research of the TCM industry often results in the extracts that feature a high purity of certain chemical components. Although these TCM extracts show higher superior medical efficacy, the patentability of them is controversial, as the physical properties of them appear to be close to naturally occurring substances.

The TCM products often pose difficulty in chemical-ingredient identification, because unlike biomedicine, TCM products, no matter the TCM formulae or extraction, contain a very complex and unstable combination of chemical ingredients.

For novelty test, TCM information exists both in the mainstream medicine and among minority groups, a large portion of which have existed as secret formulae. The question is if TCM information that exists only in the medical practice of minority peoples can still meet the novelty requirement.[13] Other factors also give rise to the problems of the novelty test of TCM inventions: for instance, since the use of TCM norms are not uniform and are different from the norms of Western medicine, it is often difficult to tell whether a TCM has been published and used before.

Inventiveness is measured by the gap between the invention and prior art, and whether such a gap may be achieved by a person skilled in the art. A challenge of the non-obviousness test in the TCM discipline is that proving medical effect is difficult. The difficulty of the non-obviousness test is that TCM is usually manufactured from a combination of raw materials of complex chemical structure. Even if it is a TCM of single extraction, it is still difficult to locate the effective ingredients and trace the medical effect. Therefore, it is hard to evaluate the inventiveness of a TCM invention from the perspective of Western pharmaceuticals. The issue of how the inventiveness test shall be applied on TCM needs to be fully explored. Similar reason

---

[13]   Xuan Li, "Novelty and Inventive Step: Obstacles to Traditional Knowledge Protection under Patent Regimes: A Case Study in China" (2007) 29 *European Intellectual Property Review*, pp. 134–139.

appears in the examination of utility requirements for TCM inventions. TCM materials, such as raw herbs, often contain toxic materials, which have caused significant concerns about the utility of TCM inventions. The qualities of TCM materials are usually influenced by natural conditions such as the weather, location, and even harvest season. Lack of disclosure of natural conditions might give rise to problems regarding the reproducibility of TCM invention. Also, the complex chemical structure of TCM often renders it difficult to prove the medical efficacy of a TCM invention.

The following parts of this chapter will focus on two areas of identification of TCM inventions and the novelty of TCM inventions to illustrate the conflicts between patent law and TCM that have been mainly embodied in practice.

3.3.2 *Identification of TCM Inventions*

In practice, when applying for a patent, patent law requires that a product be defined in the specification in a clear and precise way. Generally, two sorts of patentable subject matters are recognized in patent law: process and product.[14]

A process, in the meaning of patent law, is intangible, and can be described as "a means to an end."[15] A wide range of TCM processes can be patent subject matter, covering the techniques from the cultivation of raw materials to the manufacturing of medicines.[16] Although there are conflicting views on whether some TCM processes may be regarded as diagnostic or therapeutic, and therefore, on whether they are patentable,[17] the identification of a TCM process poses no difficulty.

In the TCM industry, product patent applications can be filed for products that are at raw-material stage and for products that are the final medicinal product. The practice of TCM is essentially guided under the principle of *Bian Zheng Lun Zhi*, which means "pattern differentiation and treatment determination."[18] Under the guidance of its theories, TCM formulae are either single or complex compositions of herbal-drug ingredients.[19] TCM treatment formulae, unlike Western medicines that have clear chemical structures or are composed of effective agents, are usually comprised of complex components of

[14] Arthur R. Miller and Michael H. Davis, *Intellectual Property Patent, Trademarks, and Copyright in a Nutshell* (West Publishing Co., 1990), p. 20.
[15] Ibid., p. 22. [16] Tonghua Liu & Shiying Xiao, The 12th Special Topic, pp. 39–40.
[17] Ibid., pp. 41–42.
[18] Scheid Volker, *Chinese Medicine in Contemporary China* (Duke University Press, 2002), p. 200.
[19] Shen Zhu and Duansheng He, *The Brief History of Traditional Chinese Medicine* (Guangxi Normal University Press, 2007), pp. 59–61.

which the chemical structure is difficult, maybe even impossible, to concisely depict.[20] These features of TCM gives rise to various problems in the identification of TCM inventions in the patent application. Because of the nature of TCM treatment formulae, in most Western countries, a TCM treatment formula is patentable as a product only if it is an extract of the authentic TCM formula.

Currently, within most patent procedures, TCM inventions are identified by three primary methods: the efficacy of compounds, their physical properties, and the product-by-process claim. Such methods have been used by countries in examination, and each of them suits certain type of TCM products.

3.3.2.1 Identifying in Terms of Chemical Structure

Naming a substance in terms of its chemical formula ensures that its disclosure is unambiguous and that there will not be any question about the nature of its construction at enforcement stage. One approach to modernizing TCM is called the "Chinese-Western medicine integrated approach."[21] In this approach, experimental methods are run on TCM products/treatments to identify their bio-effective compounds or compositions. The medicines that this method turns out fit the Western medical point of view, and some of them can be defined in terms of their chemical structures. For instance, an extract from the herbal material in black pepper that was granted a US patent is identified as a "compound for use in the treatment of skin conditions" and named in terms of its chemical formula.[22]

However, as most TCM medicines or herbal materials are very complex in chemical composition, it is difficult to locate and extract all their bio-effective chemical compounds.[23] Currently, the method of identifying by effective compounds is not widely used in TCM patent applications.

3.3.2.2 Identifying by Physical Properties

Most countries allow a substance to be defined in terms of its physical properties. For instance, the EPO patent examination guideline advises that

---

[20] Ibid.
[21] Ziea Eric & Sung Joseph, "Irritable Bowel Syndrome: A Chinese-Western Integrative Approach to Treatment," Hong Kong Jockey Club Institute of Chinese Medicine, www. hkj cicm. org/5news/3/1.asp.
[22] US Patent Number 7,361,685.
[23] Yongfeng Zheng, "An Overview of Issues in Patenting Traditional Chinese Medicine," in Taiwan Intellectual Property Office (ed.), *Mid-term Report of Patent Examination of Traditional Chinese Medicine* (2004), pp. 8–23.

a product may be defined by its "parameter" of "characteristic values," such as
the melting point of a substance, the flexural strength of steel, the resistance of
an electrical conductor, etc.[24] In some regions, this method of identification is
restricted to the situation in which the product cannot be defined in terms of
its physical structure.[25]

The Western approach to TCM research (mentioned above) has been
used to identify the effective agents of TCM treatments. Some of those
effective agents are single chemical compounds, and others are compositions of which effective compounds can be identified as the inventive-step
substance.[26] When the bioactive ingredients are identified, defining a TCM
product is essentially the task of defining its effective compounds. This is
because a composition can be defined in terms of the inventive compounds
in it.[27] The method of identification by physical properties has been widely
used as the approach to defining a compound of unknown structure.[28]
In a US-granted patent, described as a "pharmaceutical composition for
the treatment of cardiovascular and cerebrovascular disease," the composition consisted of effective compounds of which the physical properties were
also described.[29] However, as some of the compounds, for instance, the
salvianolic acid B, are complex in structure, various parameters, like wave-
length, mobile phase, and theoretic plates, were used to describe their
physical properties.[30]

However, in TCM treatments, the effective compounds are not clear, since
their chemical compositions are so complex that it is difficult to identify the
bioactive compounds among them.[31] Because the effective compounds of
a TCM treatment are difficult to identify, an approach to defining the physical
properties of the medicine as a whole has been introduced in Taiwan and
Mainland China. The Taiwan examination guideline for TCM declares that
a TCM extract may be defined by the description of its physical properties,

[24] Chapter III, para. 4. 11 of Guidelines for Examination in the European Patent Office (2010).
[25] For instance, in European countries and in Taiwan.
[26] Essentially, a composition is the invention within the compound, that is, its inventive step. See
     Philip W. Grubb, *Patents for Chemicals, Pharmaceuticals and Biotechnology: Fundamentals
     of Global Law, Practice and Strategy*, 3rd edition (Oxford University Press, 2003), pp. 226–227.
[27] Ibid., pp. 226–227.   [28] Ibid., pp. 220–221.
[29] US Patent Number 7,438,935. The invention is composed of four herbal components: Radix
     Saldix Miltiorrhizae extract, Radix Notoginseng extract, Radix Astragali extract, and Borneol
     or oil of Lignum Dalbergiae Odoriferae. Each extract was defined in terms of its effective
     compounds.
[30] Ibid.
[31] Renping Zhang, "Review and Prospect of Patent Protection of TCM in Taiwan (Part 1),"
     Intellectual *Property Rights Monthly*, Nov. 2001, pp. 62–86.

chemical properties, or other characteristics.[32] The physical or chemical properties include molecular weight, melting point, ultraviolet spectrum, molten point, etc.[33] Those indexes can be used in association with the fingerprint[34] of the extract to give a full overall illustration of the physical and chemical characteristics of a TCM medicine treatment.

Although the bioactive compounds are not identified, this method probably suits the features of TCM, which takes a systemic approach to the treatment of disease. The complexity of the chemical composition and of the chemical reactions among them are important in the TCM treatment/product. Identification of the main components of a TCM treatment/product suits the special features of TCM.

3.3.2.3 Identifying the Product-by-Process Subject

The *Manual of Patent Examining Procedure* (MPEP), administered by the USPTO, advises that a product-by-process application defines a product by its method of production.[35] This mode of application for patent is still a product application, but its claim to patentability is based solely on that it is a process. That is, it is a patentable product inasmuch as it is a process. In practice, the product-by-process claim has been widely used in identification of TCM inventions. For example, in a patent for "Qianqianxian TCM capsule (搴千癣中药胶囊)" (a TCM medicine for ringworm removal)[36] granted in China, the applicant defined this TCM compound for the treatment of psoriasis as a medicine that consisted of the materials Cotex dictamni (60 percent), Indigo naturalis (10 percent), Misha (10 percent), saffron (6 percent), Bezoar (6 percent), Manis pentadactyla (16 percent), Zaocys dhumnades (26 percent), and centipede (10 percent), and was made through the processes of preparation, extraction, mixing, weighing, and end-product filling.

The filing of a product-by-process application is the suitable means of seeking to patent products that cannot be identified by their physical structures. In practice, product-by-process applications have been filed frequently pursuant to pharmaceutical and chemical inventions.[37] The need in the

---

[32] Section 3.3.1.3 of Taiwan Patent Examination Guideline 2009, Part 2, Chapter 12 "Inventions relating to Traditional Chinese Medicine" (Chapter 12).

[33] Ibid.

[34] The fingerprint of the extract records the types of chemical component contained in the extract.

[35] Section 2113 of USPTO *Manual of Patent Examining Procedure, 8th Edition (2010).*

[36] Chinese Patent Number 02132580.4.

[37] Mark D. Passler, "Product-By-Process Claims: Majority of the Court of Appeals for the Federal Circuit Forgets Purpose of the Patent Act" (1994) 49 *University of Miami Law Review*, pp. 233–255. (Passler reveals that in 1990, the average research cost to pharmaceutical

pharmaceutical industry of an application of this kind is perfectly justified, because enormous sums of money (reaching millions and billions of dollars) have to be invested in the research of pharmaceutical and chemical drugs, many of which cannot be defined by structure.

In practice, controversy about product-by-process as a patentable subject matter is centered on two main issues: whether patent application filed as product-by-process can be restricted to subject matter that cannot be identified other than as a process; and whether a patent granted on the basis that a subject matter is a process limits the patent's protection-scope to that process, without extending it to the product, or *vice versa*. The nub of this controversy is the "necessity rule."

THE NECESSITY RULE. The necessity rule established that the product-by-process application can be made only when a product cannot be properly defined nor distinguished from prior art, otherwise than by reference to the process of producing it. This rule was followed in many countries and regions, for instance, in Europe, Mainland China, and Taiwan. In the US, the rule was brought down in the *re Painter* case.[38] However, after that, a number of cases departed from that judgment.[39] In 1974, the USPTO modified its Examination Manual, which had stated that the product-by-process application is permitted, so long as it satisfies the requirement of Section 112 (the "definiteness" requirement) of the Patent Act.[40] It was not until then that the rule of necessity was officially abolished in the US with regard to the product-by-process mode of patent application.

The effect of the rule of necessity in the product-by-process application was essentially to constrain the scope of the patent granted by excluding the product from that patent's protection, on the ground that it *is* possible to define the product by other means. The reasonable expectation of what of an invention is actually covered by patent would be better met if applicants were encouraged to define the product for which they seek a process patent by

companies of discovering one new chemical compound was USD 230 million, and only one of every 5,000 or 10,000 of the compounds eventually entered the market.)

[38] Lawrence A. Hymo & Richard A. Anderson, "Product-By-Process Claims: Time for Reexamination" (1993) 3 *The Federal Circuit Bar Journal*, pp. 132–150.

[39] These are some of the departing cases: *In re Pilkington*, 411 F. 2d 1345 (CCPA 1969), the court stated that Congress has placed no limitation on how an applicant claims his invention; *In re Hughes*, 496 F. 2d 1216, 1218 (CCPA 1974), the court recognized the right of the applicant to define the product by process, even though it could have been defined in terms of structure and characteristics; *In re Steppan*, 394 F. 2d 1013, 1019 (CCPA 1967), the court pointed out that the rule of necessity is not supported by the patent statute.

[40] Section 706.03(e) of MPEP (version 1974).

describing its physical structures. This will also benefit the patent construction[41] of courts, and it will discourage applicant use of the product-by-process claim as a hedge against the possibility of the invalidation of an application for patent protection of the product itself.[42]

However, the abandonment of the rule of necessity will also impose a heavy burden on an applicant who has to prove that in no way, other that by its process of production, can the patent subject be identified. As most TCM treatments are complex in structure and can be identified only in terms of their production process, this burden imposes particularly heavily on TCM patent applications.

LIMITATION OF THE SCOPE OF PROTECTION. Although it is agreed that the patentability of a product for which application is made as a product-by-process application is solely decided on the basis of the product itself, it is not clear in the patent examination manual of any country whether the production process would have the effect of limitation in the infringement test.

The rationales of both sides can be observed in two US cases,[43] *Scripps Clinic v. Genentech Inc.*[44] and *Atlantic Thermoplastic Co v. Faytex Corp.*[45] In *Scripps*, the patent owner, Scripps Clinic, held the patent for the protein Factor VIII:C, a patent that was awarded pursuant to a product-by-process application of which the subject was chromatographic absorption. The respondent, Genentech Inc., later produced the protein using the recombinant-DNA techniques process. The court ruled that Scripps Clinic's protein patent had been infringed, despite the fact that Genentech Inc. had manufactured it in a different process. The *Scripps* case was decided in 1991. Six months later, however, the Federal Circuit overruled that judgment.

The *Atlantic* case was about a shock-absorbing innersole that had been granted patent on a product-by-process application. Atlantic Thermoplastic sued the respondent, Faytex Corp, for manufacturing the innersole. This time, the court rejected the infringement allegation on the ground that although Atlantic Thermoplastic's production process is within the limit of its patent,

---

[41] Gregory S. Maskel, "Product-By-Process Claim Construction: Revolving the Federal Circuit's Conflicting Precedent" (2006) 17 *Fordham Intellectual Property, Media & Entertainment Law Journal*, pp. 115–152.

[42] *In re Hughes*, 496 F. 2d 1216, 1218 (CCPA 1974).

[43] In fact, before the two cases, no Federal Circuit case had addressed the issue of whether a process would constitute a limitation of the product-by-process claim. Passler, "Product-By-Process Claims: Majority," pp. 233, 246.

[44] *Scripps Clinic v. Genentech Inc.*, 927 F. 2d 1565, 1583.

[45] *Atlantic Thermoplastics Co v. Faytex Cor.* note 257, 834, 838, 839.

Faytex Corp did not infringe Atlantic Thermoplastic's patent since its manufacturing method was different from the one for which Atlantic Thermoplastic
had been awarded a patent. In later district court cases, some courts followed
the judicial decision in *Scripps*, and others that in *Atlantic*.

The rationale of the *Scripps* case was that the patentability of a product filed
by a product-by-process application should be decided solely on the product
instead of on the process of its production.[46] The court held that patentability
and infringement should be examined on the same standard, and that therefore, process is no limitation in an analysis that seeks to determine
infringement.[47] Diverging from the view in the *Scripps* decision, the
Atlantic court, having examined a number of Supreme Court cases and the
academic literature,[48] deemed that even though the patentability of a subject
filed as a product-by-process application was decided with reference to the
product itself,[49] the product-by-process patent would not be infringed unless
the same process is used in the production of another product.[50]

The criticism was leveled that if the production process imposes no limitation on the scope of right, problems arise at the application-construction stage.
To focus solely on the product is to ignore the intention of an application by
passing over the part of it that describes process.[51] The result is a breach of the
general rule that "every limitations and its equivalent" of a patent has to be
represented in the behavior of the respondent.[52]

A practical problem also arises when the product cannot be defined adequately in terms of its physical properties. It is then difficult to know what the
product really is and concomitantly difficult to decide when the patent
granted pursuant to it is infringed.[53] However, if process is construed as
limitation, then the product-by-process application becomes a *de facto* application for the patenting of the manufacturing process.[54] The product-by-
process application was supposed to be incentive for industries to seek patent
protection for new products that are difficult to define in terms other than their
process of production. The introduction of the product-by-process application
came as a relief from the general rule of identification and is said to be
a "pragmatic adjustment to the needs of science, not law."[55] Undoubtedly,

[46] *Scripps Clinic v. Genentech Inc.*, 1565, 1583.   [47] Ibid.
[48] *Atlantic Thermoplastics Co v. Faytex Cor*, 838–843.   [49] Ibid., pp. 834, 845.   [50] Ibid.
[51] Maskel, "Product-By-Process Claim Construction," p. 115.
[52] *Smithkline BeechamCorp. v. Apotex Corp.* (Fed. Cir. 2004). Judge Newman's dissenting
judgment at 1321.
[53] Maskel, "Product-By-Process Claim Construction."
[54] This is especially true in the determination of infringement, given the fact that in most
jurisdictions a process patent will also cover the product that is directly made by it.
[55] *Smithkline BeechamCorp. v. Apotex Corp.*

the *Scripps* approach that ignores the process limitation can widen the scope of protection, and provide industry with better incentive to generate invention.[56]

The technical features of TCM lie mainly in the types and proportions of the materials used in a composition.[57] Thus, disclosure of the composition of materials is important in establishing that a composition is an invention. However, in infringement disputes that occur about TCM inventions, it often appears that a respondent has made a minor modification to the original combination and marketed it as a medicine for the same medical purpose as that of the patented TCM composition. As minor modification to a TCM combination will not change the medical effect of the final medicine significantly, recognition of process limitation by the infringement test would create a major hurdle in the enforcement of patents awarded to TCM inventions.

It is proposed that the principle of equivalence should be applied to determine whether an infringement has occurred when two TCM products present with the same combinations, albeit that one of them is slightly different.[58] This principle, guided by TCM theory, would facilitate a determination of whether two medicines with similar combinations have the same medical effect, and can be regarded as the same medicine.[59]

It is odd that this controversy has arisen, because the product-by-process claim came into existence to facilitate application for the patenting of a product[60] that can be defined only in terms of its production processes. The product-defining production process was not intended to be the subject of the patent application. That is, the subject of the application for patent was meant to be the product; the production process was "in the picture" only to define that product. (When a product is such that it cannot be defined by a description of its physical properties or its function, it is defined in terms of the processes of its production.) Although the product-by-process application

---

[56] Maskel, "Product-By-Process Claim Construction."

[57] Renping Zhang, Review and Prospect of Patent Protection of TCM in Taiwan (Part 1), Nov. 2001.

[58] Yun You, "Patent Protection of Complex TCM Formula and Infringement Analysis," PhD thesis, China Academy of Traditional Chinese Medicine Science (2003), pp. 48–50.

[59] Ibid.

[60] Although it is not settled in US case law whether the scope of protection should be restricted to the process of production, there is no conflict on the point that the subject matter of a product-by-process claim is the product. See e.g. *Atlantic Thermoplastics Co. v. Faytex Corp*, 970 F. 2d 1279 (Fed. Cir. 1992) at 845. In that case, the court noted that a product-by-process should be examined in association with the product itself, even though it decided that the "process" language of the claim should limit the scope of protection to the process.

is certainly helpful in the identification of a product's inventiveness, it has certainly given rise to confusion.

All controversies about the product-by-process application have a common root in the deficiency of the patent application, which is that although it is an application for the patenting of a product, it does not disclose what that product actually is.[61] This gives trouble first to the patent constructions of the courts,[62] which face the task of working out what the product is by reading through production-process specification notes that then may not reveal the structural or physical properties of the product. Therefore, the courts, as evidenced in the US, sometimes deem that the limitation of the scope of right is to the process, and at other times, that the product is included in that scope.[63]

This deficiency of the product-by-process application also results in an unclear distinction between the product that is made by means of the patent-protected process and the same product manufactured in a different process. A patent examiner may have an idea of what had been made by the patented process, but would have difficulty with telling the difference between the two products, one of which was made by a process other than the patented one. Clearly, these problems will challenge the whole patent system, both at the patent examination level and in courts. It is, therefore, not surprising that the United States Court of Customs and Patent Appeals (CCPA) has "consistently stated" that the general rule in patenting a product is to describe its physical structure, not its manufacturing process.[64]

3.3.3 Novelty of TCM Inventions

Under patent law, the novelty test seeks to ascertain that the technology for which a patent application is filed is distinguished from any prior art.[65] The examination for novelty considers the patent subject from various angles: its public use, publication, previous patent application, and public knowledge of it by other means. An application will be rejected for lack of novelty if the

[61] Newson Gary, "Product-by-Process Patent Claims: Arguing for a Return to Necessity and Reduction in the Scope of Protection" (2008) 40 *Arizona State Law Journal*, pp. 327–349.
[62] Maskel, "Product-By-Process Claim Construction," p. 115.
[63] It was argued that the US courts' lack of consensus on the construction of the product-by-process claim lies in the fact that sometimes the process may be more important to identify than the product, while at other times it is not more important. Thus, the courts tend to construe product-by-process as a limitation to the scope of right when little information is offered on what the product is. See Maskel, ibid.
[64] *Atlantic Thermoplastics Co.* v. *Faytex Corp*, 970 F. 2d 1279 (Fed. Cir. 1992).
[65] Miller and Davis, Intellectual Property Patent.

technology is in public use, there is published information about it, or it has been made known to the public by any other means. Three issues that relate to the novelty test of TCM inventions are worth discussion: novelty of classic TCM formulae, novelty of secret TCM formulae, and categorization of TCM terms.

3.3.3.1 Classic TCM Formulae

The classic TCM formulae are those ancient TCM prescriptions that are recorded in the classic medical books. Although their exact scope has not yet been decided,[66] those formulae are regarded as the essential basis of TCM development and innovation. Having a long history of clinical trials that proves their medical effectiveness, the classic TCM formulae are now becoming the focus of modern pharmaceutical companies, which may either produce medicines according to the those formulae, or base their new drug research on them. For instance, the use of the TCM formula *niu huang jie du pian* (牛黄解毒片) has more than 800 years of history and is still used for treating fever. As the SFDA website shows, more than 700 drug companies in China have been producing drugs developed on the basis of the ancient formulae.[67]

Regarding patent-law theory, a large part of the classic TCM formulae are in the public domain, and therefore, have lost novelty. However, recent practice of patent law showed that a certain number of classic formulae have been patented if the curing effect of the TCM was modified from "Zheng (症)" (a description of illness under TCM theory) to "Bing (病)" /disease (a description of illness under the Western medical theory). Such cases often appear in jurisdictions outside of China. For instance, the US granted a patent pursuant to a therapeutic agent for treating ulcerative colitis, which is in fact the classic TCM formula *jia-wei-xiao-yao-san* (加味逍遥散).[68] In the above US patent, called "therapeutic agent for treating ulcerative colitis," the traditional TCM formula, *jia-wei-xiao-yao-san* (加味逍遥散), was claimed by the Japanese company Teikoku Seiyaku Co. Ltd. The contribution of the inventor company, Teikoku Seiyaku Co. Ltd, was that it discovered that this TCM formula has the medicinal capacity to cure ulcerative colitis.[69] However, such usage of

---

[66] Yanhua Zhou, "Research on the Protection Method of Classic Formula Involving Traditional Knowledge," Master's thesis, Beijing University of Traditional Chinese Medicine, at 5.

[67] Search results from the SFDA website, http://app1. sfda. gov. cn/datasearch/face3/base. jsp?ta bleId=25&tableName=TABLE25&title=国产药品&bcId=11810289009972394373148681445, February 8, 2009.

[68] "Therapeutic agent for treating ulcerative colitis," US patent no. 6586022.   [69] Ibid.

jia-wei-xiao-yao-san (加味逍遥散) has long been common knowledge for TCM practitioners in China. Only the medical function was described in the terms and theories of TCM.[70] Therefore, although the combinations of classic TCM formulae are widely known to TCM practitioners, these formulae may still be patentable if their disease-curing capacities are "re-invented" (and thereby acquire a "novelty" status) in the terminology of Western medicine.

The above relationship between the above "Zheng (症)" and "Bing (病)" /disease has become part of the more general debate in China regarding the bio-piracy of traditional Chinese medicine. The Chinese people regard the classic TCM formulae as intellectual property that was accumulated by generations of Chinese medical practitioners. However, with modern technological methods, Western pharmaceutical companies conduct research on knowledge gleaned from the classic formulae, and come up with new forms or understandings of the traditional Chinese medicine. The Chinese government has tried to take legislative actions to protect the traditional knowledge of TCM. In the latest version of the PRC Patent Law enacted in 2008, Article 26 requires that a patent applicant shall disclose in the application documents the direct and original sources of any genetic resource, which is the basis of the applied invention.[71] It is further provided that a patent application shall be rejected if it is developed on the basis of the genetic recourses that were acquired by means in violation of laws or administrative regulations.[72] Although lack of supplementary rules regarding the improper acquisition of the generic resource, Article 26 opens the possibility in PRC Patent Law that a future administrative regulation may provide supplementary rules of obtainment of medical resources and thus restrict the development of Western pharmaceuticals on the basis of classical TCM formulae.

3.3.3.2 Secret TCM Formula

The novelty test of the subject (an invention, etc.) of a patent application is based on the comparison of that subject and the prior art in its area of practice. A technology will lose novelty status if it has been used publicly, or made known to the public. However, "secret use" is a different matter and is not regarded as disclosure to the public. A technology may still be regarded as new

---

[70] Chaohui Chen and Hong Zhen, "Reviewing Patent Protection of TCM from the US Patent Practices" (2006) 1 *China Traditional Patent Medicine*, pp. 125–143.
[71] Article 26 of PRC Patent Law (2008).   [72] Article 5, ibid.

even if it has been used in public practice for a long time, so long as its nature has not been publicly disclosed. Given the extreme complexity of the chemical components of a TCM drug, its technical features are not apparent even to the observer of its use. A final TCM product is usually the result of the processing of multiple raw materials. The formula of that product is not evident in the final product.[73] Many TCM formulae are kept as secret to various extents. Many individual TCM practitioners in China have their own formulae for the treatment of certain diseases. A valuable formula may have been in individual medical families' private practices for generations and been kept by strict rules from exposure to the public. Usually, a formula may pass to the sons of the family.[74] However, the situation for the medical knowledge kept in some minority groups of China is more complex in terms of secrecy. For such knowledge, instead of been kept with a single family, a large part of them have been developed, delivered, and thus known within a small circle of aboriginal people. Take one example: in the Tibetan tradition, knowledge of a secret prescription may be taught only in the religious temples, and the monks are the only people who know the formulae. Many other formulae may be administered only within the family, which makes the family the collective owner of particular formulae.

Naturally, a question arises about whether an individual practitioner can apply for patent for a secret formula that is actually practiced by a group of people, and about whether a secret formula owned by particular members of an ethnic group, and administered only within that ethic group, is "public use,"[75] and therefore without novelty value. Most countries' patent laws recognize the novelty status of secret technology, although it is not clear how large the scope of the use of a technology can be for that use to remain a "secret use."[76] But secret use is not a universal guarantee that the owner of a technology will not lose the right to make an application for its protection by patent. In the US, that a technology has been in secret use by one person does not bar others from applying for a patent of the same technology, and the secret user of a technology may lose the right to apply for the patent if he or she does not apply within one year of the date of his having invented that

---

[73] Xiaoling Tian, "Research on the Patent Protection of Complex TCM Formula" (2007) 186 *Journal of Southwest University for Nationalities*, pp. 56–73.

[74] "Traditional Chinese Medicine: From Secret Formula to Patents," *CRI Online*, http://gb2. ch inabroadcast. cn/773/2003–6-9/136@249271. htm, February 24, 2009.

[75] Taiwan Intellectual Property Office (eds.), *Mid-term Report of Patent Examination of Traditional Chinese Medicine*, at 63.

[76] This is especially the case for the secret held by a small group of people, for instance secret information kept within a family, because the patent law is unclear on whether a small group of people constitutes the knowing by the public.

technology.[77] For traditional Chinese medicine, the obvious response is that the history of the legal meaning of "public use" has to be explored, and that the social and economic value of the investigation of the secret medical formulae has to be taken into consideration in a refined legal definition of "public use."

3.3.3.3 Categorization of TCM Terms

There is no norm that regulates the TCM system of classification of medicinal herbal ingredients. In the medical books, the same herbal material may have different names, while the same name may refer to different herbal materials.[78] This situation is problematic in a quest to determine the novelty of an herbal medicine, for the patent examiner has to be able to recognize the names of the herbal materials in a medicine if he or she is to reach a conclusion about the novelty of the medicine for which a patent application is made.

The problem is further enlarged when a TCM patent application names herbs by their botanical (Latin-derived) names or common English names. It is the common practice of international patent application to name thus. Understandably, the name of an herb will be different in the Chinese *pinyin* from the botanical name awarded to it by the Latin-derived system of naming plants, and from its common English name. For example, the popular herbal plant *jin yin hua* (金银花) is "silver flower" in English, and its botanical name is *flos Lonicerae*.[79] It is therefore difficult to determine the presence or absence of "close prior art" in the use of a plant for medicinal purposes when the patent examiner has to search Chinese TCM publications for possible prior art that would either defeat or confirm the novelty status of the TCM-product subject of the patent application under examination. Similar issue appears in the different naming of symptoms in TCM and in Western medicine. For instance, the TCM term *shang huo* (上火) means "having body fire." In TCM theory, "body fire" is the broad concept that encompasses a number of symptoms. For instance, "body fire" (*huo* 火) can refer to body-heat caused by fever, to mouth ulcer, to a sore throat, or even to an agitated state of mind.[80] It is often impossible to find a term in Western medicine that

---

[77] Title 35 – Patents, United States Code Section 102.

[78] Renping Zhang, Review and Prospect of Patent Protection of TCM in Taiwan (Part 1), Nov. 2001. For instance, the herb *he shou wu* may appear as the names *chi shou wu*, *di jing*, *hong nei xiao*, or *xiao du geng* in different TCM books. Also, *da huang* names both the herbs *chuang jun* and *yang di geng*. See the previously cited article. See also Wikipedia, http://en .wikipedia.org/wiki/Herb_(Meanings_of_Terms.

[79] Wikipedia website, http://en. wikipedia. org/wiki/Herb_(Meanings of_Terms.

[80] Yongcan Chen, "How to Understand 'Shanghuo' in TCM," 39 Health Website, www. 39. net /mail/qikanshow/jhwz/101596. html.

corresponds perfectly with the meaning of a TCM term. A TCM medical term will normally have a broad meaning that encompasses several concepts that are distinct in Western medicine.[81]

In practice, the TCM synonym can often hinder the granting of a patent. In June 1999, an applicant applied for a patent "Chinese Patent Drug for Quick Eradication of Haemorrhoids" (patent No. 99109930.3). The State Intellectual Property Office (SIPO) turned down this patent application in July 2003. The reason was that a key component in the patent, the "toad herb" in the patent corresponded to two TCM components: the Potentilla chinensis and Limnophila chinensis (two components share a common name). Therefore, the component in the patent could not be defined.[82] The applicant then changed the "toad herb" in the patent into "salvia plebeia" and submitted a new application. The applicant reckoned that "salvia plebeia" was included in the "toad herb." SIPO turned down the patent application again and pointed out that "toad herb" and "salvia plebeia" were two different herbs. Therefore, the applicant filed an appeal to the Board of Patent Appeals and Interferences. After having reviewed the materials submitted by the applicant as well as related TCM literatures, the Board of Patent Appeals and Interferences eventually rejected the application. The reason was that the "toad herb" was neither explicit nor equivalent to "salvia plebeia." Therefore, this patent could not be enforced by the technicians in the relevant field.[83]

Efforts to clarify and unify the use of TCM terms have been required of academic circles, and they have been productive. TCM terms can be now be arranged in five categories: *zheng ming* (正名), *fang ming* (方名), *tu ming* (土名), *bie ming* (别名), and *su ming* (俗名).[84] Books and dictionaries have been published to cross-reference the different names. For instance, the *Dictionary of TCM Names*[85] has now collected over 4,000 terms from folklore and TCM publications, and has organized them into their common *zheng ming* (正名) category. Several other lexicons with the same purpose include *Dictionary of TCM Names*,[86] *Dictionary of the Commonly-Used Bynames of TCM*,[87] and

[81] Ibid. [82] The decision to the appeal reexamination, No. 5679. [83] Ibid.
[84] Fengdao Tao, "Standardisation of TCM Terminology and TCM Formula" (2006) 24–5 *Xinjiang Journal of Traditional Chinese Medicine*, pp. 35–47.*Zheng ming* (正名) refers to the terms with official recognition; *fang ming* (方名) refers to the terms historically used in some TCM formulae; *tu ming* (土名) or *su ming* (俗名) refer to the locally used terms thathave not been widely accepted; *bie ming* (别名) refers to all the names that are not officially recognized).
[85] Yanwen Li (ed.), *Dictionary of TCM Names* (People's Medical Publishing House, 2004).
[86] Yongmin Cai (ed.), *Dictionary of TCM Medicine* (China Press of Traditional Chinese Medicine, 2006).
[87] Congyang Ye (ed.), *Changyong Zhongyao Sucha Shouce* (China Medical Science Press, 2006).

Handbook of the Names of Popular TCM Medicines.[88] These lexicons are sound
as references for checking the differences among TCM medicines. However,
their publication is not enough to organize the chaos in which TCM terminology still finds itself.[89]

Some government-led projects have also focused on this issue. In Taiwan,
the categorization of TCM terms was included in the Five-Year Agenda for
TCM Development, which planned to establish a database to collate the
TCM terms used in the various academic journals, and to give them the Latin-
derived botanical names in common use in the botany discipline.[90]
The Taiwan Agenda was finished in 2006, and has been a valuable guide of
academic TCM research and patent practice ever since. In Mainland China,
the *Chinese Pharmacopoeia* also contains comprehensive TCM medical
materials. It consists of three volumes, and it addresses the national standards
of traditional Chinese medicine in Volume 1, chemical medicine in
Volume 2, and bio-medicine in Volume 3. Volume 1 is about the medical
standards of TCM, and has a comprehensive collection of TCM medical
materials tagged with the name/term in use for each, and its origins, typical
prescriptions, storage conditions, etc.[91] Although the TCM terms of the
Chinese Pharmacopoeia do not have a legal derivation, there is no doubt
that it enjoys special authority: The PRC Drug Administration Law declares
that the medical standards specified in the *Chinese Pharmacopoeia* are the
legally binding standards of medicines marketed in China.[92] The terms of the
China Pharmacopoeia therefore impose the usage that guides TCM practice.
Recently, some efforts have been made by SIPO to bridge the Chinese terms of
TCM and the Latin-derived botanical/biological terms: The SIPO database
has put the Latin names under the Chinese common names of the key plant/
animal components that would typically occur in a TCM patent.[93]

3.4 REMEDIES TO THE INCOMPATIBILITIES BETWEEN
TCM AND PATENT LAW

The general conclusions can be drawn from the above discussion that the
patent law is, to a considerable degree, inimical to the interests of the TCM

---

[88]   Xiaojie Yu (ed.), *Tongyong Yaoming Chadui Shouce*, 2nd edition (People's Military Medical
       Publishing House, 2007).
[89]   Ibid.   [90]   Ibid.   [91]   *Chinese Pharmacopoeia*, Volume 1, 2005.
[92]   Article 32 of Regulation of the Medical Administration of the PRC, promulgated by NPC
       on September 20,1984.
[93]   The database of SIPO http://59.151.99.133/tcm_patent/chineseversion/medicine_ch/chsearch
       .asp

industry. Although patent law applies uniformly to every industry, patent policy can be adjusted according to the specific characteristics of an industry.[94] As noted above, there is considerable friction between patent policy in some jurisdictions and TCM. In view of this, urgent consideration should be given to how patent policy might be adjusted to better accommodate the characteristics of TCM.

Taking the two issues discussed above as examples, there is sufficient leeway for the introduction of the industry-tailored patent policy to make the patent practice more adaptable to TCM invention. To remedy the problems in the identification of TCM inventions, the reform can be introduced that patent practice shall give wider recognition of the product-by-process claim, the defect of which can be further remedied by proper construction of the patent claims under the doctrine of equivalence. Also, to find ways to reduce the conflicts between TCM and patent law in the novelty test, more scientific research may be carried out to find out the correspondence between the "Zheng (症)" in TCM and the "Bing (病)"/ disease in Western medicine, in order to prevent the patenting of classic TCM formulae. Further more, given the situation that the tremendous number of TCM formulae that exist in secrecy in folk culture, acknowledgment of the novelty of the products and processes of this portion of the TCM would be beneficial. That acknowledgment would also have the worthy effect of enabling their patentability. Making the secret TCM formulae patentable without demanding the full disclosure of their contents would also contribute to their preservation, for it would encourage their owners to file patent applications.

Furthermore, it shall be kept in mind that patent is only one form of intellectual property right, not the only right, in protection of TCM innovations. Patent law obviously cannot protect all TCM IP: Many TCM formulae already developed and acknowledged by the general public are deemed by the patent laws of a number of jurisdictions to lack novelty, and are therefore considered not patentable. Other TCM secret formulae that are formally elevated as items of national heritage are better protected by coercive national legislation designating them as trade secrets. Therefore, the TCM industry is well advised to consider forms of IPR protection other than patent for its innovations, especially the trade secret protection.

---

[94]   D. Burk and M. Lemley, "Policy Levers in Patent Law," (2003) 7 *Virginia Law Review*, pp. 1577–1696.

In the end, to resolve the friction in the relationship of the TCM industry and patent-policy/law is beyond the power of law alone. The friction is due in most part to the different natures of the medical cultures of TCM and Western medicine. A key task is to convert TCM into a culture easily understood by, and therefore acceptable to, the people for whom Western medicine is the dominant culture. This is a prerequisite of cross-cultural communication. Mutually informed communication has an important role.[95]

---

[95] Chuyuan Li, "Renaissance of TCM: World Standards Shall Be Geared with TCM," (2010) http://health.sohu.com/20100208/n270152770.shtml.

4

Industry-Specific Study of Patent Law and Innovation in China's Telecommunications Industry

Limeng Yu

4.1 INTRODUCTION

The purpose of the patent system is to promote innovation by granting exclusive rights to inventions.[1] Article 1 of the Patent Law of the People's Republic of China (hereafter, Patent Law) states that its aim is '[to] promote the progress of science and technology and the development of economy and society'.[2] Believing that patents can positively promote innovation, China has set about building up a pro-patent environment, using the patent as an important indicator for innovation.[3] This has been supported at both a legislative and an administrative level.

Besides the Patent Law, interpretations by the Supreme People's Court emphasizing patent protection have been issued to guide the judicial process. For example, the Notice of the Supreme People's Court on Issuing the Opinions on Several Issues Concerning Intellectual Property Trials Serving the Overall Objective under the Current Economic Situation states that 'scientific and technological innovations are the core competitiveness of enterprises, and strengthening patent protection plays the most direct and important role in promoting scientific and technological advancement and independent innovation'.[4]

---

[1]   Dan L. Burk and Mark A. Lemley, 'Policy Levers in Patent Law' (2003) 89 *Virginia Law Review* 1575–1696, 1580.

[2]   Standing Committee of the National People's Congress, 'Patent Law of the People's Republic of China (2008 Amendment)' (Order No. 8 of the Chairman of the People's Republic of China; Issued on 27 December 2008).

[3]   To enhance the enforcement of patent law and strengthen the patent protection is the topic of the fourth amendment of China's patent law. See e.g. Jianguo Zhao, 'Conference of Patent Law Amendment in Nanjing', 10 July 2013. www.sipo.gov.cn/zscqgz/2013/201310/t20131023_836461.html.

[4]   The Supreme Peoples' Court, Notice of the Supreme People's Court on Issuing the Opinions on Several Issues concerning Intellectual Property Trials Serving the Overall Objective under the Current Economic Situation (Order No. 23 of the Supreme People's Court; issued and effective on April 21, 2009).

Policies have also been designed by the central government and local governments to enhance patent protection. For example, on 5 June 2008 China's State Council (hereafter State Council) issued the Notice of the State Council on Issuing the Outline of the National Intellectual Property Strategy (Outline of IP Strategy)[5] which is aimed at 'improving China's capacity to create, utilize, protect and administer intellectual property, making China an innovative country and attaining the goal of building a moderately prosperous society in all respects'.[6] In order to implement the Outline of IP Strategy, the Chinese State Intellectual Property Office (SIPO) released the Notice of the State Intellectual Property Office on Issuing the National Patent Development Strategy (2011–2020),[7] which states that, by 2015, 'patent applications should have increased to two million per year while the transaction amount of patent trade should have increased to 100 billion [CN¥] per year'.[8] Local governments, such as Beijing, Shanghai and Shenzhen, accordingly provide financial assistance to encourage patent applications.[9]

Numerous patent applications have been filed in response to the pro-patent legislation and policies. In 2009, China ranked the fifth among the Patent Cooperation Treaty (PCT)[10] filing countries and regions,[11] with a strong growth rate of 29.7 percent and 7,946 international applications.[12] Two Chinese telecommunications manufacturers, Huawei Technologies Co., Ltd.[13] and ZTE Corporation,[14] have been leading the way as top PCT applicants, with ZTE as the top PCT applicant with 3,906 published applications

---

[5] The State Council. Notice of the State Council on Issuing the Outline of the National Intellectual Property Strategy (Order No.18 [2008]; issued and effective on 05 June 2008), 21 June 2008.

[6] The State Council. The Outline of IP Strategy, No.18 [2008]

[7] SIPO, Notice of the State Intellectual Property Office on Issuing the National Patent Development Strategy (2011–2020) (Order No.126 [2010]; issued and effective on 26 October 2010).

[8] SIPO, National Patent Development Strategy, No.126 [2010].

[9] See e.g. Shanghai Intellectual Property Administration. The Patent Subsidy Policy of Shanghai, www.sipa.gov.cn/gb/zscq/node3/node34/userobject1ai9492.html.

[10] Article 3 of the PCT defines PCT application as 'Applications for the protection of inventions in any of the Contracting States may be filed as international applications under this Treaty'. See Article 3, Chapter 1 of the PCT, www.wipo.int/pct/en/texts/articles/a3.htm.

[11] Filing countries and regions mean the country or region where a PCT applicant is from.

[12] WIPO, 'International Patent Filings Dip in 2009 Amid Global Economic Downturn', 8 February 2010, www.wipo.int/pressroom/en/articles/2010/article_0003.html.

[13] Huawei ranked the first in 2008 with 1,737 PCT applications, see WIPO, 'Global Economic Slowdown Impacts 2008 International Patent Filings', 27 January 2009, www.wipo.int/press room/en/articles/2009/article_0002.html.

[14] ZTE, Company overview, wwwen.zte.com.cn/en/about/.

in 2012.[15] China has become one of the world's fastest growing telecommunications markets and operates the world's largest fixed (wired line) and wireless telecommunications network.

The support from the authorities and the increase in patent applications show that patents have been perceived as a way to incentivize innovation as well as a sign that innovation is occurring in China.

This chapter investigates whether China's patent law system is truly capable of promoting innovation from an industry-specific perspective. More specifically, this chapter discuss whether China's patent law system has been made to meet the needs of technological innovation in China's telecommunications industry (CTI), how the application of flexible legal provisions that are open to interpretation – those concerning 'technical solutions' and 'persons skilled in the art' – interacts with the innovation characteristics of CTI. This chapter argues that, although the flexible legal provisions of China's Patent Law have provided substantial discretion to judges and patent examiners to take into account industry-specific innovation characteristics in theory, the application of China's Patent Law overlooks the industry-specific nature of China's Patent Law as well as the innovation characteristics of CTI.

4.2 THE ROLE OF CHINA'S PATENT LAW SYSTEM IN CTI: A THEORETICAL INVESTIGATION

4.2.1 *The Chinese Approaches*

Current studies focusing on the role of the patent law system in CTI have not connected innovation characteristics with the legal provisions. They mainly involve two aspects: (a) studies on the relationship between the patent law system and telecommunications standards which include research on patent pools,[16] standard-essential patents (SEPs)[17] and principles related to the litigation and licensing of SEPs; and (b) the legislative impact of the Patent Law on CTI.[18] However, few of these studies correlate the innovation characteristics of CTI and China's patent law system.

---

[15]   WIPO, 'PCT Yearly Review 2013', in WIPO Economics & Statistics Series, p. 34, www.wipo .int/edocs/pubdocs/en/patents/901/wipo_pub_901_2013.pdf.
[16]   See e.g. Ping Zhang, 'Antitrust Regulations Against Patent Pool' (2007) 29 *Modern Law Science* 97.
[17]   See e.g. Chengjian Wu and Zhangxiao, 'On Injunctive Relief for Standard-Essential Patents' (2013) 2 *China Patents & Trademarks* 21.
[18]   See e.g. Xiaoming Guo, Jianfeng Shen and Haibo Wang, 'The Influence of the Third Amendment of China's Patent Law on China's Communication Industry' (2009) *Electronics Intellectual Property* 28.

Besides academic research, SIPO has also issued some studies based on its patent data. These studies mainly pay attention to (a) the function of patents in promoting indigenous innovation in China; and (b) the guidelines for patent examination. For example, some studies of SIPO analyse the patent pressure from leading foreign companies and how this damages innovation in CTI.[19] Some studies focus on how to apply the Patent Law in patent examinations. For example, an article examining the criterion of means-plus-function patent claims uses the telecommunications industry as an example to illustrate the examining criterion of 'means plus function' without highlighting the features of the telecommunication technologies.[20]

4.2.2 *Burk and Lemley's Industry-Specific Theory*

Burk and Lemley set out systematic industry-specific studies to explore how patent protection works in the innovation of different industries. This has been termed the 'industry-specific theory'.[21] Burk and Lemley's industry-specific studies on patents and innovation are concerned with correlating the industry-specific nature of US patent law to industry-specific innovation. In Burk and Lemley's industry specific theory, the application of the industry-specific nature of patent law is comprised of two parts: (a) in theory, the patent system has provided substantial discretion to the courts; and (b) in application, the courts may make decisions which take into account the industry-specific innovation characteristics.[22] Inspired by this theory, this chapter aims to explore whether the application of flexible legal provisions of China's patent law system considers the innovation characteristics of CTI and encourages inventions, by directly analyzing the interaction between China's patent law system and the technological characteristics of innovation of CTI.

4.3 THE INNOVATION CHARACTERISTICS OF CTI

A telecommunication is defined by the International Telecommunication Union (ITU)[23] as '[a]ny transmission, emission or reception of signs, signals,

[19] Lei Wang, 'The Impact and Significance of patent in China', *Mobile Telecommunication Technology Innovation*, January 2010, 97–104, p. 27.
[20] Peng Zhang, 'Opinions on interpreting the patent claims – from the perspective of industries in China', (2010) 7 *China Patent & Invention*, 97–101. www.chinaiprlaw.cn/file/2010051316941.html
[21] Yahong Li, *Imitation to Innovation in China: The Role of Patents in Biotechnology and Pharmaceutical Industries* (Cheltenham, UK: Edward Elgar, 2010), p. 13.
[22] Dan L. Burk and Mark A. Lemley, *The Patent Crisis and How the Courts Can Solve It* (Chicago, US: University of Chicago Press, 2009), p. 95.
[23] See the introduction to ITU on its website, available at www.itu.int/en/about/Pages/default.aspx.

writings, images and sounds or intelligence of any nature by wire, radio, optical or other electromagnetic systems'.[24] Telecommunications equipment and systems are needed to realize the transmission, emission and reception to provide telecommunication services to network subscribers. Accordingly, equipment manufacturers, network carriers and terminal manufacturers make up the main part of the telecommunications industry. With the development of numerous other telecommunications services, service providers and distributors have also become involved in the telecommunications industry.

Based on the above concept and structure of telecommunications industry, this section summarizes two technological characteristics of CTI. The first characteristic is the interconnection and interoperability of telecommunications technologies, which means that telecommunications equipment and systems can connect and work with each other.[25] These are required to realize the transmission, emission and reception of telecommunication information. Technical specifications of telecommunications standards are drafted to promote the harmonious development and efficient operation of technical facilities, as well to make international telecommunication services efficient, useful and available to the public.[26] For example, the standard-setting organization, the 3rd Generation Partnership Project (3GPP), uses a system of parallel 'releases' (technical specifications) to list features and parameters needed for 2G, 3G and 4G.[27]

Incremental innovation is the second technological characteristic of innovation in CTI, which means that Chinese telecommunications companies closely follow leading innovation information regarding new inventions in order to get dependent patents that can be used as bargaining chips to obtain cross-licences.[28] The incremental innovation is reflected by the improvement based on the existing leading technologies. In CTI, these improvements are evident from (a) the follow-on position in the activities of setting telecommunications standards; and (b) the way that Chinese companies obtain patent licences from foreign companies.

As for the activities of setting telecommunications standards, among the leading standard-setting organizations (SSOs), both the Chinese Standard Development Organization (SDO) and Chinese companies are in a follow-

---

[24] ITU. ITU specification Rec. ITU-R V.662-3, p 6. Clause 1.06 of the English version, www.itu .int/dms_pubrec/itu-r/rec/v/R-REC-V.662-3-200005-W!!PDF-E.pdf.

[25] ITU. Interconnection and Interoperability, World Conference on International Telecommunications (Dubai, 2012), www.itu.int/en/wcit-12/Documents/final-acts-wcit-12.pdf.

[26] Ibid.   [27] 3GPP, Releases, www.3gpp.org/specifications/releases.

[28] Yahong Li, Imitation to Innovation in China, p. 53.

on stage. Qualcomm, Ericsson and Nokia lead the standard-essential patent owners in 3GPP[29] based on the Global System for Mobile Communications (GSM).[30] Furthermore, Qualcomm, Nokia and Motorola lead the standard-essential patent owners in the 3rd Generation Partnership Project 2 (3GPP2)[31] based on code division multiple accesses (CDMA).[32] Although time division synchronous code division multiple access (TD-SCDMA) is considered to be the indigenous innovation of CTI, Chinese companies only own about 7 percent of the core patent technology of TD-SCDMA.[33]

As for the Chinese telecommunications companies, they have signed licence agreements with leading foreign companies because they are in a follow-on stage regarding technological innovation – Chinese telecommunications companies usually perform R&D in a follow-on mode focusing on the improvement of existing technologies. Even though it is considered as the leading telecommunications company with a large patent portfolio, the Chinese telecommunications equipment manufacturer, Huawei, paid 0.22 billion USD for patent licence fees in 2011.[34] This is mainly because Huawei focuses on the improvement of existing designs and engineering realization. Besides Huawei, Chinese telecommunications companies have extensively paid licence fees to the leading companies in the global telecommunications industry. For example, ZTE has signed a patent licence agreement with Microsoft for its usage of Microsoft's patents in ZTE's mobile phones running Android systems.[35]

[29] 3GPP is known as an 'Organizational Partner' and provides 3GPP members with a stable environment in which to produce technical reports and specifications that define the third generation technologies.
[30] The Global System for Mobile Communications (GSM) is the second-generation (2G) telecommunications technology featured in the digital cellular networks used by mobile phones. The network of GSM is based on time division multiple access (TDMA).
[31] 3GPP2 is a collaborative third-generation (3G) telecommunications specifications-setting project comprising North American and Asian interests and is tasked with developing global specifications.
[32] As for the patent ownership of 3GPP and 3GPP2, see David J. Goodman and Robert A. Myers, '3g Cellular Standards and Patents, the Wireless Networks' (2005), Proceedings of 2005 IEEE Wireless Communications and Networking Conference, p. 418–419.
[33] Yan Hui, 'The 3G Standard Setting Strategy and Indigenous Innovation Policy in China: Is TD-SCDMA a Flagship?' DRUID Working Papers No.07-01, 2007 (JEL codes: O31, L96, ISBN: 978-87-7873-229-3), p. 2. The working paper is also available at www3.druid.dk/wp/20070001.pdf.
[34] Xiaoxing Wang and Yufeng Xiao, 'Unaffordable Defeat: Trapped ZTE Aims to Find a Way out by Filing Litigation against Ericsson in China', 13 April 2011, *Southern Metropolis Daily*, http://tech.sina.com.cn/t/2011-04-13/05005397632.shtml.
[35] Bill Rigby, 'China's ZTE signs Android patent license with Microsoft', 23 April 2013, www.reuters.com/article/2013/04/24/us-microsoft-zte-patent-idUSBRE93N03W20130424.

Admittedly, both of the two innovation characteristics of CTI may exist in the telecommunications companies of other countries when they stand in the similar technology levels and business markets to Chinese telecommunication companies. To focus on the interaction of China's telecommunications innovation and China's patent law, this chapter only analyses the innovation characteristics of CTI and China's patent law.

4.4 APPLICATION OF LEGAL PROVISIONS TO THE INNOVATION CHARACTERISTICS OF CTI

4.4.1 *Flexible Legal Provisions Responding to the Innovation Characteristics of CTI*

The legal provisions that may respond to the innovation characteristics of CTI will be analysed based on the following Chinese laws relating to patents: national law (the Patent Law);[36] administrative regulation (Detailed Rules for the Implementation of the Patent Law of the People's Republic of China (2010 Revision) (hereinafter referred to as the Detailed Rules for the Implementation));[37] and administrative rules promulgated by SIPO (Guidelines for the Examination of Patents in the PRC (2010) (the Guidelines)).[38] In addition, this paper will also examine the function of the Operating Rules of Patent Examination (Division of Substantial Examination) (the Operating Rules)[39] in patent prosecution which is the internal working guidebook issued by SIPO for providing detailed illustration to guide the patent substantial examination following the Guidelines.[40]

As for the characteristics of interconnection and interoperability, China's patent law system does in fact offer a certain amount of discretion for protecting different types of technologies. This can be seen in the fact that the concept of a 'technical solution' is used to define the term invention in

---

[36] Standing Committee of the National People's Congress. Patent Law, Order No.8 of the Chairman of the People's Republic of China.

[37] The State Council, 'Detailed Rules for the Implementation of the Patent Law of the People's Republic of China' (2010 Revision) (Order No.569 of the State Council; Issued on 01 September 2010), www.wipo.int/wipolex/en/details.jsp?id=6504 #.

[38] SIPO, 'Guidelines For Patent Examination (2010)' (Order No.55 of SIPO; Issued on 21 January 2010), www.sipo.gov.cn/zhfwpt/zlsqzn/sczn2010eng.

[39] SIPO, 'The Operating Rules of Patent Examination' (A Separately Published Part for Substantial Examination) (Revised Version in 2011) (Beijing: Intellectual Property Publishing House, 2011). The Introduction to the Operating Rules is available at www.siptc.com/html/news/2013-7/1518.html.

[40] See the preamble of the Operating Rules, available at www.doc88.com/p-377360168442.html.

Article 2.2 of the Patent Law: 'any new technical solution relating to a product, a process or an improvement thereof'.[41] This means that those interpreting China's patent laws are able to be flexible when responding to technological innovation by CTI, given that a technical solution is defined by the Guidelines as 'an aggregation of technical means employing natural law to solve a technical problem . . . a solution that does not adopt technical means to solve a technical problem and thereby does not achieve any technical effect in compliance with the laws of nature does not constitute a subject matter as defined in Article 2.2 [of the Patent Law]'.[42]

The interaction between China's patent law system and innovation by CTI will be examined in the context of invention patents; specifically the legal provisions concerning technical solutions in Article 2.2 and the illustrating provisions of Article 2.2 in the Guidelines and the Operating Rules.

As for the other characteristics, China's patent law system is able to respond to the incremental innovation of CTI – the Patent Law has provided the discretion in Article 22.3 for assessing the inventiveness and the Guidelines refer to the person skilled in the art to assess the inventiveness of a patent application. In this way, the level of technological expertise of the person skilled in the art is associated with the technologies of CTI. The Guidelines define such a person as 'a fictional person who is presumed to be aware of all the common technical knowledge and have access to all the technologies before the filing date or the priority date in the technical field to which the invention pertains, and have capacity to apply all the routine experimental means before that date'.[43]

The level of technological expertise of the person skilled in the art may vary from industry to industry and it is the key benchmark for assessing the 'substantive features and represents progress' in judging the inventiveness of inventions. The third paragraph of Article 22 (Article 22.3) of the Patent Law states that 'Inventiveness means that, as compared with the technology existing before the date of application the invention has prominent substantive features and represents a notable progress and that the utility model has substantive features and represents progress.'[44]

Besides, flexible legal provisions concerning DOE are used to interpret the scope of patent rights in patent disputes. Patent disputes settlement in China is made up of a judicial track and an administrative track. The flexibility in the

[41]   Standing Committee of the National People's Congress. Patent Law, Order No.8 of the Chairman of the People's Republic of China.
[42]   SIPO, 'Guidelines for Patent Examination', p. 129.   [43]   Ibid., p. 194.
[44]   Standing Committee of the National People's Congress. Patent Law, Order No.8 of the Chairman of the People's Republic of China.

legal provisions concerning DOE that can respond to incremental innovation in CTI is also granted by the concept of the person skilled in the art. This is because Article 30 of Notice of the Higher People's Court of Beijing on Guidelines for Determining Patent Infringement states that: 'to judge whether the sued technical solution falls in to the patent of a plaintiff the judge should compare all the technical features of the patent claim declared by the plaintiff with all the technical features of the sued technical solution'.[45]

If the level of technological expertise of the person skilled in the art is high, the patent scope is easy to interpret to cover the sued technical solution.

Further, the interpretation of the Supreme People's Court shows how to assess patent infringement by using the DOE. Article 7 of the Interpretation of the Supreme People's Court on Several Issues concerning the Application of Law in the Trial of Patent Infringement Dispute Cases[46] states that '[w]here the alleged infringing technical solution contains technical features identical or equivalent to all the technical features described in a claim, the people's court shall determine that it falls into the scope of protection of the patent . . .'[47]

Article 17 of Several Provisions of the Issues Concerning Applicable Laws to the Trial of Patent Controversies defines what the term equal characteristics mean: 'characteristics that use similar means, realize similar functions and achieve similar effects as the technological characteristics indicated in the claims, and that the ordinary technological personnel of this field may think out without creative work'.[48]

It can be seen that the 'ordinary technological personnel of this field'[49] is the reason why the DOE may allow a certain amount of discretion when considering innovation characteristics of CTI. The level of technological

[45] The Higher People's Court of Beijing Municipality. Notice of the Higher People's Court of Beijing on Guidelines For Determining Patent Infringement (Document No.301 [2013] of The Higher People's Court of Beijing Municipality, issued and effective on 4 September 2013). 9 October 2013. The Chinese text is available at http://bjgy.chinacourt .org/article/detail/2013/10/id/1104565.shtml.

[46] Supreme People's Court. Interpretation of the Supreme People's Court on Several Issues Concerning the Application of Law in the Trial of Patent Infringement Dispute Cases (Interpretation No. 21 [2009] of the Supreme People's Court, issued on 28 December 2009, effective on 1 January 2010), www.court.gov.cn/spyw/mssp/201006/t20100630_6513.htm.

[47] Supreme People's Court. Several Issues Concerning the Application of Law in the Trial of Patent Infringement Dispute Cases, Interpretation No. 21 [2009].

[48] Supreme People's Court. Several Provisions of the Supreme People's Court on Issues Concerning Applicable Laws to the Trial of Patent Controversies (Interpretation No. 21 [2001] of the Supreme People's Court, issued on 22 June 2001, effective on 1 July 2001; revised by Interpretation No. 9[2013] of the Supreme People's Court, effective on 15 April 2013), www .wipo.int/wipolex/en/text.jsp?file_id=199492.

[49] The Chinese term of the 'the ordinary technological personnel of this field' is the same as 'the person skilled in the art' – and this chapter uses 'the person skilled in the art' consistently.

expertise of the person skilled in the art can be affected by the innovation characteristics of CTI.

4.4.2 Constraints on the Application of Legal Provisions to the Interoperability of CTI

This section discusses the interaction between the flexible legal provisions that are open to interpretation concerning technical solutions and the inventions of CTI. By specifically analyzing the application of these legal provisions to inventions involving signals,[50] computer programs and business methods of CTI, this section argues that they are restricted in their ability to respond to the requirement of innovation in CTI. The constraints from China's patent law system on the application of these flexible legal provisions for accommodating telecommunication technologies may act to discourage inventions.

4.4.2.1 Interaction between Flexible Legal Provisions and Signals

In China, there has been little discussion over whether signals are patentable because the Guidelines and the Operating Rules have excluded signals from patent protection. The Guidelines state that 'smell, signal, such as sound, light, electricity, magnetism, and wave, or energy do not constitute a subject matter as provided in Article 2.2'.[51] The Operating Rules further explain that signals are excluded from the subject matter protected by Article 2.2 for the reason that the signal cannot constitute a product.[52]

The problem is that there is no definition for the word 'product' in China's patent law system. Its meaning can be roughly deduced from the Guidelines where it defines product claim and process claim: 'according to their nature, claims are divided into two basic types, namely, claims to a physical entity and claims to an activity, which are simply referred to as product claims and process claims respectively'.[53] The Guidelines state that product claims relate to a physical entity, such as articles, substances, materials, tools, apparatus and equipment.[54] However, this does not take into account the technological development and diversity of information and communication technologies.

Moreover, neither the Guidelines nor the Operating Rules have defined what signals are. The ITU defines the signal as 'a physical phenomenon one or

---

[50] 'Signals' in this chapter means electronic signals, optical signals and electromagnetic signals, which are used in the signalling process technologies of telecommunications area.
[51] SIPO, Guidelines for Patent Examination, p. 129.   [52] Ibid., p. 5.   [53] Ibid., p. 129.
[54] Ibid., p. 157.

more of whose characteristics may vary to represent information'.[55] Therefore, the type of signals depends on the information that the signals convey. For telecommunications technologies, the type of signals, depending on the transmission type of current telecommunications technologies, comprises electronic signals, electromagnetic signals, optical signals and digital signals.[56] If signals, per se, can be patented, which means signal claims are admitted as product claims in a patent application, a broad protection may be granted to encourage innovation. Moreover, signal claims may enable patent owners to use the broad patent protection against infringers who produce and transport telecommunications with the signals. Due to the interconnection and interoperability of telecommunications innovation, the signal patents may cause barriers, thus preventing competitors from entering the same market.

This chapter does not argue that signals should be directly protected by China's patent law system as products but that the Guidelines and Operating Rules constrain the patent examiners' discretion in assessing whether or not an invention can claim for patent protection with signal claims. The patent examination of a signal invention is an example that shows the constraints found in the Guidelines and the Operating Rules. The reason for excluding the signals from patent protection is that they are not products. The Guidelines and the Operating Rules have provided a clear definition neither of a product nor of the standards for defining a product. This situation can be compared with the jurisdictions of the EU and the US where, although the patent protection for signals is controversial, signals are not directly excluded. Patent examiners and judges are allowed to use their discretion when assessing signal claims.

In the EU, the EPC (2013) does not exclude signals from the category of 'patentable subject matter'. The limitations on patentable subject matter are set out in Articles 52 and 53 of EPC (2013), and Article 52 is relevant to the question of whether a signal is patentable.[57]

According to the Article 52, the EPC (2013) does not define the concept of invention. However, the Board of Appeal in the European Patent Office (EPO) held that 'technical character' was an implicit requisite of an 'invention'.[58]

---

[55]   ITU. ITU specification Rec. ITU-R V.662-3, p 6.
[56]   http://en.wikipedia.org/wiki/Signal_(electrical_engineering).
[57]   European Patent Office. European Patent Convention (version of September 2013). http://doc uments.epo.org/projects/babylon/eponet.nsf/0/00EoCD7FD461CoD5C1257C060050C376/$Fi le/EPC_15th_edition_2013.pdf.
[58]   Board of Appeal in the EPO. Case Law of the Boards of Appeal – 1.1. Technical character of an invention. www.epo.org/law-practice/legal-texts/html/caselaw/2016/e/clr_i_a_1_1.htm.

The patentability of signals should depend on whether technical traits exist. The Guidelines for Examination in the European Patent Office takes signals as the example of apparatus claims for protecting computer programs: '[s]uch claims directed at computer-implemented inventions may e.g. take the form of ... following T 1173/97, the computer program itself as well as the physical media carrying the program (see T 424/03), i.e. computer program product claims, such as "data carrier", "storage medium", "computer readable medium" or "signal".'[59]

Furthermore, the case T163/85 issued by the Official Journal of the European Union (hereinafter referred to as the OJ)[60] states that '[a] colour television signal characterized by technical features of the system in which it occurs, i.e., in which it is being generated and/or received, does not fall within the exclusions of Article 52(2) (d) and (3) EPC and is regarded as an invention within the meaning of Article 52(1) EPC'.[61]

As for the US patent laws, section 101 of Chapter 10 of Title 35 of the United States Code (35 USC §101) states that 'Whoever invents or discovers any new and useful process, machine, manufacture, or composition of matter, or any new and useful improvement thereof, may obtain a patent therefor, subject to the conditions and requirements of this title.'[62]

Therefore, signals are not directly excluded from the patent law of the United States. For example, the USPTO granted Samsung Electronics a patent[63] where claim 109 of the patent defined a frequency-multiplexed signal.[64]

However, the United States Court of Appeals for the Federal Circuit (CAFC), in *re Nuijten*,[65] held that 'The claims on appeal cover transitory electrical and electromagnetic signals propagating through some medium, such as wires, air, or a vacuum. Those types of signals are not encompassed by any of the four enumerated statutory categories: process, machine, manufacture, or composition of matter.'[66]

---

[59]   EPO. Guidelines for Examination in the European Patent Office (September 2013), Part G – Chapter II-5. http://documents.epo.org/projects/babylon/eponet.nsf/0/6c9c0ec38c2d48df c1257a21004930f4/$FILE/guidelines_for_examination_2013_en.pdf.

[60]   See the archive of OJ at www.epo.org/law-practice/legal-texts/official-journal.html.

[61]   The Boards of Appeal of European Patent Office. Colour Television Signal, Case Number T163/85. www.epo.org/law-practice/case-law-appeals/recent/t850163ex1.html.

[62]   35 USC §101, www.law.cornell.edu/uscode/text/35/112.

[63]   The application No. is US 5500739 A.

[64]   Stephen G. Kunin and Bradley D. Lytle, 'Patent Eligibility of Signal Claims' (2005) 87 *Journal of the Patent and Trademark Office Society* 991–1001, p. 997.

[65]   CAFC. In Re Petrus A.C.M. Nuijten, Serial No. 09/211,928, www.uspto.gov/web/offices/com /sol/fedcirdecision/06-1371.pdf.

[66]   *In Re Petrus A.C.M. Nuijten*, Serial No. 09/211,928 (2006), p 8.

The majority of the CAFC judges in *re Nuijten* clearly decided that electromagnetic signals could not constitute patentable subject matter within any of the four categories of 35 USC §101. The controversy arises over whether a signal can constitute patentable subject matter within 35 USC §101 – manufacture. The majority held that various definitions of manufacture addressed 'articles' or 'manufacture' as being tangible articles or commodities. A transient electric or electromagnetic transmission does not fit within the definition of 'manufacture' because the manufacture is considered as tangible articles or commodities.[67] Linn, a Circuit Court judge, concurred in part and dissented in part, stating that 'in determining the scope of patentable subject matter, we must reconcile cutting-edge technologies with a statute, the language of which dates back to the beginning of the Republic'.[68] Linn argued that "Claim 14 is directed to a 'manufacture' because the signal is, in the broad sense discussed above, an 'article' ... Put differently, it is a product of human 'art' or ingenuity; it is an application of technology to provoke some purposeful transformation in the real world".[69]

The dissenting opinion shows that whether or not a signal is tangible is not the critical criterion for defining whether it is patentable. Judging whether a signal falls into any one of the four categories of 35 USC §101 is merely a metaphysical exercise. The majority opinion and the dissenting opinion of this case show that the patentability of signals is controversial in the US.

From the above situations in the EU and the US, it is possible to see that signals are not directly excluded from the patent protection. The assessment of the patentability of signals is done on a case-by-case basis. Discretion over the assessment is not constrained by rules of the patent law systems in either jurisdiction. If signals are patentable, signals can be protected by product claims. If the scope of what is patentable were to be enlarged, more patent protection would be provided and more new technology would be published.

The reality, however, is that, through the guidelines, China's patent law system excludes signals from being patentable subject matter. The Operating Rules explain why signals cannot constitute a product as defined in patent law, although neither Patent Law nor the Guidelines clearly define what a 'product' is. The subject matter of a patent leads the innovation direction of an invention. The scope of patent protection for signals is different to the scope of patent protection for the technical solution using signals. In this situation, inventors are not encouraged to study the technologies directly associated with signals and disseminating related technologies.

[67] Ibid., p. 16.   [68] Ibid., p. 20.   [69] Ibid., p. 19.

This chapter suggests that the Guidelines clarify the legal standards of assessing signal inventions instead of using bright-line rules to directly exclude the signals from the subject matter of invention. Article 2.2 of the Patent Law defines the term invention within the concept of technical solution. The product or process referred to in this article is an expression of the technical solution. The Guidelines may further define what a product is or provide criteria of assessing product inventions. Accordingly patent examiners are able to assess the patent applications involving signals from the perspective of assessing technical solutions instead of rejecting a patent claim based solely on the Guidelines stating that 'smell, signal, such as sound, light, electricity, magnetism, and wave, or energy do not constitute a subject matter as provided in Article 2.2'.[70] For example, technical problems, technical means and technical effects should be used to assess the patentability of signals based in Article 2.2 and to assess whether a signal is a technical solution.

4.4.2.2 Application of Legal Provisions to Inventions Involving Computer Programs

This section discusses the constraints made by the Guidelines and the Operating Rules on the patent examination of inventions involving computer programs. The Guidelines define a computer program as: 'a coded instruction sequence which can be executed by a device capable of information processing, e.g. a computer, so that certain results can be obtained, [e.g.,] a symbolized instruction sequence, or a symbolized statement sequence, which can be transformed automatically into a coded instruction sequence'.[71]

The Ninth Chapter of Part II of the Guidelines, 'Some Provisions on Examination of Invention Applications Relating to Computer Programs', further sets out the patentability requirements for computer programs: 'If a claim merely relates to an algorithm, or mathematical computing rules, or computer programs per se, or computer programs recorded in mediums (such as tapes, discs, optical discs, magnetic optical discs, ROM, PROM, YCD, DVD, or other computer-readable mediums), or rules or methods for games, etc., it falls into the scope of the rules and methods for mental activities and does not constitute the subject matter for which patent protection may be sought.'[72]

The Ninth Chapter of Part II of the Guidelines states that computer programs per se and the mediums recording the computer programs fall into the category of 'rules and methods for mental [intellectual] activities'

---

[70] SIPO, 'Guidelines For Patent Examination', p. 129.   [71] Ibid., p. 305.   [72] Ibid., p. 305.

and these inventions cannot obtain patent protection.[73] Computer programs used for solving technical problems with technical means, thereby obtaining technical effect, may fall into the invention defined by Article 2.2 of the Patent Law.[74]

The computer program is widely used in telecommunications, from chips of mobiles to network construction. For example, the computer program can be used for encryption, improving the efficiency of telecommunications devices and measuring performance of telecommunications networks. For inventions related to computer programs in CTI, the computer programs are usually used for improving the performance of telecommunications devices and the structure or the shape of the devices seldom changes. Because of this, an apparatus claim is required to reward the patent owner by directly protecting the product performing the computer program. If apparatus claims for protecting computer programs can be granted, patent owners may compare the allegedly infringing product directly with the apparatus claims of computer programs.

However, the provision of the Guidelines on the apparatus claims for computer programs requires that the component of the apparatus claims should follow the flow of the computer program step by step. The Guidelines set requirements for drafting applications: 'for apparatus claim drafted on the basis of computer program flow completely ... each component in the application for the apparatus must completely correspond to a step of the computer program flow'.[75] This is why the apparatus claims for performing the computer programs are called 'virtual apparatus' claims.[76] Moreover, the Guidelines emphasize that each component of the apparatus should correspond to each step of the computer program flow. In this way, the Guidelines state that these components should only be considered as the functional module for performing the computer program instead of a real hardware or device in the invention.[77]

In contrast, the US and the EU grant apparatus claims directly in order to protect the technical solutions performing the computer program without creating a 'virtual apparatus'.[78] The Guidelines for Examination in the EPO provide that the examples of allowable claim types comprise 'a computer program [product] adapted to perform said method – a computer-readable

---

[73] Ibid., p. 306.   [74] Ibid., p. 307.   [75] Ibid., p. 322.
[76] See e.g. Baohai Sun, 'Legal Issues on the "Virtual Apparatus" Claims Related to Computer Programs', The fourth part of the conference proceedings of the fourth Annual Conference and the fourth intellectual property forum, All-China Patent Attorneys Association, http://cpfd .cnki.com.cn/Article/CPFDTOTAL-ZHZL201307004026.htm.
[77] SIPO, 'Guidelines For Patent Examination', p. 322.   [78] Ibid., p. 307.

storage medium/data carrier comprising said program'.[79] Moreover, the Manual of Patent Examining Procedure of the US states that '[t]he statutory requirements for computer-implemented inventions are the same as for all inventions'.[80] A patent family[81] filed by Nokia entitled 'Method, Apparatus, Communications System, Computer Program, Computer Program Product and Module'[82] can be taken as an example. Table 4.1 compares the apparatus claims for protecting the invention related to computer programs of the patent family. The claims derive from the same technical solution but the claims in the patent application filed in China are presented differently, and thereby they obtain different patent scope compared with the patent scope granted by the EU and the US.

As mentioned above, in telecommunications, computer programs are usually combined with the devices to improve the performance of devices. In this situation, if the telecommunications devices performing the computer programs change in structure or shape, the devices should be protected as apparatus claims. However, the Guidelines state that the apparatus perform-ing the computer program should be modules matching each step of the computer program, and that, in practice, the modules cannot be interpreted as any physical entity. It is still hard to compare the allegedly infringing product to the so-called 'virtual apparatus'. Constrained by the Guidelines, the technical solutions used in practice cannot be disclosed and disseminated, and the scope of patent rights for the same technical solution may be different in China compared with the EU and the US.

4.4.2.3 Application of Legal Provisions to Inventions Involving Business Methods

Telecommunications services are linked in to the daily life of subscribers. Business methods are used widely in telecommunications. In CTI, for exam-ple, the various telecommunications services include making payments, loca-tion, and remote medical care. Due to the convergence between information

---

[79] See, www.epo.org/law-practice/legal-texts/html/epc/2010/e/ar52.html, at Part F – Chapter IV-5.

[80] The United States Patent and Trademark Office. Manual of Patent Examining Procedure (8th Edition, 9th Revision, August 2012), www.uspto.gov/web/offices/pac/mpep/s2161.html#d oe213447, Section 2161.01.

[81] EPO, 'About Patent Families', www.epo.org/searching-for-patents/helpful-resources/first-time -here/patent-families/about.html.

[82] This patent application was firstly filed to Finland and the patent applications filed to EU (EP20070858371), US (11/961,027) and China (200780048419.2) claimed the priority of the application filed to Finland.

TABLE 4.1 *Comparison of Patent Claims Protecting Computer Programs*

China Application No. CN 200780048419.2	Claim 22. A data process apparatus, comprising: a module for receiving a request for a radio connection; a module for checking at least one of: subscriber information, a service request and terminal information; and a module for directing, on the basis of at least one of: the subscriber information, service request and terminal information, data to be delivered via the requested radio connection to different network elements of a communications system.
EU Application No. EP20070858371	Claim 24. A computer program product encoding a computer program of instructions for executing a computer process for data processing, the process comprising: receiving a request for a radio connection; checking at least one of: subscriber information, a service request and terminal information; and directing, on the basis of at least one of: the subscriber information, service request and terminal information, data to be delivered via the requested radio connection to different network elements of a communications system.
US Application No. US 11/961,027	Claim 24. A computer program product encoding a computer program of instructions for executing a computer process for data processing, the process comprising: receiving a request for a radio connection; checking at least one of: subscriber information, a service request and terminal information; and directing, on the basis of at least one of: the subscriber information, service request and terminal information, data to be delivered via the requested radio connection to different network elements of a communications system.

technologies and communication technologies, many Internet services are integrated into mobile phones. This section aims to explore whether the discretion that the Patent Law allows for responds adequately to the innovation related to business methods.

In China, the business method per se cannot be protected by the Patent Law; according to Article 25.1(2), 'the following subject matter will not be granted patent rights: ... (2) rules and methods for intellectual activities ...'[83]

---

[83] Standing Committee of the National People's Congress. Patent Law, Order No.8 of the Chairman of the People's Republic of China.

The Guidelines state that '[b]ecause [rules and methods for intellectual activities] do not use technical means or apply the laws of nature, nor do they solve any technical problem or produce any technical effect, they do not constitute technical solutions'.[84] According to the Guidelines, if there are other technical features besides the 'rules and methods for intellectual activities', inventions will be further examined under Article 2.2 of the Patent Law which means that the invention should be assessed as to whether it is a technical solution.[85]

Further, item (1) of Section 4.2, 'Rules and Methods for Mental [intellectual] Activities' in Chapter 1 of Part II of the Guidelines stipulates that, if a claim or the whole content, except the subject matter of the claim, concerns only rules and methods for mental (intellectual) activities, no patent will be granted.[86] Meanwhile, item (2) states that if the claim contains technical features other than rules and methods for mental (intellectual) activities, the claim, viewed as a whole, will not be excluded from patentability by Article 25.[87] From the instructions in the Guidelines, it can be seen that when assessing whether an invention falls within the category of 'rules and methods for mental [intellectual] activities' of Article 25.1(2) of the Patent Law, it is necessary to consider the whole technical solution including technical problems, technical means and technical effects according to the Guidelines.

The main constraint for examining inventions related to business methods is from the Operating Rules. The Operating Rules instruct patent examiners to use three methods for examining inventions involving business methods. The three examination methods divide the assessment of the technical solution by looking at three factors: technical problem, technical means and technical results, when examining whether the subject matter of a claim constitutes an invention.[88] The Operating Rules inform patent examiners that they can reject an invention by judging that the problem solved by the invention is not a technical problem. Also, patent examiners can redefine the problem solved by the invention by using their own judgement and deciding whether the redefined problem is a technical problem.

The guidance of the Operating Rules stating that patent examiners can reject a patent application merely because of a technology problem is not reasonable. This is because an invention actually reflects a whole technical solution that includes all the three factors. The three factors are interconnected. To reject an invention solely because the problem is not a technical problem may mean neglecting the technical means and the technical effects.

[84] SIPO, 'Guidelines For Patent Examination', p. 134.   [85] Ibid., p. 260.   [86] Ibid., p. 135.
[87] Ibid., p. 136.   [88] Ibid., p. 232.

Although the Operating Rules set out unreasonable rules for assessing the technical solutions for applying Article 2.2 of the Patent Law, in practice, the Patent Reexamination Board gave a different way to assess technical solutions in the reexamination decision No.53240.[89] The decision concerned a rejected application, 'Method and System for Managing the Order of Tickets' with application No. 200680050606.X. This provided 'a system for managing the production of retail tickets in accordance with a ticket order and includes a ticketing services bureau adapted to receive the ticket order and a print centre to print tickets in accordance with the ticket order'.[90] The original patent examiner rejected the patent application by stating that 'Claim 1 of the patent application aims to solve the problem related to the information of clients' orders for commodities, which is a business problem instead of a technical problem'[91] and following the analysis about technical problem, the original patent examiner gave the decision that technical means and technical effects were not involved in the patent application. The original patent examiner rejected the patent application as set out in Article 2.2 of the Patent Law. However, the Patent Reexamination Board overturned the original decision. It considered the whole solution of the patent application by taking account of the technical improvements of the patent application, 'the improvement for the existed retailing service device and related network'.[92] It stated that the methods of the patent application involved technical factors, a 'technical approach comprising "test", "search", and "remind"'.[93] The Patent Reexamination Board also confirmed that the problem this patent application solved was a technical one: 'Claim 1 enables the client and the retailer to have more real-time unrestricted information exchange and therefore the client may review the format of his or her ticket. This is a technical problem.'[94]

From the above reexamination decision, the original patent examiner followed the Operating Rules and first assessed whether a technical problem existed. However, the decision of the original patent examiner was totally

[89] Patent Reexamination Board of SIPO, 'Re-examination Decision of the Rejected Patent Application "System and Method for Managing the Order of Tickets"', Issued on 8 May 2013; No.53420 of the Re-examination Decisions), http://app.sipo-reexam.gov.cn/reex am_out/searchdoc/decidedetail.jsp?jdh=53240&lx=fs.

[90] The introduction is from the abstract of the PCT application of the invention with the published No. WO2007064939 A3. See Jeffrey P. Jooste, Sheila A. Babine and Perry Clifton Hart Jr., 'System and Method of Managing a Ticket Order'. https://patentscope.wipo.int/sea rch/en/detail.jsf?docId=WO2007064939&redirectedID=true.

[91] Patent Reexamination Board of SIPO, 'Reexamination Decision of the Rejected Patent Application "System and Method for Managing the Order of Tickets,"' No.53420.

[92] Ibid.   [93] Ibid.   [94] Ibid.

different to the Patent Reexamination Board. The Patent Reexamination Board considered the solution of the patent application as a whole and made the decision that the patent application involved a technical solution and over-turned the original rejection. The Operating Rules are working guidelines for patent examiners. Although the Patent Reexamination Board may give different decisions when deciding on the assessment of the technical solution, the Operating Rules actually constrain the discretion of patent examiners in asses-sing the technical solutions referred to in Article 2.2 of the Patent Law.

4.4.2.4 Conclusion and Recommendations

As stated in Article 2.2, the Patent Law has provided sufficient room for the discretion of judges and patent examiners: what the Patent Law protects is the technical solution. However, the Guidelines and Operating Rules further constrain the discretion of the patent examiners' application of the Patent Law in the patent prosecution. The Guidelines directly exclude signals as the subject matter of a patent. The apparatus performing computer software can only be protected as a 'virtual apparatus',[95] and the invention related to business methods of CTI can be rejected solely by analyzing a technical problem instead of assessing a technical solution as a whole. The result of these constraints is that the scope of patent rights is limited to a scope that the Guidelines want instead of what a technical solution requires.

These aforementioned constraints have not responded positively to the interconnection and interoperability of innovation of CTI. The interconnec-tion and interoperability of innovation make telecommunications innovation international and this increases the need for international patent protection. However, this paper does not suggest copying patent protection standards of the EU and the US. What this paper suggests is that much more attention should be paid to protecting a technical solution without adding too many administrative constraints on the discretion of the patent examiners in patent prosecution.

4.5 CONSTRAINTS ON THE APPLICATION OF LEGAL PROVISIONS TO THE INCREMENTAL CTI INNOVATION

Incremental innovation is another innovation characteristic of CTI. Incremental innovation is associated with the legal provisions that provide

---

[95] See e.g. Baohai Sun, 'Legal Issues on the "Virtual Apparatus," Claims Related to Computer Programs'.

for discretion over the use of the concept of 'person skilled in the art'. These flexible legal provisions are found in Article 22.3, which concerns inventiveness and the related information in the Guidelines and the Operating Rules on patent prosecution, as well as Article 17 of the Issues Concerning Applicable Laws to the Trial of Patent Controversies concerning the DOE in settling patent disputes.[96] This section explores how the flexible legal provisions concerning inventiveness and the DOE are applied in order to respond to the incremental innovation of CTI.

4.5.1 *The Legal Provisions Concerning Inventiveness in the Incremental Innovation of CTI*

The easy-to-access feature of the existing technology for CTI's patent application may make it harder to assess inventiveness in patent prosecution compared with other industries – the open technology standards caused by the interconnection and interoperability of telecommunications technologies make it easier for the existing technology to be found by patent examiners in patent prosecution. This situation brings to mind Rachlinski's statement that 'the more significant that the materials are to one's self-esteem, the more critical it would be to have accurately predicted the outcome'.[97]

The Guidelines say that if an invention application is non-obvious to a person skilled in the art when compared with the prior art, the invention application has substantive features.[98] The Latin *ob via*, from which the word obvious is derived, literally means 'lying in the road',[99] and in the sense of inventions it means something that would be the next logical step along a path from the problem to the solution.[100] The person skilled in the art[101] providing

---

[96] The Supreme People's Court. Several Provisions of the Supreme People's Court on Issues Concerning Applicable Laws to the Trial of Patent Controversies (Interpretation No. 21 [2001] of the Supreme People's Court, issued on 22 June 2001, effective on 1 July 2001; revised by Interpretation No. 9[2013] of the Supreme People's Court, effective on 15 April 2013), www .wipo.int/wipolex/en/text.jsp?file_id=199492.

[97] Jeffrey J. Rachlinski, 'A Positive Psychological Theory of Judging in Hindsight' (1998) 65 *The University of Chicago Law Review* 571–625, p. 584.

[98] SIPO, 'Guidelines For Patent Examination', p. 193.

[99] Paul England, 'Saint Gobain – Patron of Pharmaceutical Patentees?' (2007) 2 *Journal of Intellectual Property Law & Practice* 532–539, p. 533.

[100] John Richards, 'Obviousness and Inventive Step -New Differences?', Fordham IP Conference (2011), p. 3, http://fordhamipconference.com/wp-content/uploads/2010/08/John_Richards_Ob viousness_and_Inventive_Step_New_Differences.pdf.

[101] The 'person skilled in the art' is also known as the 'person having ordinary skill in the art' in the United States, where the abbreviation PHOSITA is used.

assessment criterion for the technology level of his or her technical field is an important factor that makes legal standards adaptive to different technologies.

This section aims to explore the interaction between the flexible legal provisions concerning inventiveness – Article 22.3 and related instructions on the application of Article 22.3 in the Guidelines – and the incremental innovation in the patent prosecution. Specifically, this paper finds that the common knowledge makes it easy for examiners to reject the patent applications of CTI in their assessments of inventiveness.

Because the Guidelines do not include a clear definition or criterion standards for common knowledge, the uncertainty of the result of patent prosecutions increases. According to the Guidelines, it is not compulsory for patent examiners to provide evidence for what is common knowledge in patent prosecution. The patent search process, in Section 3.3 of Chapter 7, Part II of the Guidelines, states that 'there is no need to make a further search if the additional features of the dependent claims fall into the common knowledge of the relevant art'.[102] Chapter 8 of Part II of the Guidelines, which regulates the procedure for the substantial examination of a patent, states that 'the common knowledge of the art cited in the Office Action by the examiner shall be accurate. Where the applicant has objections to the common knowledge cited by the examiner, the examiner shall state the reasons or provide corresponding evidence for proof.'[103] Therefore, in the patent examination process, patent examiners usually issue an office action for inventiveness including an assessment of common knowledge, without attaching any evidence to prove the common knowledge. Following the Guidelines, the patent examiner may directly make the distinguishing part of an invention fall within common knowledge without providing evidence.

Further, in the patent invalidation procedure for patent prosecution, Chapter 3, 'Examination of Requests for Invalidation' of Part IV of the Guidelines states that 'the Patent Reexamination Board may determine ex officio whether the technical means belong to common knowledge of the art, and may introduce such common knowledge evidence as those in a technical dictionary, technical manual, or textbook into the examination ex officio'.[104] This means the Patent Reexamination Board may determine that the technical means fall into common knowledge without providing any evidence. However, for the parties in the patent invalidation procedure, if one of the parties' invalidation reasons is that the technical means are common knowledge, the party should provide evidence to prove this.[105] Therefore the

[102] SIPO, 'Guidelines For Patent Examination', p. 234.   [103] Ibid., p. 274.
[104] Ibid., p. 455.   [105] Ibid., p. 503.

assessment of inventiveness is very frequently based on reference documents plus common knowledge because the Guidelines do not compulsorily require patent examiners to provide evidence for what is common knowledge.

Although remedies may exist in administrative reconsideration procedure, it increases the cost of patent applicants in patent prosecution. Article 28 of the Administrative Reconsideration Law of the People's Republic of China (hereinafter referred to as the Administrative Reconsideration Law) states

> (3) if a specific administrative act has been undertaken in one of the following circumstances, the act shall be annulled, altered, or confirmed as illegal by decision; if the specific administrative act is altered, or confirmed as illegal by decision, the applied may be ordered to undertake a specific administrative act anew within a fixed time:
>
> a. ambiguity of essential facts, and inadequacy of evidence . . .'[106]

A direct request to patent examiners to attach the evidence for holding that the technical means are common knowledge is also justified by the principle of allocating the burden of evidence – the burden of proof lies with he who declares, not he who denies.[107] Moreover, this would be cost-effective because allocating the burden of evidence to patent examiners in order to prove common knowledge may reduce the possibility of patent reexamination and administration litigation by applicants against the Patent Reexamination Board. For example, in the reexamination case of Patent CN96196073.6 'High Efficiency Sub-Orbital High Altitude Telecommunications System',[108] the patent application was rejected under the substantial examination procedure because of a lack of inventiveness. The patent examiner used the reference document WO9504407 plus common knowledge to decide that Claim 1 of CN96196073.6 was not inventive. The patentee requested reexamination before the Patent Reexamination Board. The Patent Reexamination Board upheld the decision of the CN96196073.6 case, supporting the patent examiner's assessment. The patentee then brought administrative litigation against the Patent Reexamination Board. In the court of first instance, the Patent Reexamination Board provided the evidence of common

---

[106] Standing Committee of the National People's Congress. Administrative Reconsideration Law of the People's Republic of China (2009 Amendment) (Issued on 27 August 2009).

[107] Wikipedia. Presumption of innocence. Available at http://en.wikipedia.org/wiki /Presumption_of_innocence.

[108] Patent Reexamination Board, 'High Efficiency Sub-orbital High Altitude Telecommunications System', Issued on 25 March 2003; No.FS3302 of the Re-examination Decisions).

knowledge that had not been shown in the patent prosecution. The court of first instance dismissed the evidence provided by the Patent Reexamination Board because it could not prove that the information was common knowledge. Although in the court of second instance the court supported the evidence provided by the Patent Reexamination Board, the complexity of deciding common knowledge has been clearly shown by the different assessments of common knowledge in the litigation procedure.[109]

In theory, the Patent Law has provided rooms for discretion for patent examiners' assessment of inventiveness when considering the innovation characteristics of different industries, including CTI. However, the Guidelines for instructing the patent prosecution do not consider either the innovation characteristics of CTI or the industry-specific nature of China's patent law system. Coupled with the unclear definition of common knowledge and the loose rules over using common knowledge, the Guidelines allow the patent examiners to abuse the discretion they are given when applying the legal provisions concerning inventiveness.

4.5.2 *The Legal Provisions concerning the DOE in Patent Infringement Litigation*

The doctrine of equivalent (DOE) principle applied in patent infringement litigation may also reflect the interaction between flexible legal provisions concerning the person skilled in the art and CTI innovation. The DOE is a frequently used principle for comparing the allegedly infringing product and the patent scope, and it is closely connected with the technological characteristics of innovation due to the person skilled in the art concept. This section aims to explore whether the application of the flexible legal provisions concerning the DOE respond to the incremental innovation of CTI.

In China's patent law system, the settlement of patent infringement in China is made up of a judicial track and an administrative track. The administrative approach is seldom used for invention patents in telecommunications. The swift and efficient administrative approach is suitable for settling disputes with strong evidence. The judicial track is suitable for invention patents involving complicated technological issues in the telecommunications area. Therefore, this section discusses the interaction between the flexible legal provisions related to the person skilled in the

109   Nie Chunyan, 'The Assessment of Inventiveness of the Patent Claims Regarding Information and Communication Technologies', 3 April 2008, www.lawtime.cn/info/zhuanli/zlsqfushen /2011082683355.html.

patent infringement litigation. Specifically, this section aims to take the case of *Zhejiang Holley Communication Group* v. *Shenzhen Samsung Kejian Mobile Telecommunication Technology Co., Ltd* (hereinafter referred to as *Holley* v. *Samsung*) as an example for exploring the interaction between the application of the DOE and the innovation of CTI.

Zhejiang Holley Communication Group (hereinafter referred to as Holley) was the patent licensee that obtained the exclusive licence from Zhejiang Holley Industry Group for Patent ZL02101734.4, entitled 'Method for the Communication of a GSM/CDMA Dual Mode Mobile Device'. Holley discovered that the CDMA/GSM dual mode mobile phone SCH-W579 infringed Patent ZL02101734.4. The mobile phone SCH-W579 was manufactured by Shenzhen Samsung Kejian Mobile Telecommunication Technology (hereinafter referred to as Samsung) and was sold by Dai Gang. Holley filed a lawsuit in April 2007 at Hangzhou Intermediate People's Court of Zhejiang Province requesting that Samsung stop infringing and pay RMB 50 million ($7.35 million USD) as compensation. It also requested Dai Gang to stop selling the mobile phone SCH-W579. The Hangzhou Intermediate People's Court of Zhejiang Province supported Holley's request in its court decision in December 2008.[110]

Samsung appealed to the Higher People's Court of Zhejiang Province in 2009.[111] In March 2012, the Higher People's Court of Zhejiang Province reversed the court decision issued by the first instance court.[112] The Higher People's Court of Zhejiang Province commissioned the Shanghai Science and Technology Consulting Center to make a comparison between the allegedly infringing mobile phone and ZL02101734.4. According to the technical appraisal of the Shanghai Science and Technology Consulting Center, the mobile phone SCH-W579 did not fall within the patent scope of ZL02101734.4.[113] The Higher court revoked the decision of the court of first instance and rejected all the requests of Holley.

The critical question for judging the patent infringement is whether the allegedly infringing SCH-W579 mobile phone falls within the patent scope of ZL02101734.4. In the court of first instance, the court rejected Samsung's application for the technical appraisal by a technology institution because

---

[110] *Hangzhou Intermediate People's Court of Zhejiang Province. Zhejiang Holley Communication Group* v. *Shenzhen Samsung Kejian Mobile Telecommunication Technology Co., Ltd* ([2007] No. 108 of the Judgments of the Third Civil Court).

[111] Higher People's Court of Zhejiang Province. *Hangzhou Zhejiang Holley Communication Group* v. *Shenzhen Samsung Kejian Mobile Telecommunication Technology Co., Ltd* (Appeal) ([2009] No. 83 of the Final Instance of the Intellectual Property Court).

[112] Ibid.   [113] Ibid.

the court considered that the comparison of SCH-W579 mobile phone and the claims of ZL02101734.4 was a legal issue. The court of first instance used the DOE to judge that the mobile phone fell within the patent scope of ZL02101734.4.[114] However, the court of second instance accepted Samsung's application for a technical appraisal by the Shanghai Science and Technology Consulting Center. The court of second instance found that the dual-mode communication method of Claim 1 of Patent ZL02101734.4 could be achieved by a different technical approach. SCH-W579 did not necessarily have to take the technical solution provided by Claim 1 of Patent ZL02101734.4.

From this case, it is clear that the court may use the DOE principle to assess a patent infringement or the court may agree to a technical appraisal from an independent institution. Because the patent litigation may lead to a large amount of compensation, the court is very cautious about handing down any decision on patent infringement. Moreover, the cost of patent infringement litigation is also very high. Due to the large investment in the patent litigation, the court should have been better able to use its discretion to interpret the legal provisions concerning the DOE. However, in this case the court of first instance directly applied the DOE to the different technical features that the product had without giving supporting documents or analysis. For example, the court of first instance believed that the antennas for both the GSM mode and the CDMA mode that the SCH-W579 mobile phone had could be thought out by the person skilled in the art without any creative work.[115] In a similar way to the common knowledge issue in patent prosecution, the court of first instance did not provide any evidence for the judgment concerning the DOE.[116]

With the rich resources available in patent infringement litigation, such as the support from technical experts, the court could have been able to show how the application of discretion to the legal provisions could be connected with the technologies in CTI. Compared with patent prosecution, the constraints from the Guidelines and the Operating Rules would not be present in patent infringement litigation. However, at least in this case, the court of first instance gave insufficient evidence to show that the distinguishing technical features of SCH-W579 mobile phone compared with the Claim 1 of Patent ZL02101734.4 could be thought out by the person skilled in the art without any creative work.

[114] Hangzhou Intermediate People's Court of Zhejiang Province. *Zhejiang Holley Communication Group* v. *Shenzhen Samsung Kejian Mobile Telecommunication Technology Co., Ltd*, [2007] No. 108 of the Judgments of the Third Civil Court.
[115] Ibid.   [116] Ibid.

4.5.3 *Conclusion and Recommendations*

This section has analysed flexible legal provisions in relation to two terms – inventiveness and the DOE. Both the inventiveness and the DOE are closely associated with the person skilled in the art concept. In the patent prosecution, patent examiners tend to use common knowledge that the person skilled in the art has to reject the invention patents of CTI. The Patent Law has provided discretion for patent examiners' assessment of inventiveness. However, the assessment of inventiveness in the Guidelines introduces the common knowledge for patent examiners' assessment of inventiveness. The abuse of the common knowledge makes the patent prosecution overlook the innovation characteristics of CTI. In a similar way to patent prosecution, in patent litigation judges are not using the DOE cautiously enough to judge patent infringement. The judges do not provide supporting documents to prove the salient features that exist in the allegedly infringing product that can be thought out by the person skilled in the art without any creative work.

This section suggests that the patent examiners could at least consider the incremental innovation of CTI in order to cautiously use common knowledge as the reference point to assess the inventiveness of invention patent applications of CTI. The definition and the criteria for using common knowledge should be further illustrated in the Guidelines. If common knowledge is used, the supporting documents should be attached to prove the appropriateness of common knowledge. As for the litigation, with the rich resources in patent infringement litigation, such as the support from technical experts, the court could show how the legal provisions that are open to interpretation are applied to respond to the innovation characteristics of CTI.

4.6 CONCLUSIONS

This chapter does not suggest amending the general Patent Law to be industry-specific since the Patent Law has provided sufficient discretion for patent examiners and judges in their application of the Patent Law. This chapter argues that the available discretion of the Patent Law that may respond to the innovation of CTI has been overlooked in the application of the Patent Law by rule-makers, the examiners, practitioners and judges. The constraints from the Guidelines and the Operating Rules suggest that the rule-makers have overlooked the industry-specific nature of the Patent Law and the innovation characteristics of CTI. The court, having fewer chances to apply the flexible legal provisions, has also overlooked the industry-specific nature of patent laws and the innovation characteristics of CTI.

Feldman makes the point that '[t]he law that exists at any given moment is constantly driven to adapt to changing circumstances within the framework of what has gone before'.[117] This is also the case with China's conservative patent law system, which needs to adapt to new technologies. Accordingly, this chapter suggests that the procedural regulations on the assessment of inventiveness in patent prosecution should be enhanced. For example, the patent examiners should provide evidence to prove the common knowledge that he or she uses in the inventiveness assessment. Meanwhile, the court may make good use of the sufficient resources – those especially including the technical support from the third expertise party – to interpret the flexible legal provisions concerning the person skilled in the art. The published interpretation from courts may set a model for the application of flexible legal provisions in patent prosecution even though China is not a case law country, and in this way the industry-specific nature of China's patent law system may be better realized.

---

[117]   Robin Feldman, 'Plain Language Patents' (2009) 17 *Texas Intellectual Property Law Journal* 289–304, p. 289.

5

The Legal Framework for FRAND
Enforcement in China*

Jyh-An Lee

5.1 INTRODUCTION

Information-communication-technology (ICT) innovations nowadays, such as mobile phones and tablets, typically use hundreds of standards, each with thousands of patents in it. Currently, most standard-setting organizations (SSOs) require their members to license standard-essential patents (SEPs) under fair, reasonable, and non-discriminatory (FRAND) terms.[1] SEPs cover inventions that are necessary to comply with a technical standard and are particularly important in the communications industry. Some complicated legal issues concerning SEPs and FRAND have been the focus of recent patent and antitrust scholarship. Courts and competent authorities in many jurisdictions around the world have had to cope with this series of legal problems.[2]

---

* This chapter is revised from part of a paper titled "Implementing the FRAND Standard in China" originally published in the *Vanderbilt Journal of Entertainment & Technology Law*, Volume 19, Issue 1, Fall 2016.

[1] The term FRAND is sometimes used interchangeably with RAND (reasonable and non-discriminatory). They have the same meaning in the realm of SEP licensing. See e.g. Dennis W. Carlton and Allan L. Shampine, "An Economic Interpretation of FRAND" (2013) 9 *Journal of Competition Law and Economics*, 531, p. 531 n.1; Jorge L. Contreras and Richard J. Gilbert, "A Unified Framework for RAND and Other Reasonable Royalties" (2015) 30 *Berkeley Technology Law Journal*, 1447, pp. 1453–1454; Thomas F. Cotter, "Comparative Law and Economics of Standard-Essential Patents and FRAND Royalties" (2014) 22 *Texas Intellectual Property Law Journal*, 311, p. 312; Kassandra Maldonado, Note, "Breaching RAND and Reaching for Reasonable: Microsoft v. Motorola and Standard-Essential Patent Litigation" (2014) 29 *Berkeley Technology Law Journal*, 419, p. 419 n.6.

[2] See e.g. Cotter, "Standard-Essential Patents," 312; Leon B. Greenfield et al., "SEP Enforcement Disputes Beyond the Water's Edge: A Survey of Recent Non-U.S. Decisions" (2013) 27 *Antitrust*, 50; Daryl Lim, "Standard Essential Patents, Trolls, and the Smartphone Wars: Triangulating the End Game" (2014) 119 *Penn State Law Review*, 1, p. 9; Koren W. Wong-Ervin, "Standard-Essential Patents: The International Landscape" (2014) ABA *Section of Antitrust Law* 4, www.ftc.gov/system/files/attachments/key-speeches-presentations/standard-essential_patents_the_intl_landscape.pdf [https://perma.cc/LDK4-DTKA].

As China has grown into a major market in the worldwide communications business, its public policy, court decisions, and private business strategies concerning SEPs and FRAND are likely to have a global impact in the high-technology sector.[3] The recent Chinese case *Huawei v. IDC*[4] represents an important judicial development that has drawn global attention. Like most FRAND disputes, where standard implementers claim that the patentees have breached the FRAND terms and courts are asked to determine the reasonable royalty rate,[5] the Chinese courts in *Huawei* were asked to make a substantive judgment regarding the patentee's possible violation of FRAND commitments.[6] This chapter uses the *Huawei* case as a lens to understand the legal framework of FRAND enforcement in China.

5.2 SEP AND FRAND

Standards or technical standards are "any set of technical specifications that either provide or are intended to provide a common design for a product or process."[7] Standards enable consumers to enjoy various compatible innovations, and manufacturers benefit from massive commercial opportunities.[8] Therefore, standards have become an essential part of our daily lives and the world of rapid technological innovation.[9]

SSOs are organizations whose primary activities are developing, coordinating, promulgating, and revising technical standards that are intended to address the needs of a wide range of implementers and consumers.[10] SSOs

---

[3] Daniel Sokol and Wentong Zheng, "FRAND in China" (2013) 22 *Texas Intellectual Property Law Journal*, 71, pp. 73–74.

[4] *Huawei Tech. Co. v. InterDigital Communications, Inc.* (*Huawei v. IDC*), 2013, No. 305 (Guangdong High People's Ct. 2013) (China).

[5] See e.g. Mark A. Lemley and Carl Shapiro, "A Simple Approach to Setting Reasonable Royalties for Standard-Essential Patents" (2013) 28 *Berkeley Technology Law Journal*, 1135, p. 1160.

[6] 2013 Yue Gao Fa Min San Zhong Zi No. 305.

[7] Mark A. Lemley, "Intellectual Property Rights and Standard-Setting Organizations" (2002) 90 *California Law Review*, 1889, p. 1896.

[8] See e.g. Enrico Bonadio, "Standardization Agreements, Intellectual Property Rights and Anti-competitive Concerns" (2013) 3 *Queen Mary Journal of Intellectual Property*, 22, pp. 24–25; Damien Geradin, "The Meaning of 'Fair and Reasonable' in the Context of Third-Party Determination of FRAND Terms" (2014) 21 *Georgy Mason Law Review (Special Issue)*, 919, p. 933; Jay P. Kesan and Carol M. Hayes, "FRAND's Forever: Standards, Patent Transfers and Licensing Commitments" (2014) 89 *Indiana Law Journal*, 231, pp. 237–238.

[9] See e.g. Lemley, "Standard-Setting Organizations," 1896.

[10] See e.g. ibid., 1892–1893; see also Bonadio, "Standardization Agreements," 24; Stéphanie Chuffart-Finsterwald, "Patent Markets: An Opportunity for Technology Diffusion and FRAND Licensing?" (2014) 18 *Marquette Intellectual Property Law Review*, 335, p. 347;

play an important role in promoting innovation by coordinating various demands from developers and manufacturers.[11] Implementing a standard sometimes requires employing certain patents when standard implementers cannot design around the patents or cannot choose an alternative technology to replace these patents.[12] These patents are the so-called SEPs.[13] Standardization and the market demand for interoperability enabled by standards can lead to a higher probability of infringing SEPs, on which more manufacturers need to build their products.[14] Currently, in their patent or intellectual property (IP) policies, most SSOs require their members to license any SEPs to other members on FRAND terms.[15] FRAND is designed to balance the interests of SEP holders and standard implementers by ensuring the former's fair compensation and the latter's access to the standard.[16] On the one hand, the FRAND rate should be high enough so that

Srividhya Ragavan, Brendan Murphy, and Raj Davé, "FRAND v. Compulsory Licensing: The Lesser of the Two Evils" (2015) 14 *Duke Law & Technology Review*, 83, p. 87; Daniel S. Sternberg, "A Brief History of RAND" (2014) 20.2 *Boston University Journal of Science & Technology Law*, 211, pp. 212, 223–224.

[11] See e.g. Geradin, "The Meaning of 'Fair and Reasonable'," 933; Lim, "Standard Essential Patent," 10–11.

[12] See e.g. Maldonado, "Breaching RAND and Reaching for Reasonable," 432; Ragavan et al., "FRAND v. Compulsory Licensing," 88; Maurice Schellekens, "Horizon 2020 and Fair and Reasonable Licenses" (2015) 21(8) *Computer and Telecommunication Law Review*, 234, pp. 234–235.

[13] See e.g. Jorge L. Contreras, "Fixing FRAND: A Pseudo-Pool Approach to Standards-Based Patent Licensing" (2013) 79 *Antitrust Law Journal*, 47, pp. 50–51; Lemley and Shapiro, "Setting Reasonable Royalties," 1136; Maldonado, "Breaching RAND and Reaching for Reasonable," 419; James Ratliff and Daniel L. Rubinfeld, "The Use and Threat of Injunctions in the RAND Context" (2013) 9 *Journal of Competition Law and Economics*, 1, p. 3.

[14] See e.g. Lim, "Standard Essential Patent," 20.

[15] See e.g. National Research Council (2013) *Patent Challenges for Standard-Setting in the Global Economy: Lessons from Information and Communications Technology*, p. 1; Carlton and Shampine, "Economic Interpretation of FRAND," 531–532; Contreras, "Fixing FRAND," 51, 55; Cotter, "Standard-Essential Patents," 311–312; Layne Keele, "Holding Standards for RANDsome: A Remedial Perspective on RAND Licensing Commitments" (2015) 64 *Kansas Law Review*, 187, pp. 190–191; Kesan and Hayes, "FRAND's Forever," 233, 238; Lemley and Shapiro, "Setting Reasonable Royalties," 1136–1137; Doug Lichtman, "Understanding the RAND Commitment" (2010) 47 *Houston Law Review*, 1023, p. 1025; Lim, "Standard Essential Patent," 9–10; Maldonado, "Breaching RAND and Reaching for Reasonable," 419; Ragavan et al., "FRAND v. Compulsory Licensing," 86–87; Ratliff and Rubinfeld, "Injunctions in the RAND Context," 4; Sokol and Zheng, "FRAND in China," 71.

[16] See e.g. Geradin, "The Meaning of 'Fair and Reasonable'," 922, 932–938; Kirti Gupta, "Technology Standards and Competition in the Mobile Wireless Industry" (2015) 22 *Georgy Mason Law Review*, 865, p. 868; Lim, "Standard Essential Patent," 41; Maldonado, "Breaching RAND and Reaching for Reasonable," 422–425; J. Gregory Sidak, "The Meaning of FRAND, Part II: Injunctions" (2015) 11 *Journal of Competition Law and Economics*, 201, pp. 211–212.

inventors' incentives to develop new technologies will not be hampered.[17] On the other hand, SEP holders are obliged to FRAND commitment so that implementers can legally employ the SEPs without the risk of infringement,[18] being locked-in by the SEPs,[19] or losing their standard-specific investments.[20] By balancing the implementers' interest in access to standard and inventors' incentive, FRAND plays a vital role in modern innovation policy.

It is widely believed that the purpose of FRAND terms is to prevent the "hold-up problem,"[21] wherein SEP holders withhold a license until an implementer agrees to pay an unduly high royalty rate for the patent.[22] Because implementers will have invested substantially in developing products based on the specific standard, it is quite expensive to opt out of the standard.[23] Consequently, SEP holders enjoy an advantageous position in negotiations associated with licensing the subject patents to other entities due to the SSOs' adoption decision rather than the incremental value of those patents.[24]

---

[17]   See e.g. *In re Innovatio IP Ventures, LLC Patent Litig.*, No. 11 C 9308, 2013 WL 5593609, at *11 (N.D. Ill. Oct. 3, 2013); *Microsoft Corp. v. Motorola, Inc.*, No. C10-1823JLR, 2013 WL 2111217, at *12 (W.D. Wash. Apr. 25, 2013); Sidak, "The Meaning of FRAND," 212.

[18]   Maldonado, "Breaching RAND and Reaching for Reasonable," 426.

[19]   Lim, "Standard Essential Patent," 42.

[20]   Carlton and Shampine, "Economic Interpretation of FRAND," 535–536; Contreras, "Fixing FRAND," 56–57; Lim, "Standard Essential Patent," 29; Sidak, "The Meaning of FRAND," 211–212.

[21]   Patent hold-up problems take place when a patent holder refuses to license a patent on expected terms and, therefore, holds up the progress of the diffusion of new technologies. See Robert P. Merges and Jeffrey M. Kuhn, "An Estoppel Doctrine for Patented Standards" (2009) 97 *California Law Review*, 1, pp. 10, 49.

[22]   See e.g. *Ericsson, Inc. v. D–Link Sys., Inc.*, 773 F.3d 1201, 1209 (Fed. Cir. 2014); *Microsoft Corp. v. Motorola, Inc.*, No. C10-1823JLR, 2013 WL 2111217, at *12 (W.D. Wash. Apr. 25, 2013); Rebecca Haw Allensworth, "Casting A FRAND Shadow: The Importance of Legally Defining 'Fair and Reasonable' and How Microsoft v. Motorola Missed the Mark" (2014) 22 *Texas Intellectual Property Law Journal*, 235, p. 244; Carlton and Shampine, "Economic Interpretation of FRAND," 534; Jorge L. Contreras, "A Brief History of FRAND: Analyzing Current Debates in Standard Setting and Antitrust Through a Historic Lens" (2015) 80 *Antitrust Law Journal*, 39, p. 42; Contreras and Gilbert, "A Unified Framework for RAND," 1456; Contreras, "Fixing FRAND," 49–51; Gupta, "Technology Standards and Competition," 866, 882; Keele, "RAND Licensing Commitments," 189; Mark A. Lemley and Carl Shapiro, "Patent Holdup and Royalty Stacking" (2007) 85 *Texas Law Review*, 1991, p. 1993; Lim, "Standard Essential Patent," 4, 29; Maldonado, "Breaching RAND and Reaching for Reasonable," 428; Ragavan et al., "FRAND v. Compulsory Licensing," 89–90; Sidak, "The Meaning of FRAND," 211.

[23]   See e.g. Contreras, "Fixing FRAND," 48–49; Lim, "Standard Essential Patent," 3.

[24]   See e.g. Contreras and Gilbert, "A Unified Framework for RAND," 1456; Contreras, "Fixing FRAND," 50–51; Maldonado, "Breaching RAND and Reaching for Reasonable," 428.

Although FRAND provisions are quite common in SSOs' IP policies, none of these policies define what is "fair" or "reasonable."[25] The FRAND commitment is, therefore, viewed as an "incomplete contract."[26] Although some scholars suggest the incompleteness of FRAND is necessary and desirable for negotiations between SEP holders and standard implementers,[27] controversies occasionally occur when a standard implementer fails to reach an agreement regarding the FRAND rate with the SEP holder.[28] The central disputes are primarily about whether the rates offered by the SEP holder are consistent with its FRAND commitment.[29] If not, the dispute then centers on how a court should decide the FRAND rate for both parties.[30]

5.3 BACKGROUND OF *HUAWEI V. IDC*

Huawei is a Chinese company with its headquarter in Shenzhen.[31] It is one of the largest telecommunications equipment and device producers in the

---

[25] See e.g. Rudi Bekkers and Andrew Updegrove, "A Study of IPR Policies and Practices of a Representative Group of Standards Setting Organizations Worldwide" (2012), pp. 102–103, http://sites.nationalacademies.org/PGA/step/IPManagement/PGA_072197 [https://perma.cc/A6 N7-GSNV]; Carlton and Shampine, "Economic Interpretation of FRAND," 532; Contreras and Gilbert, "A Unified Framework for RAND," 1454; Contreras, "Fixing FRAND," 51; Lemley, "Standard-Setting Organizations," 1913–1914, 1964–1965; Lichtman, "Understanding the RAND Commitment," 1031; Ragavan et al., "FRAND v. Compulsory Licensing," 90–91.

[26] See e.g. Geradin, "The Meaning of Fair and Reasonable," 922; Lim, "Standard Essential Patent," 22; Joanna Tsai and Joshua D. Wright, "Standard Setting, Intellectual Property Rights, and the Role of Antitrust in Regulating Incomplete Contracts" (2015) 80 *Antitrust Law Journal*, 157, pp. 162–164.

[27] See e.g. Richard A. Epstein, F. Scott Kieff and Daniel F. Spulber, "The FTC, IP, and SSOs: Government Hold-Up Replacing Private Coordination" (2012) 8 *Journal of Competition Law and Economics*, 1, p. 12; Geradin, "The Meaning of 'Fair and Reasonable'," 930 (arguing that such incompleteness is inevitable and beneficial).

[28] See e.g. Ichiro Nakayama and Yoshiyuki Tamura, "Denial of Injunctive Relief on Grounds of Equity: Situation in the U.S. and Japan," in Reto M. Hilty and Kung-Chung Liu (eds.), *Compulsory Licensing – Practical Experiences and Ways Forward* (Berlin: Springer, 2015) 267–290.

[29] See e.g. Contreras, "Fixing FRAND," 52–54; Fei Deng, "Determining the FRAND Rate: U.S. Perspectives on Huawei v. InterDigital," *Competition Policy International*, 12 February 2014, www.competitionpolicyinternational.com/determining-the- frand-rate-u-s-perspectives-on -huawei-v-interdigital/ [https://perma.cc/EZ6Y-363W]; Geradin, "The Meaning of 'Fair and Reasonable'," 940–41; see also Lim, "Standard Essential Patent," 5 ("When disputes occur, they reveal a stark disparity of views on the meaning of FRAND obligations."); Maldonado, "Breaching RAND and Reaching for Reasonable," 420 (describing "a flood of litigation seeking to define what constitutes reasonable royalty rates").

[30] See e.g. Lichtman, "Understanding the RAND Commitment," 1032; see also Kesan and Hayes, "FRAND's Forever," 239 ("SSOs adopt vague language requiring fairness and reasonableness, leaving it to the courts to determine what license terms would be fair and reasonable.").

[31] See e.g. Adam Pasick, "The World's Third-Largest Smartphone Maker Is Weirdly Cagey about Its Progress Outside of China," *Quartz*, July 29, 2014, http://qz.com/241746/the-worlds-third

world.[32] InterDigital Communications (IDC)[33] is a non-practicing entity (NPE)[34] whose business model is primarily based on licensing patents for 2G, 3G, and 4G devices, and the IEEE802 standard, rather than the manufacture of products.[35] In September 2009, IDC joined an SSO, the European Telecommunications Standards Institute (ETSI), and committed to licensing its SEPs on FRAND terms.[36] IDC also owns SEPs in China's wireless communications standards (WCDMA, CDMA2000, and TD-SCDMA standards).[37] Since November 2008, Huawei has had several negotiations with IDC regarding the license royalties for those SEPs.[38]

IDC first sued Huawei and other telecommunications companies, including Nokia and ZTE, in the US Federal District Court of Delaware and the International Trade Commission (ITC) in 2011 and 2012, claiming infringement of its 3G telecom patents.[39] In addition to damages claims, IDC sought

-largest-smartphone-maker-is-weirdly-cagey-about-its-progress-outside-of-china/ [https://perma .cc/98EB-EMX4]; Andrew Stevens, "China's Silicon Valley," CNN, September 23, 2016, htt p://money.cnn.com/2016/05/20/technology/china-tech-huawei-campus-life/ [https://perma.cc /9GC5-66HR].

[32] "Huawei," Wikipedia, https://en.wikipedia.org/w/index.php?title=Huawei&oldid=700203172 [https://perma.cc/77SZ-J8UD].

[33] It should be noted that there were four defendants in this case: InterDigital Communications, Inc.; InterDigital Technology Corporation; InterDigital Patent Holdings Inc.; and IPR Licensing Inc., which are affiliated with one another. In this chapter, following the term used in the *Huawei* decision, I use "IDC" to denote all four of these defendants. See 2013 Yue Gao Fa Min San Zhong Zi No. 305.

[34] NPEs or patent assertion entities (PAEs) are companies that profit from asserting patents without making or selling products. See e.g. John R. Allison, Mark A. Lemley, and David L. Schwartz, "Our Divided Patent System" (2015) 82 *The University of Chicago Law Review*, 1073, p. 1129; Christopher A. Cotropia et al., "Unpacking Patent Assertion Entities (PAEs)" (2014) 99 *Minnesota Law Review*, 649, p. 650; Stefania Fusco, "Markets and Patent Enforcement: A Comparative Investigation of Non-Practicing Entities in the United States and Europe" (2014) 20 *Michigan Telecommunication and Technology Law Review*, 439, pp. 443–444; Camilla A. Hrdy, "Commercialization Awards" (2015) 2015 *Wisconsin Law Review*, 13, p. 35; Eric Rogers and Young Jeon, "Inhibiting Patent Trolling: A New Approach for Applying Rule" (2014) 11.12 *Northwestern Journal of Technology and Intellectual Property*, 291, p. 293; Aria Soroudi, "Defeating Trolls: The Impact of Octane and Highmar on Patent Trolls" (2015) 35 *Loyola of Los Angeles Entertainment Law Review*, 319, p. 320.

[35] See 2013 Yue Gao Fa Min San Zhong Zi No. 305.   [36] Ibid.   [37] Ibid.

[38] See e.g. Guangliang Zhang and Gary Zhang, "A Review of Huawei v IDC," Managing Intellectual Property, March 27, 2015, www.managingip.com/Article/3440420/A-review-of -Huawei- v-IDC.html [https://perma.cc/58Z2-KFWD].

[39] US patent numbers 7349540, 7502406, 7536013, 7616070, 7706332, 7706830, and 7970127. See 2013 Yue Gao Fa Min San Zhong Zi No. 305. On December 19, 2013, ITC ruled that IDC's alleged patents are either invalid or not infringed. See "Certain Wireless Devices with 3G Capabilities and Components Thereof," Inv. No. 337-TA-800, 19 December 2013 (Notice), http://usitc.gov/secretary/fed_reg_notices/337/337_800_notice12192013sgl.pdf [https://perma .cc/TK3C-YUWM].

not only preliminary and permanent injunctions from the district court but also exclusion orders from ITC against Huawei.[40] In December 2011, Huawei, in turn, filed two lawsuits against IDC in the Shenzhen Intermediate People's Court.[41] In the first lawsuit, Huawei alleged that IDC had been abusing its dominant market position through a number of unlawful practices, such as differentiated pricing, tying-in, and refusal to deal.[42] Huawei claimed damages of RMB 20 million.[43] In the second case, Huawei sued IDC for violating its FRAND obligations.[44] The first case was primarily associated with China's Anti-Monopoly Law, whereas the second dealt with a more fundamental issue regarding the legal mechanism to enforce FRAND commitment and judicial determinations of the FRAND rate.

The Shenzhen Intermediate People's Court ruled on February 4, 2013, that IDC had violated its FRAND obligations.[45] On October 16, 2013, the Guangdong High People's Court (the *"Huawei* court") upheld the Shenzhen Intermediate People's Court's decision regarding IDC's violation of its FRAND obligation.[46] This *Huawei* decision is of great importance to understand judicial practices with regard to FRAND-encumbered SEPs in China.

5.4 THE FRAND OBLIGATION UNDER CHINESE LAW

Jurisdictions may have quite different approaches to the legal effect of a FRAND commitment.[47] One of the notable issues in *Huawei* is the determination of an appropriate legal basis for Huawei to claim a FRAND rate against IDC. In all cases involving FRAND and SEPs, standard implementers need to find an enforcement mechanism to hold SEP holders to their obligation to license such patents under FRAND terms. In this case, IDC argued

---

[40]   2013 Yue Gao Fa Min San Zhong Zi No. 305.
[41]   See CPI, "Huawei v. InterDigital: China at the Crossroads of Antitrust and Intellectual Property, Competition and Innovation," Competition Policy International, December 3, 2013, www.competitionpolicyinternational.com/huawei-v-interdigital-china-at-the-crossroads -of-antitrust-and-intellectual-property-competition-and-innovation/ [https://perma.cc/RL8L -SBKR].
[42]   Huawei Jishu Youxian Gongsi Su Jiaohu Shuzi Tongxin Youxian Gongsi [*Huawei Tech. Co. v. InterDigital Communications, Inc. (Huawei v. IDC)*], 2011 Shen Zhong Fa Zhi Min Chu Zi No. 858 (Shenzhen Interm. People's Ct. 2011) (China).
[43]   Ibid.
[44]   Huawei Jishu Youxian Gongsi Su Jiaohu Shuzi Tongxin Youxian Gongsi [*Huawei Tech. Co. v. InterDigital Communications, Inc. (Huawei v. IDC)*], 2011 Shen Zhong Fa Zhi Min Chu Zi No. 857 (Shenzhen Interm. People's Ct. 2011) (China).
[45]   See CPI, "Huawei v. InterDigital."   [46]   Ibid.
[47]   Kesan and Hayes, "FRAND's Forever," 233.

Jyh-An Lee

that its FRAND commitment was just an invitation for license negotiation, rather than an obligation to form the contractual relationship.[48] As such, IDC denied any legally binding bases for FRAND and contended that the courts could not create the contractual relationship between the two parties.[49] Huawei, on the other hand, insisted that IDC was obliged to license its SEPs under FRAND terms, no matter whether that was based on contract, their FRAND commitment, or the doctrine of fairness and good faith in Chinese law.[50] The courts, therefore, had to look into all these claims and explore whether there was an appropriate legal basis for SEP holders' FRAND commitments in China.[51]

5.4.1 *Contract between SEP Holders and Implementers*

Some scholars attempt to view a FRAND commitment as an implied license to all implementers so that patent holders have "a contractual claim for royalty, not a cause of action for patent infringement that might result in an injunction, treble damages, and attorneys' fees."[52] Chinese IP scholar Cui Guobin likewise suggests that it is possible that IDC and Huawei had already entered into a license agreement before negotiation.[53] He interprets IDC's FRAND commitment to ETSI as an offer, and Huawei could accept the offer by notifying IDC of its plan to implement the subject standard.[54]

As a FRAND pledge does not include a specific license fee or royalty rate, it cannot be an offer made by SEP holders.[55] For example, a Dutch court made it clear in a 2012 decision that a SEP holder's FRAND commitment to SSOs does not constitute a license between the SEP holder and standard implementers.[56] Similarly, in *Huawei*, both first-instance and second-instance courts ruled out the possibility that Huawei requested a FRAND

---

[48] Huawei Jishu Youxian Gongsi Su Jiaohu Shuzi Tongxin Youxian Gongsi [*Huawei Tech. Co. v. InterDigital Communications, Inc. (Huawei v. IDC)*], 2013 Yue Gao Fa Min San Zhong Zi No. 305 (Guangdong High People's Ct. 2013) (China).

[49] Ibid.   [50] Ibid.

[51] Zhong Lun Law Firm, "Seeking Injunctions for Standard Essential Patents in China," Lexology, March 3, 2016, www.lexology.com/library/detail.aspx?g=d2c6e034-3544-4b6e-bb29-55be99235ffe [https://perma.cc/9FDT-68UV].

[52] See e.g. Lemley, "Standard-Setting Organizations," 1925.

[53] Cui Guobin, "Standard-Essential Patents and Injunctive Relief," in Stefan Luginbuehl and Pater Ganea (eds.), *Patent Law in Greater China* (Cheltenham: Edward Elgar Publishing, 2014) 340–362.

[54] Ibid., 348–349.

[55] Maurice Schellekens, "Horizon 2020 and Fair and Reasonable Licenses" (2015) 21.8 *Computer and Telecommunication Law Review*, 234, p. 239.

[56] Cotter, "Standard-Essential Patents," 318.

licensing rate based on its contract with IDC.[57] The courts stated that there was no contractual relationship between Huawei and IDC, and such a relationship would only be formed after they reached a consensus over the license rates and other licensing terms.[58] In other words, there was no contractual basis for Huawei to claim a FRAND licensing rate against IDC.

5.4.2 Contract with Third-Party Beneficiaries

The other option for enforcing FRAND commitment is to define IDC's agreement with ETSI as a contract with third-party beneficiaries.[59] Put more clearly, this approach suggests that IDC entered into a binding contractual commitment with ETSI, agreeing to license its SEPs on FRAND terms,[60] and Huawei is a third-party beneficiary of IDC's commitments to ETSI.[61] A contract with third-party beneficiaries has been common practice to cope with FRAND-encumbered SEPs in the US.[62] Two court decisions in the United States provide examples of this approach.[63] In *Microsoft* v. *Motorola*,[64] the US court held that Microsoft was a third-party beneficiary of Motorola's FRAND commitments to the Institute of Electrical and Electronics Engineers (IEEE) and ETSI, which were enforceable contracts. Therefore, Microsoft was entitled to sue for breach of the FRAND contract.[65]

---

[57] Huawei Jishu Youxian Gongsi Su Jiaohu Shuzi Tongxin Youxian Gongsi [*Huawei Tech. Co.* v. *InterDigital Communications, Inc. (Huawei v. IDC)*], 2013 Yue Gao Fa Min San Zhong Zi No. 305 (Guangdong High People's Ct. 2013) (China).

[58] Ibid.   [59] Cui, "Standard-Essential Patents and Injunctive Relief," 349.

[60] The contractual nature of FRAND commitment has been recognized by numerous court decisions and academic articles in the United States. See e.g. *Microsoft Corp.* v. *Motorola, Inc.*, 696 F.3d 872, 878 (9th Cir. 2012); *Research in Motion Ltd.* v. *Motorola, Inc.*, 644 F. Supp. 2d 788, 797 (N.D. Tex. 2008), *Ericsson, Inc.* v. *Samsung Elecs. Co.*, No. 2:06-CV-63, 2007 WL 1202728, at *1 (E.D. Tex. Apr. 20, 2007); Cotter, "Standard-Essential Patents," 313, 315–319; Keele, "RAND Licensing Commitments," 194–196; Lemley and Shapiro, "Setting Reasonable Royalties," 1141; Mark A. Lemley, "Ten Things to Do about Patent Holdup of Standards (and One Not To)" (2007) 48 *Boston College Law Review*, 149, pp. 155–158; Ragavan et al., "FRAND v. Compulsory Licensing," 93–94; Ratliff and Rubinfeld, "Injunctions in the RAND Context," 4; Sidak, "The Meaning of FRAND," 210; Sternberg, "A Brief History of RAND," 225.

[61] Yang Li and Nari Lee, "European Standards in Chinese Courts – A Case of SEP and FRAND disputes in China," in Nari Lee, Niklas Brunn and Mingde Le (eds.), *Governance of Intellectual Property Rights in China and Europe* (Cheltenham: Edward Elgar Publishing, 2016), 266–286.

[62] See e.g. Jorge L. Contreras, "A Market Reliance Theory for FRAND Commitments and Other Patent Pledges" (2015) *Utah Law Review*, 479, pp. 483–484; Ragavan et al., "FRAND v. Compulsory Licensing," 98–99.

[63] *Microsoft Corp.* v. *Motorola, Inc.*, 864 F. Supp. 2d 1023, 1033 (W.D. Wash. 2012); *Apple, Inc.* v. *Motorola Mobility, Inc.*, 886 F. Supp. 2d 1061, 1083 (W.D. Wis. 2012).

[64] *Microsoft*, 864 F. Supp. 2d at 1033.   [65] Ibid.

As the district court's Judge Robart noted, "[the FRAND] commitments are clearly designed to benefit potential licensees of Motorola's standard essential patent by ensuring that such patents are readily accessible to everybody at reasonable rates."[66] The court thus rejected Motorola's statement that the IEEE and International Telecommunications Union (ITU) commitments were merely unilateral offers to negotiate reasonable and non-discriminatory (RAND) licenses.[67] Motorola was, therefore, obliged to grant Microsoft a FRAND license, not permitted merely "to engage in bilateral, good-faith negotiations leading to [F]RAND terms."[68] In *Apple, Inc.* v. *Motorola Mobility, Inc.*,[69] Judge Crabb similarly concluded that, by committing to FRAND terms to ETSI and IEEE, Motorola had made a contractual commitment to license its SEPs on FRAND terms to third-party beneficiaries, including Apple. If the SEP holder's FRAND commitment constitutes a binding contract, then it becomes crucial for the court to carefully read the language of SSOs' Intellectual Property Right policies so that it can determine what an SEP holder's FRAND obligations are.

According to Chinese contract law, parties may agree that one party shall perform its obligation to a third party.[70] Based on the majority and authoritative interpretation of Chinese contract law, a third party can claim the contractual right against the obligor although it is not a contracting party[71] and although the third party's right is not independent from the original contracting parties.[72] In *Huawei*, some Chinese scholars suggest that, although the contractual relation took place between ETSI and IDC, Huawei, as a third-party beneficiary, could still request a FRAND rate from IDC.[73] However, it should be noted that China derived its civil law,

---

[66]   Ibid.   [67]   Ibid., 1032.

[68]   *Microsoft Corp.* v. *Motorola, Inc.*, No. C10-1823JLR, 2012 WL 4827743, at *6 (W.D. Wash. Oct. 10, 2012).

[69]   *Apple, Inc.* v. *Motorola Mobility, Inc.*, 886 F. Supp. 2d 1061, 1085 (W.D. Wis. 2012).

[70]   Contract Law of the People's Republic of China (promulgated by Nat'l People's Cong., Mar. 15, 1999), art. 64, 1999 PRC Contract Law (China) ("Where the parties prescribed that the obligor render performance to a third person, if the obligor fails to render its performance to the third person, or rendered non-conforming performance, it shall be liable to the obligee for breach of contract.").

[71]   See e.g. Mo Zhang, *Chinese Contract Law: Theory and Practice* (Leiden: Martinus Nijhoff Publishers, 2006), p. 319; Cui, "Standard-Essential Patents and Injunctive Relief," 350–351.

[72]   See e.g. Hector L. MacQueen, "Third Party Rights in Contract: A Case Study on Codifying and Not Codifying," in Lei Chen and C.H. (Remco) van Rhee (eds.), *Toward a Chinese Civil Code: Comparative and Historical Perspective* (Leiden: Martinus Nijhoff Publishers, 2012), 309–333.

[73]   Cui, "Standard-Essential Patents and Injunctive Relief," 349–350.

including contract law, from the German system.[74] Therefore, the way that German courts and scholars interpret contract law has a significant impact on Chinese contract law.[75] In Germany, the courts have made it clear that SEP holders' FRAND commitments do not grant other SSO members a right to obtain a license, and the FRAND commitment is nothing but an invitation for third parties to make offers.[76] In *Huawei*, IDC also cited a German court decision to dissuade the court from holding that Huawei was a third-party beneficiary to the contract between IDC and ETSI.[77] Although the *Huawei* court did not view Huawei as a third-party beneficiary, it did not explain that decision.[78] One possible explanation is that in Chinese contract law, contracting parties cannot impose any obligation on the third and a third-party beneficiary will obtain purely benefit without any obligation. The third party only receives obligor's performance and is not subject to any contractual obligation.[79] However, in the SEPs scenario, standard implementers still need to pay SEP holders a royalty based on FRAND terms. Therefore, such arrangement cannot be a contract with third-party beneficiary under Chinese law.

5.4.3 Doctrines of Fairness and Good Faith

The *Huawei* court eventually ruled that the legal basis for Huawei to request that IDC provide a FRAND rate was the doctrine of fairness and good faith prescribed in the General Principles of Civil Law and Chinese Contract Law.[80] The court also identified three statutes from these two bodies of law as the legal basis for Huawei's FRAND claim against IDC:[81]

---

[74] See e.g. Zhu Jingwen and Han Dayuan (eds.), *Research Report on the Socialist Legal System with Chinese Characteristics* (Singapore: Enrich Professional Publishing, 2013), vol. 3, p. 51; Zhang Xiaoyang, *Chinese Civil Law for Businesses* (Hong Kong: Open University of Hong Kong Press, 2013) pp. 21, 30; Zhang, *Chinese Contract Law*, p. xi; Tianshu Zhou and Mathias Siems, "Contentious Modes of Understanding Chinese Commercial Law" (2015) 6 *George Mason Journal of International Commercial Law*, 177, pp. 179–180.

[75] See e.g. Jianlin Chen, "Challenges in Designing Public Procurement Linkages: A Case Study of SMES Preference in China's Government Procurement" (2013) 30 *UCLA Pacific Basin Law Journal*, 149, p. 179; Perry Keller, "Sources of Order in Chinese Law" (1994) 42 *American Journal of Comparative Law*, 711, pp. 718–719; Wang Liming, "An Inquiry into Several Difficult Problems in Enacting China's Uniform Contract Law" (1999) 8 *Pacific Rim Law & Policy Journal*, 351, pp. 354–355, 385.

[76] Cotter, "Standard-Essential Patents," 318.

[77] 2013 Yue Gao Fa Min San Zhong Zi No. 305.   [78] Ibid.

[79] Contract Law of the People's Republic of China (promulgated by Nat'l People's Cong., Mar. 15, 1999), art. 64, 1999 PRC Contract Law (China).

[80] 2013 Yue Gao Fa Min San Zhong Zi No. 305.   [81] Ibid.

(1) Article 4 of the General Principles of Civil Law: "In civil activities, the principles of voluntariness, fairness, consideration for equal value, and good faith shall be observed."[82]
(2) Article 5 of the Chinese Contract Law: "The parties shall observe the principle of fairness in defining each other's rights and obligations."[83]
(3) Article 6 of the Chinese Contract Law: "The parties shall observe the principle of good faith in exercising their rights and fulfilling their obligations."[84]

The *Huawei* court ruled that IDC's FRAND obligation to Huawei could be established by applying the three Articles to construct the scope and effect of IDC's FRAND commitment.[85] It is not surprising that the *Huawei* court applied the General Principles of Civil Law and Chinese Contract Law to solve the issues surrounding FRAND-encumbered patents because intellectual property (IP) laws in China have always been viewed as part of the civil law system, and relevant civil code can, therefore, be applied to IP disputes,[86] not to mention that the *Huawei* dispute originated from IDC's contracts with SSOs.[87] As in most civil law countries, fairness and, especially, good faith are overriding principles that govern all private activities in China.[88] "Good faith" in Chinese refers to "honesty" (*chengshi*) and "faithfulness" (*xinyong*).[89] It implies the reasonable expectations of the parties, a proper balance of different interests, and the reasonable commercial standard for fair dealing.[90] The implementation

---

[82] General Principles of the Civil Law of the People's Republic of China (promulgated by the Nat'l People's Cong., Apr. 12, 1986), art. 4, 1986 PRC Civil and Commercial Laws (China).

[83] Contract Law of the People's Republic of China (promulgated by Nat'l People's Cong., Mar. 15, 1999), art. 5, 1999 PRC Contract Law (China).

[84] Contract Law of the People's Republic of China (promulgated by Nat'l People's Cong., Mar. 15, 1999), art. 6, 1999 PRC Contract Law (China).

[85] 2013 Yue Gao Fa Min San Zhong Zi No. 305.

[86] See e.g. Liming Wang, "The Systematization of the Chinese Civil Code," in Chen and van Rhee (eds.), *Toward a Chinese Civil Code*, 21–28.

[87] See above p. 160 and notes 35–37.

[88] See e.g. Ejan Mackaay, *Law and Economics for Civil Law Systems* (Cheltenham: Edward Elgar Publishing, 2013), pp. 432–433; Zhang, *Chinese Contract Law*, 75–76; Zhu and Han, "Socialist Legal System with Chinese Characteristics," 17; Reinhard Zimmermann and Simon Whittaker, *Good Faith in European Contract Law* (Cambridge: Cambridge University Press, 2000), 49–56; Chunlin Leonhard, "A Legal Chameleon: An Examination of the Doctrine of Good Faith in Chinese and American Contract Law" (2010) 25 *Connecticut Journal of International Law*, 305, p. 306; Wang Liming and Xu Chuanxi, "Fundamental Principles of China's Contract Law" (1999) 13 *Columbia Journal of Asian Law*, 1, p. 16; Saul Litvinoff, "Good Faith" (1997) 71 *Tulane Law Review*, 1645, pp. 1646–1647, 1655.

[89] See e.g. Bing Ling, *Contract Law in China* (Hong Kong: Sweet & Maxwell Asia, 2002), pp. 49–50, 52; Zhang, *Chinese Contract Law*, 26.

[90] See e.g. Ling, *Contract Law in China*, 54.

of this principle requires parties to ensure fairness in civil activities and to avert the abuse of rights.[91] Therefore, Chinese scholars view the principle of fairness as "subsumed under the principle of good faith."[92] Moreover, FRAND rightfully echoes the principle of fairness in Chinese law as fairness is an essential component of a FRAND commitment.

Although the *Huawei* court did not specify, based on the doctrine of good faith, the duty that IDC as a SEP holder owed to a standard implementer, it is generally accepted in China that parties during the negotiation stage should bear the duties of loyalty, honesty, non-deception, confidentiality, and most importantly, duty to keep promises.[93] If the court viewed IDC's offer as excessively high, it could rule that the company violated good faith doctrine by breaking its FRAND promise.

From a comparative perspective, some US scholars have proposed to establish a mechanism to enforce FRAND commitments based on promissory or equitable estoppel doctrine. This would similarly require the patent holder's promise or statement and the standard adopter's reliance.[94] These proposals, however, were not adopted by the US courts: promissory estoppel is the American common law approach to deciding whether to impose precontractual liability in the absence of an agreement.[95] Nonetheless, the concept of estoppel does not exist in China and other civil law systems.[96] Therefore, experiences from other civil law jurisdictions are noteworthy for the discussion of FRAND enforcement in China, especially with the view whether they similarly apply the doctrine of good faith in FRAND disputes. The Tokyo District Court in Japan, whose civil law jurisdiction has had a huge influence on the Chinese private law regime,[97] once recognized that the principle of

---

[91] See e.g. Hui Zheng, "Overview," in Yuanshi Bu (ed.), *Chinese Civil Law* (Oxford: Hart Publishing, 2013), 1–6.

[92] See e.g. Ling, *Contract Law in China*, 50.

[93] See e.g. Wang Liming and Xu Chuanxi, "Fundamental Principles of China's Contract Law" (1999) 13 *Columbia Journal of Asian Law*, 1, pp. 16–19. In some other jurisdictions, courts will also hold parties liable if the party "breaks off negotiations in a manner contrary to precontractual good faith." See Martijn W. Hesselink, "The Concept of Good Faith," in Ewoud Hondius (ed.), *Toward a European Civil Code* (Nijimegen: Kluwer Law International, 2011) 619–650.

[94] See e.g. Contreras, "Market Reliance Theory," 516–517, 521–523; Kesan and Hayes, "FRAND's Forever," 263–264; Lemley, "Standard-Setting Organizations," 1918; Sidak, "The Meaning of FRAND," 223–224.

[95] See e.g. Nadia E. Nedzel, "A Comparative Study of Good Faith, Fair Dealing, and Precontractual Liability" (1997) 12 *Tulane European and Civil Law Forum*, 97, pp. 128–136.

[96] See e.g. David V. Snyder, "Comparative Law in Action: Promissory Estoppel, the Civil Law, and the Mixed Jurisdiction" (1998) 15 *Arizona Journal of International & Comparative Law*, 695, p. 695.

[97] See e.g. Zhang, *Chinese Contract Law*, xi.

good faith should be applied to parties engaging in contract negotiations, including those involving FRAND-encumbered SEPs.[98] The Tokyo District Court, therefore, ruled that SEP holders should honestly disclose appropriate information to substantiate their offers upon the request of standard implementers.[99]

SEP holders such as IDC, on the other hand, may always argue that based on freedom of contract, they should have freedom to enter into a license agreement, the freedom to choose with whom to sign the license agreement, and the freedom to decide the content and form of a license agreement.[100] However, the freedom of contract is limited by the principle of good faith[101] because of policy concerns arising from asymmetric bargaining power or unfair clauses.[102] Additionally, technical standard and FRAND-encumbered SEPs involve not only the private interests of both parties but also the public interest. The principle of good faith in China was designed precisely to balance the interests of the parties and society.[103] Therefore, a FRAND violation may be an appropriate case in which to apply the doctrine of good faith.

5.4.4 *SAIC's Provisions*

The State Administration for Industry and Commerce (SAIC) in China recently issued the Provisions of the State Administration for Industry and Commerce on Prohibiting the Abuse of Intellectual Property Rights to Preclude or Restrict Competition (Provisions). These were issued on April 7,

---

[98] See e.g. Herbert Hovenkamp, Mark Janis, Mark Lemley, and Christopher R. Leslie, *IP and Antitrust: An Analysis of Antitrust Principles Applied to Intellectual Property Law* (Austin: Aspen Publishers, 2016), § 48.5d1 n.191.1 (citing Tokyo district court cases); Cotter, "Standard-Essential Patents," 325–326; Ichiro Nakayama and Yoshiyuki Tamura, "Denial of Injunctive Relief," 286.

[99] Cotter, "Standard-Essential Patents," 326.

[100] See e.g. General Principles of the Civil Law of the People's Republic of China (promulgated by the Nat'l People' Cong., Apr. 12, 1986), 1986 PRC Civil and Commercial Laws, art. 4 ("In civil activities, the principles of voluntariness, fairness, making compensation for equal value, honesty and credibility shall be observed."); Contract Law of the People's Republic of China (promulgated by Nat'l People's Cong., Mar. 15, 1999), art. 4, 1999 PRC Contract Law (China) ("A party is entitled to enter into a contract voluntarily under the law, and no entity or individual may unlawfully interfere with such right."); Ling, *Contract Law in China*, 43; Zhang, *Chinese Contract Law*, 25.

[101] See e.g. Ling, *Contract Law in China*, 49–50.

[102] See e.g. Maud Piers, "Good Faith in English Law – Could a Rule Become a Principle?" (2011) 26 *Tulane European and Civil Law Forum*, 123, pp. 161–162.

[103] See e.g. Ling, *Contract Law in China*, 53–54; Zhang, *Chinese Contract Law*, 76.

2015, and came into effect on August 1 in the same year.[104] The third paragraph of Article 13 of the Provisions defines a SEP as a "patent which is essential to the implementation of such standard."[105] More importantly, the second paragraph of the same Article may become a legal basis for standard implementers to claim FRAND terms against SEP holders in the future:

Businesses with dominant market position shall not, without justification, engage in the acts below to exclude or restrict competition in the process of setting and implementing standards:

1. when participating in the formulation of the standards, deliberately not disclosing information on its rights to the standards developing organization, or explicitly waiving its rights, but claiming its patent rights to the implementers of a standard after the standard involves the patent.

2. once the subject patent becomes a standard-essential patent, [the patent holder] will violate the fair, reasonable and non-discriminatory (FRAND) principle, by precluding or restricting competition, such as refusal to license, tying products, or imposing other unreasonable terms.[106]

Although the violation of Article 13 constitutes an independent ground for anti-monopoly liability,[107] it has made it clear that SEP holders bear the FRAND duty to standard implementers. Therefore, it is possible that standard implementers will establish their FRAND claims against SEP holders based on Article 13 of the Provisions. Nevertheless, it should be noted that, because the Provisions are designed according to the Anti-Monopoly Law,[108] they are primarily based on antitrust and competition law concerns. Only businesses

---

[104] Provisions on Prohibiting the Abuse of Intellectual Property Rights to Preclude or Restrict Competition (promulgated by the St. Administration for Industry and Commerce, 7 April 2015, 1 August 2015), www.kangxin.com/en/index.php?optionid=927&auto_id=726 [https://perma.cc/JC2N-Y8XJ] (China).

[105] Provisions, art. 13.   [106] Ibid.

[107] Article 14 of the Provisions states: "Where an operator is suspected of abusing the intellectual property rights to exclude or constraint competition, the administration for industry and commerce shall perform the investigation in accordance with the Anti-monopoly Law and the Provisions of the Administrations for Industry and Commerce on the Procedures for the Investigation and Penalties of Monopoly Agreement Cases and Abuse of Dominant Market Position Cases." Provisions, art. 14. Article 17(2) of the *Provisions* stipulates: "If an operator's abuse of intellectual property rights to exclude or restrict competition constitutes an abuse of dominant market position, the administration for industry and commerce shall order the operator to stop the illegal act, confiscate the illegal income, and impose a fine of not less than 1% but not more than 10% of annual sales of the previous year." Provisions, art. 17(2).

[108] "In order to protect fair market competition, encourage innovation, and stop operators from abusing intellectual property rights to exclude or restrict competition, the Provisions on the Prohibition of the Abuse of Intellectual Property Rights to Exclude or Restrict Competition (hereinafter referred to as the 'Provisions') are formulated in accordance with the Anti-monopoly Law of the People's Republic of China (hereinafter referred to as the 'Anti-monopoly Law')." Provisions, art. 1.

with "dominant market position" will be charged with FRAND obligations. This requirement does not exist for most of the scenarios in which SEP holders bear FRAND duties. Moreover, the examples of FRAND violations provided in the Provisions, such as refusal to deal or tying arrangement, are also typical antitrust violations. It is uncertain whether SEP holders' excessive pricing or initiating injunctive relief will fall into the scope regulated by Article 13. In this respect, Article 13 might focus only on cases that implicate anti-monopoly law concerns.

On the other hand, Article 13 of the Provisions may occasionally include cases beyond normal FRAND disputes, where both SEP holders and standard implementers are affiliated with the same SSO and SEP holders have made FRAND commitments to the organization concerned. Although Article 13 does mention the standard setting process, it does not require that SEP holders have previously made any FRAND commitment, nor does it require that either the SEP holder or the standard implementer should be a member of an SSO.[109]

Moreover, the State Intellectual Property Office (SIPO) and the National Standardization Administration of China (SAC) recently jointly released the (Provisional) Administration Regulations of National Standards Involving Patent (Provisional Regulations), which have come into effect since January 1, 2014.[110] According to Article 10 of the Provisional Regulations, if the patent holder refuses to license it under FRAND terms, the patent cannot be included in non-mandatory national standards.[111] Article 15 further stipulates that if the compulsory national standard must involve the patent whose owner refuses to license under FRAND terms, the SAC, SIPO, and relevant authorities will negotiate a solution with the holder.[112] However, the Provisional Regulations have limited purview, as the subject standards must involve Chinese national standards.[113] Unlike the Provisions mentioned in previous paragraphs, the Provisional Regulations do not establish legal liability for FRAND violations, but rather provide a signal of potential government intervention into the FRAND negotiations associated with SEPs for national standards. Therefore, commentators suggest that the Provisional Regulations "leave a number of definitional and procedural ambiguities."[114]

---

[109] Provisions, art. 13.   [110] Provisions, art. 24.   [111] Provisions, art. 10.
[112] Provisions, art. 15.   [113] Provisions, art. 2.
[114] National Research Council, "Patent Challenges for Standard-Setting in the Global Economy," 12.

5.4.5 SPC's Interpretation

On March 21, 2016, the Supreme People's Court (SPC) in China issued the Interpretation (II) of the Supreme People's Court on Several Issues concerning the Application of Law in the Trial of Patent Infringement Dispute Cases (Interpretation), which has been in effect since April 1, 2016.[115] SPC's judicial interpretations have been viewed as important normative documents in the legal and economic development in China;[116] therefore, the above-mentioned Interpretation may substantially influence the judicial practice in patent litigation.

Article 24 of the Interpretation provides SPC's view on FRAND. Sections 1 and 3 of Article 24 stipulate the "negotiation before litigation principle" in FRAND disputes. According to Section 1, SPC does not support the defense raised by the alleged infringer that it does not need to obtain a license from SEP holder to practice the subject SEP.[117] Section 3 stipulates that licensing terms should be negotiated by SEP holder and the alleged infringer, and parties may request people's courts determine the licensing terms if no consensus can be reached from the negotiation.[118]

Section 2 of Article 24 provides a defense for standard implementers in patent litigation initiated by the SEP holder. According to Section 2, SEP holder's request to prevent the implementer from practicing the subject SEP is not validated if (1) parties fail to reach a license agreement because the SEP holder violates its FRAND obligation during the preparation of the standard and its negotiation with the implementer, and (2) the implementer does not commit any obvious fault.[119] This Section provides standard implementers with significant advantage over SEP holders' claim for infringement. The later will not be able to use injunction or litigation to force the former to accept licensing terms that are against the FRAND commitment during the negotiation.[120] However, Section 2 is not a direct legal basis for standard implementers to enforce SEP

---

[115] Zuigao Renmin Fayuan Guanyu Shenli Qinfan Zhuanliquan Jiufen Anjian Yingyong Falv Ruogan Wenti De Jieshi II [Interpretation (II) of the Supreme People's Court on Several Issues concerning the Application of Law in the Trial of Patent Infringement Dispute Cases] (issued by Sup. People's Ct., Mar. 31, 2016, effective April 1, 2016) (China), www.court.gov.cn/fabu -xiangqing-18482.html [https://perma.cc/FSG9-CDKF].

[116] See e.g. Eric C. Ip, "The Supreme People's Court and the Political Economy of Judicial Empowerment in Contemporary China" (2011) 24 *Columbia Journal of Asian Law*, 367, p. 403.

[117] Interpretation (II) of the Supreme People's Court on Several Issues concerning the Application of Law in the Trial of Patent Infringement Dispute Cases, art. 24, § 1.

[118] Interpretation (II) of the Supreme People's Court on Several Issues concerning the Application of Law in the Trial of Patent Infringement Dispute Cases, art. 24, § 3.

[119] Interpretation (II) of the Supreme People's Court on Several Issues concerning the Application of Law in the Trial of Patent Infringement Dispute Cases, art. 24, § 2.

[120] Ibid.

holders' FRAND obligation. It is at most a defense, rather than a legal right, that standard implementers can raise against SEP holders' injunction or infringement claims. Nonetheless, it is not yet clear if SPC aimed to define FRAND commitment as a "covenant not to sue" or an action with other legal effect in this Interpretation.[121] It is worthwhile to observe how Chinese courts implement Section 2 of Article 24 in the Interpretation in the future.

5.5 CONCLUDING REMARKS

Innovation typically builds on earlier technologies. FRAND plays a critical role in this cumulative process and is necessary to enhance innovation. With the FRAND requirement, inventors can recoup from their investment in SEP related innovation, whereas implementers are able to innovate based on the subject standard without being held up. Put differently, FRAND encourages both innovation in standards and innovation built upon standards. Any policy that breaks the balance of interests of standard inventors and implementers may chill innovation. Consequently, patent hold-ups will harm the benefits of standardization and threat innovation surrounding standards.

Huawei is certainly a benchmark case, in which China has carved out its own enforcement mechanism for FRAND with strong civil-law characteristics, which deviates from the continental European civil-law approach. The *Huawei* court ruled that good faith, rather than the contractual relationship, was standard implementers' legal basis to enforce FRAND commitments against SEP holders. China is not alone with such developments, as the Japanese courts have similarly established FRAND obligation based on good faith doctrine. In the short run, the outcome of applying good faith doctrine to enforce FRAND seems to be similar to that of the third-party beneficiary approach in the US because courts in both jurisdictions have recognized the enforceability of FRAND commitment. New innovations will be fostered based on standard implementation. In the long run, good faith doctrine may become an important part of China's innovation policy that fits its own needs because the application of this doctrine will reflect local business practices, norms, or even moral standards. With the fast-growing innovative capabilities in the country and more similar litigations emerging in the future, the Chinese courts will certainly have more chances to develop its own good faith doctrine associated with innovation, competition, SEP holders' injunctive action, excessive pricing, and abuse of right.

---

[121] See e.g. Kesan and Hayes, "FRAND's Forever," 289.

PART II

REFORM OF THE PATENT SYSTEM AND INNOVATION IN HONG KONG

6

The Role of Patents in the Economic Development of Hong Kong

Frank Charn Wing Wan

6.1 INNOVATION, INTELLECTUAL PROPERTY, AND INNOVATION IN A CAPITALIST SOCIETY

Innovative and creative industries depend heavily on intellectual property (IP) protection to safeguard investment spent on research and development (R&D), especially in a highly competitive business environment. In Hong Kong, creative and innovation-based industries, such as media, entertainment, electronics, semiconductor, and the information and communication technology industries that provide the infrastructure for Hong Kong's service-oriented industries, have all benefitted from IP protection. While IP protection is important for the innovative industry, the issue of how IP may affect the processes of economic development is complex and also depends on other market factors. This chapter examines how patent protection and other non-IP factors, such as the Hong Kong government's economic policy and Hong Kong's unique business environment, may affect the process of development of the innovative industry.

Joseph A. Schumpeter observed[1] that in a free market economy, market competition drives firms to create new methods of production and transportation through innovative forms of industrial organization in order to reduce the marginal costs of the goods (e.g. Li & Fung Limited – a global supply chain manager), and to develop new products that either create a new market (smartphone) or bring down the market leaders overnight (e.g. digital camera). Only the efficient and creative firms (e.g. Apple Inc.) will be selected and will survive in the market, and those non-innovative firms will be eliminated (e.g. Nokia phones). Schumpeter coined this survival of the fittest process as 'creative destruction', which is a natural outcome in a capitalist economic

---

[1] J.A. Schumpeter, *Capitalism, Socialism and Democracy* (Harper & Row, 1942).

system. Schumpeter considered perfect competition to be antithetical to innovation. Such *ceteris paribus* assumption has been used in all economic modelling and poses some difficulties for the verification of creativity. Although intellectual efforts are valuable to society, there is low incentive to create or innovate because knowledge is easily free-ridden by others. Keith E. Maskus points out that 'society has a dynamic interest in avoiding this outcome by providing defined property rights in information'.[2] Paul Romer[3] suggests that 'innovators must anticipate a period of monopoly rents to justify the sunk costs of innovation'. As perfect competition does not allow creators to recoup their sunk costs, a public intervention such as the establishment of institutions for IP rights (IPRs) is needed to incentivize creativity. In short, although pricing at marginal cost in a perfectly competitive market structure would maximize consumer welfare from a static perspective, it would curtail any incentive for investing in the creation of new knowledge. Protection of creative and innovative ideas in the form of IPRs is needed to recoup the initial investment costs or the sunk costs of investment, and to provide a solution to the problem created by the public good (non-rivalrous and non-excludable) characteristics of creative and innovative ideas.

The Clinton administration's Treasury Secretary Lawrence Summers, a former Harvard economics professor, has summed up the above points well. In his speech 'The New Wealth of Nations' before business executives in 2000, he said that

> ... the only incentive to produce anything is the possession of temporary monopoly power – because without that power the price will be bid down to marginal cost and the high initial fixed costs cannot be recouped. So the constant pursuit of that monopoly power becomes the central driving thrust of the new economy. And the creative destruction that results from all that striving becomes the essential spur of economic growth. In that sense, if the agricultural and industrial economies were Smithian – the new economy is Schumpeterian.[4]

The public good nature of information goods (that are non-rivalrous and non-excludable) encourages free-riding, which leads to market failure. The government must intervene and prevent this market failure by providing

[2] K. E. Maskus, *Intellectual Property Rights in the Global Economy* (Washington, DC: Institute for International Economics, 2000), p. 29.
[3] P. Romer, 'Endogenous Technological Change, Part Two' (1990) 98 *Journal of Political Economy*, pp. 71–102.
[4] US Treasury Press Release, 'The New Wealth of Nations' Remarks by Treasury Secretary Lawrence H. Summers, Hambrecht & Quist Technology Conference San Francisco (2000), www.treasury.gov/press-center/press-releases/Pages/ls617.aspx.

a monopoly property-like protection system to encourage people to invest in the creation of new knowledge and to enable the creators/investors to recoup their sunk costs. The IP system effectively gives an inventor a monopoly for a fixed term of years to recoup the sunk costs of development and to eliminate the risk of failure by new technology being adopted into the market. This serves as an incentive to stimulate R&D, which ultimately benefits society with new products. The IP protection is said 'to internalize the externality by giving the firm a property right over the invention and/or creativity'.[5]

Therefore, the objective of IP protection is to promote investment in new knowledge, technology, and innovation; and to encourage the owners of such new knowledge technology and innovation to make and sell newly developed goods and services. Strong IP protection may enable innovators to protect their competitive advantage over competitors, which will encourage investment in innovation and creativity. Competitors will introduce competing technologies and products in the market when it is clear that they can make money from investing in IPRs. On the other hand, an absence of IP protection would create an external negative dynamic. Firms would be less willing to invest in research and development, as the risk in competitive appropriation is very high.

6.2 FROM A COLONY TO A SAR: A BRIEF HISTORY OF HONG KONG

Hong Kong was a former British colony for the period between 26 June 1843, the date on which Sir Henry Pottinger proclaimed the founding of the Colony of Hong Kong, and 1 July 1997, the date on which British rule in Hong Kong ended and the sovereignty of Hong Kong was returned to Mainland China. Under Article 5 of the Hong Kong Basic Law (hereafter, Basic Law), Hong Kong is a special administrative region of China, and will continue to maintain and enjoy its present capitalist economic system and legal, business, and monetary systems for the next 50 years, up to 2047. Under this unique design of 'one country, two systems', Hong Kong has complete economic and civil freedom but not political freedom unless and until the selection of the chief executive under Article 45 of the Basic Law and the selection of all the legislative members under Article 68 of the Basic Law by way of universal suffrage are implemented. The 'Executive-Led System' was adopted in Hong Kong before and after the return of Hong Kong's sovereignty to Mainland China and has a clear bias towards the business community.

---

[5] N. Gregory Mankiw, *Principles of Economics*, 4th edition (Mason, OH: Thomson South – Western, 2007), p. 209.

Geographically, Hong Kong is strategically located at the doorway to Mainland China. Hong Kong is also one of the global financial centres, and it is the second largest capital market in Asia. However, the wealth of Hong Kong society is built primarily on the services industry, which represents about 93 per cent[6] of the GDP, and only about 1.5 per cent[7] comes from the manufacturing sector.

Hong Kong has a strong commitment to comply with international IP treaties and conventions and has an IP system comparable to those in Western countries.[8] In addition, Hong Kong has a corruption-free government, a strong and independent legal profession, effective law enforcement agencies, and a well-respected independent judicial system that is based on the common law system. Hong Kong has high business integrity and ethical standards, and has state of the art technology and market information that are freely accessible to the public. Being a key financial centre in the world, Hong Kong has always been able to access capital markets freely. Hong Kong also has excellent research universities and institutions. Therefore, Hong Kong appears to have all the key elements for establishing and developing one of the most innovative centres. However, Hong Kong has not become an innovation centre, and the subsequent section will explores the weaknesses and strengths of Hong Kong in attracting investment, both local and foreign, for the innovative industry.

6.3 HONG KONG'S ECONOMIC DEVELOPMENT

Before the 1950s, Hong Kong was just a fishing village. Its main economic activity was to serve as an *entrepôt* for the import and export of goods into

---

[6] Table 036 on Gross Domestic Product by economic activity, published by Census and Statistics Department of Hong Kong SAR government indicates that the services sector accounted for 92.7 per cent, 93 per cent, 93.1 per cent, 93 per cent, and 92.9 per cent of GDP for the years of 2009, 2010, 2011, 2012, and 2013 respectively, www.censtatd.gov.hk/hkstat /sub/sp250.jsp?tableID=036&ID=0&productType=8.

[7] Table 4.4 of Hong Kong Monthly Digest of Statistics July 2015, published by Hong Kong government: the manufacturing sector accounted for 1.6 per cent, 1.5 per cent, and 1.4 per cent of GDP for the years of 2011, 2012, and 2014 respectively, www.statistics.gov.hk/pub/B10100022 015MM07B0100.pdf.

[8] This is best illustrated by the statement made by Denise Yue Chung-Yee, J.P. Secretary for Trade and Industry, who informed the Legislative Council (LegCo), on the second reading of the Intellectual Property (World Trade Organization Amendments) Bill 1995 on 24 April 1996, that '[t]he objective of the Bill is to render the intellectual property regime in Hong Kong compatible with the standards and requirements in the Agreement on Trade-Related Aspects of Intellectual Property Rights or the TRIPS Agreement in short. This Agreement is one of the multilateral agreements under the World Trade Organization (WTO). Hong Kong, as a full member of the WTO, is obliged to comply with the Agreement.'

Mainland China and other parts of the world. However, the change of government regime in Mainland China after 1949 led to the influx of skilled labourers and entrepreneurs, particularly from Shanghai, into Hong Kong. The immigration transformed Hong Kong into a manufacturing base for light industries such as textile, clothing, and plastic. Manufacturing-based revenue represented about 26 per cent of the GDP in the 1970s.[9] This represents the first phase of post-war economic development.

Facing severe competition from other cheap labour exporting countries and expensive quota systems structured for the exporting of textile products out of Hong Kong, industrialists were forced to move their manufacturing of traditional industries, or the so-called sunset industries, to other cheap labour and low cost production countries in other parts of Asia. As Mainland China, under Deng Xiaoping's leadership, adopted its open-door policy for foreign investment in the early 1980s, Hong Kong's indus-trialists began moving their manufacturing bases to the Pearl River Delta region of South China to take advantage of the cheap labour and land cost offered. The manufacturing-based revenue in Hong Kong has seen steady decline from about 23.7 per cent of the GDP in 1980 and 22.1 per cent in 1985, to 17.6 per cent in 1990 and then further down to about 6.5 per cent in 1997,[10] representing only about 1.4 per cent by 2013.[11] Ever since the 1980s, Hong Kong has not been considered an ideal place for manufacturing. Nevertheless, industrialists still choose Hong Kong as their key business centre because of its well-established and efficient banking system and its ability to access world financial and capital markets, much less its low taxes and simple tax structure.

As society in Hong Kong accumulated wealth from the first phase of economic development, Hong Kong became a capital and services-oriented market that focuses more on tourism, logistics supplies, and the expansion of importing and exporting facilities such as container depots and the airport to cope with the ever-growing demand for the shipment of goods out of the Pearl River Delta region of China. In 1996,[12] 83 per cent of GDP came from services,

---

[9] 2000 Gross Domestic Product, published by the Census and Statistics Department of Hong Kong Special Administrative Region on March 2001 Chapter 5, at p. 111 (that provides the GDP information between 1965–2000): the percentage distribution of gross domestic product at current factor cost by the manufacturing sector were 30.9 per cent, 26.9 per cent, and 25.1 per cent for the years of 1970, 1975, and 1980, respectively.

[10] Ibid., see Table 12 on DEP by economic activity (1980–1999) on page 68.

[11] See note 7 above.

[12] 1996–1997 Budget Speech 'Building Our Prosperous Future', paragraph 7 (under the heading of 'A Tradition to Success') by the Financial Secretary the Hon Donald Tsang on Wednesday, 6 March 1996, www.budget.gov.hk/1996/budget.htm.

compared to 67 per cent in 1980.[13] This represents the second phase of economic development. The percentage of GDP from the services industry remained about 90 per cent into the 2000s (88.1 per cent GDP in 2002, 92.9 per cent in 2007, and 93.1 per cent in 2011).[14]

Hong Kong has struggled to enter into the third phase of economic development, trying to jump-start an innovative and value-added industry since 1997. As the Hong Kong government believes that innovation and technology are the drivers of the next phase of economic development, the key is to enhance the competitiveness of the innovative industry. So far, there has not been much progress partly due to Hong Kong's 'positive non-interventionism economic policy'.

6.3.1 Sir Philip Haddon-Cave's Positive Non-interventionism Economic Policy

Hong Kong has adopted a positive non-interventionist policy or 'small government, big market' as its economic policy since 1961. Such policy was introduced by the fifth Financial Secretary John Cowperthwaite, who was a disciple of laissez-faire economics. He said in his first budget speech in 1961, 'In the long run, the aggregate of decisions of individual businessmen, exercising individual judgment in a free economy, even if often mistaken, is less likely to do harm than the centralized decisions of a government, and certainly the harm is likely to be counteracted faster.'[15] This is a pro-business economic policy. The idea is that the role of the Hong Kong government is to facilitate trade and business transactions and to encourage entrepreneurship to seek profits. The government would only intervene in the market if there was a market failure. This means that the government simply provides a level playing field for business and entrepreneurship. It also means that the government would not attempt to plan any allocation of public resources to the private sector. Cowperthwaite believed that it was important to allow Hong Kong to adjust and respond to market changes by the sums of market forces. Despite the change of Hong Kong's economic structure shifting from a manufacturing to services-oriented economy since the 1980s, the

---

[13] Table 2–1 of the First Report of the Chief Executive's Commission on Innovation and Technology published in September 1998, www.itc.gov.hk/en/doc/First_report_98_(eng).pdf.

[14] See Table 4.7 on page 108 of 2013 edition of Hong Kong Annual Digest of Statistics published by the Census and Statistics Department of Hong Kong Special Administrative Region. See also note 6 above.

[15] Quoted in Andrew Craig-Bennett, 'J. J. Cowperthwaite and the Hong Kong Economic Miracle', 19 July 2010. http://gwulo.com/node/6190.

government has maintained the same economic policy and remained unwilling to subsidize R&D in the private sector.

Mr Donald Tsang, Hong Kong's former Chief Executive, repeated his stance to maintain the same economic policy by stating that

> one of my key economic strategies is to encourage entrepreneurship and fair competition under the principle of 'Big Market, Small Government' ... In the face of rapid changes in the world and on the Mainland, we must take a proactive but at the same time pro-market approach and see how we could provide a platform and foster an environment that would best support economic development.[16]

Having adopted the positive non-interventionist economic policy since 1961, the government simply lacks the expertise, knowledge, skills, and ability to invest in the emerging technology sector.

6.3.2 *The Hong Kong Government's Innovation and Technology Policy*

It is against the above backdrop that Hong Kong's innovation and technology policy has been shaped. Before 1997, there was no such innovation and technology policy in place in Hong Kong other than an annual allocation of HK $250 million available to all different industries in the form of an Industrial Support Fund since 1994.[17] This was 'partly because pre-1997 governments had little incentive to develop long-term high-tech capabilities, given the foreseeable takeover of Hong Kong by China'.[18] As the amount allocated to each industry was not high enough to drive it forward and the fund was distributed to different industries rather than selected and focused ones, the policy failed at the end of 1997. Business people at that time always joked that 'High-tech haaiye (揩野), Low-tech laauye (捞野)'[19] or 'low-tech made good profits and high-tech created financial disaster' due to the high failure rate of high-tech firms.

---

[16] Hong Kong Government Press Release, 'Big Market, Small Government', 18 September 2006, www.ceo.gov.hk/archive/2012/eng/press/oped.htm.

[17] Suzanne Berger and Richard K. Lester, eds., *Made by Hong Kong* (Oxford University Press, 1997), p. 71.

[18] Axel Gelfert, 'Before Biopolis: Representations of the biotechnology discourse in Singapore' (2013) *East Asian Science, Technology and Society* 7.1, pp. 103–123, 105.

[19] Wong Y. C. Richard, 'Regulation, Rent Seeking Innovation and Economic Growth (2015)'. *Hong Kong Economic Journal*; see 'For Years Businessmen in Hong Kong Chimed: "High-Tech Hi-Yeah, Low-Tech Lo-Yeah!"', 16 December 2015, http://wangyujian.hku.hk /?p=6436&lang=en.

The situation began to change when Mr C. H. Tung, Hong Kong's first chief executive, who had a vision of building up innovation and technology capacity, appointed Professor Chang-Lin Tien, a NEC (Nippon Electric Company) distinguished professor of engineering from the University of California, Berkeley, to chair the Innovation and Technology Commission in March 1998. The Commission's task was to make Hong Kong a regional innovation centre because Hong Kong's services industries were facing fierce competition from other countries such as Singapore. The aim was to move Hong Kong to a new phase of economic development by transforming it into a knowledge-based economy.[20]

Following the recommendations from Professor Tien's reports,[21] the Hong Kong government set up a HKD 5 billion Innovation and Technology Fund to support advancement in the innovative and technological industry; to establish the Applied Science and Technology Research Institute (ASTRI) in January 2000 to serve as the R&D centre for information and communication technologies; and later to promote innovation and technological development through an Innovation and Technology Commission on 1 July 2000. The Innovation and Technology Commission's

> approach in promoting innovation and technology development is underpinned by five core strategies: providing world-class technology infrastructure for enterprises, research institutions and universities; offering financial support to stakeholders in the industry, academia and research sector to develop and commercialize their R&D results; nurturing talent; strengthening science and technology collaboration with the Mainland and other economies, and fostering a vibrant culture of innovation.[22]

The Hong Kong Science and Technology Parks were established in Sha Tin next to the Chinese University of Hong Kong in May 2001 in order to provide 'one-stop infrastructural support services to technology-based companies and activities'.[23] In addition, the Innovation and Technology Commission also invited three overseas biotechnology experts from Silicon Valley to conduct

[20]   Executive Summary of the first report of the Chief Executive's Commission on Innovation and Technology published in September 1998. www.itc.gov.hk/en/doc/First_report_98_(eng) .pdf.

[21]   The Second and Final Report of the Chief Executive's Commission on Innovation and Technology was published in October 1999. www.itc.gov.hk/en/doc/Second_and_Final_rep orts_99_(Eng).pdf.

[22]   Innovation and Technology Commission, HKSAR government, 'The Fact sheet on Innovation and Technology', May 2015, www.gov.hk/en/about/abouthk/factsheets/docs/tech nology.pdf.

[23]   Ibid.

a snapshot study on the biotechnology capabilities of Hong Kong in September 2000: namely, Sir Colin Dollery, Senior Consultant to SmithKline Beecham Pharmaceuticals from the United Kingdom; Professor Savio Woo, director of the Institute for Gene Therapy at New York University; and Dr Kenneth Fong, founder and president of Clontech Laboratories, Inc.[24] The study acknowledged that the old economic policy needed to be readjusted to cope with the new phase of economic development, especially to strengthen the ties and promote cooperation between Hong Kong and Mainland China's innovative industries. The experts' report has never been released to the public. Interestingly enough, the Hong Kong government released a press release endorsing a new strategy of innovation and technology policy after the conclusion of public consultation on 10 December 2004[25] indicating that it has identified 13 focus areas[26] in which Hong Kong's industry has comparative advantages. However, biotechnology was not included in the list. In 2006, the Innovation and Technology Commission set up research centres for five focus areas, namely automotive parts and accessory systems; information and communications technologies; logistics and supply chain management enabling technologies; nanotechnology and advanced materials; and textiles and clothing.[27] Furthermore, the Hong Kong government injected a further HKD 5 billion into the Innovation and Technology Fund in February 2015.[28]

It is believed that some sort of government leadership is needed to facilitate the change of economic structure from the second phase to the third phase of Hong Kong economic development. The problem is that it would be the market rather than the government that would have the knowledge and expertise to determine the path of economic development based on its unique

---

[24] Hong Kong Government Press Release on Snapshot study on local biotechnology capabilities in progress published on 21 September 2000, www.info.gov.hk/gia/general/200009/21/0921228.htm.

[25] 'Government Endorses New Strategy of Innovation and Technology', Hong Kong Government Press Release, 10 December 2004, www.info.gov.hk/gia/general/200412/10/1210221.htm.

Also 'Report on Public Consultation on the New Strategy of Innovation and Technology Development', Innovation and Technology Commission of the Hong Kong Government, January 2005, www.itc.gov.hk/en/doc/consultation/R-New_strategy_consultation-180105.pdf.

[26] Ibid.
(a) Advanced Manufacturing Technologies (b) Automotive Parts and Accessory Systems (c) Chinese Medicine (d) Communications Technologies (e) Consumer Electronics (f) Digital Entertainment (g) Display Technologies (h) Integrated Circuit Design (i) Logistics/Supply Chain Management Enabling Technologies (j) Medical Diagnostics and Devices (k) Nanotechnology and Advanced Materials (l) Opto-electronics and (m) Textile and Clothing.

[27] See note 22 above.   [28] Ibid.

history, industrial strength, social and investment cultures. Despite all these efforts made by the government, Hong Kong has made little headway towards the next phase of economic development, let alone any increase in contribution made by the innovative industry to the GDP.[29]

6.3.3 *A Proposal to Establish an Innovation and Technology Bureau*

The government's first attempt to table the proposal for the establishment of an Innovation and Technology Bureau before the LegCo was unsuccessful as the chief executive's proposal for restructuring the government organization failed and was rejected by the LegCo in April 2012. In the Chief Executive's policy address on 15 January 2014,[30] he stated that he would reinitiate the establishment of an Innovation and Technology Bureau. However, the Chief Executive's proposal was put on hold, as the LegCo did not have time to consider it before the end of the LegCo session in July 2014. The second attempt failed before the Financial Committee of the LegCo because of filibustering by pan-democratic legislative councillors on 14 February 2015.[31] The government reintroduced the proposal before the LegCo in June 2015 but the proposal was put on hold again on 18 July 2015 due to filibustering.[32] The Finance Committee of the LegCo finally approved the budget to establish the Innovation and Technology Bureau (ITB) on 6 November 2015, and the ITB was formally established on 20 November 2015.[33] Despite the support of the manufacturing sector, it took the government more than three years to get approval from the LegCo to set up the ITB partly because of political reasons and partly because the government has failed to project to the public

---

[29]   Wang Shengwei, 'HK Needs to Boost Research and Development', 15 April 2015, *China Daily Asia*, www.chinadailyasia.com/opinion/2015-04/15/content_15250809.html.

[30]   Chief Executive Policy Address states '. . . The new bureau will be responsible for formulating policies and promoting the development of innovation and technology as well as information technology (the portfolio is hereafter referred to as innovation and technology) in Hong Kong, and coordinating relevant efforts within the Government', 15 January 2014, p. 11, www .policyaddress.gov.hk/2014/eng/pdf/PA2014.pdf.

[31]   The government's press release on 'LQ6: Assessment of the Performance of the Government and Principal Officials', 25 March 2015, www.info.gov.hk/gia/general/201503/25/P2015032504 37.htm.

[32]   Hong Kong Government, 'CE Regrets Pan-Dems' Filibustering', 18 July 2015, www.news.gov .hk/en/categories/admin/html/2015/07/20150718_132646.shtml. Also see, Tony Cheung 'Filibuster delays Innovation and Technology proposal', *South China Morning Post*, 3 July 2014, www.scmp.com/news/hong-kong/article/1545117/filibuster-delays-innovation-and -technology-bureau-proposal.

[33]   The Government Press Release, 20 November, 2015, www.info.gov.hk/gia/general/201511/20 /P201511200739.htm.

the way forward; instead the government has consolidated the various innovative units and industrial funding supports under one roof. In Hong Kong, the
failing rate of technology companies is high, and none are willing to take the
risk unless the government is willing to share the risk by providing adequate
funding support for the downstream development of technology and translat-
ing it into products or services. More importantly, some industrialists perceive
that the ITB would only focus on the IT and communication sectors, and it
would duplicate the ASTRI's effort in the same areas. It has been suggested
that the Hong Kong government should explain how its economic policy
might help drive the development of innovative industry, and the role that
could be played by the ITB in shaping the future of the innovative industry in
Hong Kong. Nevertheless, the establishment of the ITB marks the beginning
of the change of Hong Kong's economic era of 'positive non-intervention'
towards adopting a more proactive approach to support the local industries.
The problem is that the Hong Kong government, with little entrepreneurial
spirit and expertise, could invest in the wrong type of information or invention;
and the competition from the private inventors for the limited government
fund may lead to rent-seeking activities.

6.4 INNOVATION, PATENTS AND ECONOMIC DEVELOPMENT

6.4.1 Hong Kong's Patent System and Patenting Trend

The World Intellectual Property Indicator published by the World
Intellectual Property Organization (WIPO) in 2014 indicates that Mainland
China, a low-income country, received the most patent applications (825,136)
in 2013, followed by the US (571,612), a high-income country. 'Resident
applications accounted for almost all the growth in China.'[34] Hong Kong
received a total of 6,564 standard patent applications of which 92 came from
residents,[35] and it also received 552 short-term patent applications, of which 312
applications were made by residents.[36] Being a high-income country, the
US remains the world's largest investor in R&D with investments totalling
USD 465 billion or 2.8 per cent of its GDP in 2014.[37] Mainland China
overtook the European Union in terms of R&D spending as GDP percentage,

---

[34] WIPO 'Patent Applications by Office and Origin' 2013, pp. 47–50, and also Table A 47
indicating that 885,226 applications were made by residents of China, www.wipo.int/ipstats
/en/wipi/.
[35] Ibid., Table A 48 on page 51.   [36] Ibid., Table A 49 on page 55.
[37] www.chinadailyasia.com/opinion/2015-04/15/content_15250809.html.

with China spending 1.98 per cent of GDP compared to 1.97 per cent of the joint economic output of the 28 member states of the European Union.[38]

The number of standard patents granted by the Hong Kong Intellectual Property Department was; 5,035; 6,564; 5,932; 5,963; and 5,698 for the years of 2012, 2013, 2014, 2015, and 2016 respectively.[39] The numbers of short-term patent applications for the same period were 645, 552, 587, 702 and 762 respectively.[40] The number of standard patents granted per year has remained more or less the same since 2005, in which there were 6,518 applications. This statistic represents more than double than standard patents granted in 1996.

The percentage of GDP spent on R&D in Hong Kong was 0.5 per cent in 2000 and gradually increased to 0.79 per cent in 2009.[41] The percentage of Hong Kong's GDP spent on R&D were 0.75 per cent, 0.72 per cent, 0.77 per cent, 0.75 per cent, 0.72 per cent, and 0.73 per cent for the years of 2007, 2008, 2009, 2010, 2011, and 2012, respectively.[42] In comparison, Mainland China's spending on R&D represented 1.76 per cent, 1.84 per cent, and 1.98 per cent of GDP for the years of 2010, 2011, and 2012, respectively; and Singapore's represented 2.05 per cent, 2.23 per cent, and 2.10, respectively, for the same period.[43] This indicates that Hong Kong has fallen behind on investment of R.&D.

It appears that the ratio of patent applications filed by local residents to the total number of applications filed in a given country might serve as an

[38] Patrick Boehler, 'China Spending More than Europe on Science and Technology as GDP Percentage', *South China Morning Post*, 21 January 2014, www.scmp.com/news/china-insider /article/1410178/china-spending-more-europe-science-and-technology-gdp-percentage.
OECD reported that GDP expenditure on R&D in 2012 was USD 257 billion in China, USD 397 billion in the United States, USD 282 billion for the EU and USD 134 billion in Japan, 12 November 2014, www.oecd.org/newsroom/china-headed-to-overtake-eu-us-in-science -technology-spending.htm.

[39] 'Statistics of Standard Patents Granted (by Countries of Origin/Region of Proprietors) Calendar Yearly Report', Intellectual Property Department of the Hong Kong Government,' 2016, www.ipd.gov.hk/eng/intellectual_property/ip_statistics/2016/ip_statistics_std_patent _granted_e.pdf.

[40] 'Statistics of Short-Term Patent Applications Filed (by Countries of Origin/Region of Applicants) Calendar Yearly Report', Intellectual Property Department of the Hong Kong Government, 2016,
www.ipd.gov.hk/eng/intellectual_property/ip_statistics/2016/ip_statistics_short_patent_ap pl_e.pdf.

[41] Trading Economics on Research and Development Expenditure (% of GDP) in Hong Kong, www.tradingeconomics.com/hong-kong/research-and-development-expenditure-percent-of-gdp -wb-data.html.

[42] 'Hong Kong Annual Digest of Statistics' 2014 edition published by the Consensus and Statistics Department of Hong Kong SAR government, Table 10.1 on page 289.

[43] Data on Research and Development expenditure (% of GDP) published by the World Bank. http://data.worldbank.org/indicator/GB.XPD.RSDV.GD.ZS.

indicator of the amount of investment and spending in R&D in a given country. A higher percentage of GDP could relate to more money spent on R&D, and would therefore lead to a higher number of patent applications from local residents. The economic miracle of South Korea in successfully building up an innovative industry illustrates this point well, given that it incurred 3.73 per cent and 4.04 per cent of GDP on research and development expenditures in 2011 and 2012, respectively,[44] and its ratio of patent applications filed by local residents to the total number of application for Korea is 159,978 out of 204,589, or 78.2 per cent[45] (as compared with the ratio of patents granted 95,667 out of 127,330, or 75.1 per cent)[46] in 2013. The ratio for Hong Kong is 226 out of 13,916, or 1.62 per cent[47] (as compared with the ratio of patent granted 92 out of 6,564, or 1.4 per cent).[48] This can be compared to the ratio for Singapore of 1,143 out of 9,722, or 11.75 per cent[49] (as compared with the ratio of patent granted 393 out 5,575, or 7 per cent).[50] The percentage of GDP spent on R&D for Singapore is about 2.1 per cent, compared to about 0.75 per cent for Hong Kong.

With a view to fostering the development of Hong Kong as a regional IP trading hub, the Hong Kong government introduced the Patents Amendment Bill 2015 to establish an original grant patent (OGP) system that allows a patent applicant to apply for a standard patent directly in Hong Kong without first obtaining a patent from a designated office outside Hong Kong while retaining the existing reregistration system on 30 October 2015. The bill was passed on 2 June 2016 with a commencement date yet to be fixed.[51] Apparently, the new route encourages the local inventors to file their own patent applications in Hong Kong while the old reregistration route would be favoured by foreign patent applicants unless Hong Kong is the main market for the patented goods.

Innovation and creation of new knowledge and technology are the key factors in developing a knowledge-based economy. Hong Kong must develop an economic policy that provides incentive to encourage investment in R&D in the private sector other than simply providing an Industrial Support Fund and other infrastructures such as the OGP system because there is no way the government could know and choose the right winner.

---

[44] Ibid.   [45] See WIPO 'Patent Applications by Office and Origin', Table A47 on page 49.
[46] Ibid., Table A48 on page 52.   [47] Ibid., Table A47 on page 47.
[48] Ibid., Table A48 on page 51.   [49] Ibid., Table A47 on page 49.
[50] Ibid., Table A48 on page 53.
[51] For more details on the Amendment Bill, see Chapter 7 of this book. See also, Bills Committee of the LegCo on the Patents Amendment Bill 2015, www.legco.gov.hk/yr15-16/en glish/bc/bco2/general/bco2.htm.

6.4.2 *The Landscape of Hong Kong's Innovative Industry*

The population of Hong Kong was about 7.33 million in 2015.[52] Hong Kong has excellent research-oriented universities, research institutions, and a rich tradition in scientific excellence through the work of individual scientists; an effective IP law and enforcement agency; an independent impartial and credible judicial system that safeguards the integrity of commercial and financial transaction, protects individual civil rights and liberty, and is applied equally and uniformly to all walks of life; the third largest capital market in Asia; a stable currency and no foreign exchange control on money flows into and out of Hong Kong; free flow of up-to-date information; and a strong entrepreneurial culture. These are also the key factors for developing an innovative industry. However, as observed above, the positive non-interventionist economic policy has been the dominant ideology of Hong Kong governance since 1961. The Hong Kong government primarily 'serves the interests of bourgeoisie by facilitating the accumulation of the capital',[53] lacks a cohesive innovation and technology strategy, and has failed to provide a conducive environment that stimulates and actuates innovation and entrepreneurship. The establishment of the ITB might guide Hong Kong into a new economic era, but the Hong Kong deep-rooted investment culture – high return on a short-term investment with limited risk[54] – remains the key obstacle for Hong Kong to move in this new direction.

Since the transition from traditional labour-intensive manufacturing indus-tries to services-oriented phases of economic development in the 1990s, Hong Kong people accumulate wealth from the profit made in Mainland China and invest into real estate and stock markets. The investment culture in Hong Kong can be described as follows: the citizens wish to make quick profit instead of investing in R&D to upgrade the manufacturing industries, and they are not used to investing in intangible property such as IPRs and technology. More importantly, the conservative attitudes of financial institutions do not support high-risk businesses and ventures. Unlike Silicon Valley, there is no venture capital funding available to support early-stage start-up companies due to Hong Kong's small local market. Hong Kong's investment culture favours a quick return on investment and an exit plan, and revenue model for any business must be short, usually about three years. For these reasons,

---

[52] The Census and Statistics Department on Estimated Statistics on Population (2016), www
       .censtatd.gov.hk/hkstat/sub/so20.jsp.
[53] Barry Clark, *Political Economy: A Comparative Approach*, 2nd edition (Conneticut: Praeger
       Publishers, 1998), p. 114.
[54] Hong Kong investors prefer to buy stocks and real property.

Hong Kong's investors are normally conservative and try to avoid investing in a firm that has uncertainty or risk on the return of their investment.[55]

Even though most inventions come from research oriented universities, there has been a weak link between industry and university in Hong Kong, which leads to poor collaboration between academic and industry.[56] This is not surprising given the very low level of manufacturing activities in Hong Kong and investment in R&D, as reflected in the relatively fewer number of standard patent applications by local residents as compared to other developed countries.

In sum, Hong Kong does not have a favourable business environment for start-up companies because of a lack of sufficient investment and technical support from the government, financial institutions, venture capitals, industries, and academia. However, one should not lose sight of the presence of insignificant manufacturing capacity in Hong Kong. The government needs to think beyond and make Hong Kong place for attracting global R&D activities from multinational corporations. However, tax in Hong Kong is already very low, and further tax breaks on investment on R&D would not be a key enticing factor for multinational companies to consider moving their R&D to Hong Kong. This is made more complicated by the fact that Hong Kong is one of the most expensive places to work and live, making Hong Kong a less attractive place for multinational companies. On the contrary, some of the local companies have taken advantage of the opportunities offered by other countries to set up their R&D centres where the most qualified technical experts are readily available.[57] In addition, the Hong Kong Science and Technology Parks Corporation operates incubation programs[58] to assist early-stage technology start-up companies by providing incubatees with financial packages, free office and laboratory facilities, technical management, business support, and IP management that address

---

[55] Oswald Chan, 'A Date with An Angel', *China Daily USA*, 12 July 2013: '. . . Hong Kong still lacks the list of successful tech companies to lure more individual investors to become confident enough to provide angel funding. Moreover, the robust property and stock markets in the city also divert individual investors' away from angel investment. In the US Silicon Valley and San Francisco Bay Area, the middle class generally are more willing to provide angel funding', www.chinadailyasia.com/business/2013-07/12/content_15077971.html.

[56] Professor Chan Ching Chuen, Honorary Professor, The University of Hong Kong, stated in the 13 April 2015 morning session at The CAE-HKAES Joint Summit on Innovation and Technology Industry in Hong Kong and the Pearl River Delta (PRD), that about 10 per cent of RGC funded research was being tested, translated, and applied in the industry.

[57] VTech Holding Limited 2014 Annual Report, p. 8.: R&D centres in Canada, Germany, Hong Kong and China and it spends on average 3.1 % annual sales on R&D in 2014, www.vtech.com/wp-content/uploads/2015/03/AR2014_eng.pdf.

[58] Hong Kong Science and Technology Park website: www.hkstp.org/hkstp_web/en/what-we-do/nurture-technology-talents/incubation-programme/Incu-Tech/incu-tech-programme/.

some of the issues discussed above. However, Hong Kong's investment culture makes it difficult to secure financial support to continue their business model to the next phase of development. These are the non-IPRs variables that have and will continue to constrain the progress of development of the innovative industry in Hong Kong.

There has been significant frustration in attempting to move Hong Kong to the third phase of economic development. Now the process requires the most optimistic policymakers to remain optimistic and cautious with regards to the prospect. Hong Kong's effort to become an innovation and technology centre is continually challenged due to smaller talent pools, lack of venture capital financing, fewer resources in general, the absence of industrial support, and its small manufacturing base. There is a real concern about the lack of capability to translate innovative and technological concepts into practical commercial application.

Besides setting up an efficient patent application system and effective enforcement against infringers by civil courts, Hong Kong government should make an effort to create a favourable business environment for both technopreneurs and investors, and for attracting multinational corporations to set up R&D centres in Hong Kong. Owing to the economic integration with Mainland China, any innovation and technology policy must take Mainland China's role into consideration. It is important to build a strong technopreneur culture, technical and management skills, and mindsets to help bring technology into commercial application; to promote public-private-academic collaboration; to build up a strong private investor base to support early start-ups; and to define and focus R&D priorities in response to Chinese, regional, and international opportunities. Multinational corporations and foreign investors will come to Hong Kong once it has experienced an industrial cluster effect armed with the Chinese market.

6.4.3 *The Rule of Parallel Filing of Patents in Mainland China*

Hong Kong has a very unique role to play in furthering the development of Mainland China because of close economic ties between Mainland China and Hong Kong. If Mainland China becomes a source of innovative technology, the technology can be transferred to Hong Kong, which has all the key elements for a successful innovative industry. If Hong Kong technopreneurs would like to either have their products manufactured or market their products in Mainland China, they would need a patent to protect the fruits of their creation. Therefore, the technopreneurs must develop a strategy to manage their patent and other IP portfolios for Mainland China and global markets. This strategy is especially important for those products that have relatively short product life-cycles and technopreneurs should focus or prioritize on those countries that have strong patent protection regimes.

It is imperative to take note that foreign patentees who have filed the first patent application in a country that is a member of the Paris Convention may only file both the standard invention and utility model patents via the Paris Convention route rather than through the Patent Cooperation Treaty (PCT) or European Patent Office (EPO) routes (both PCT and EPO only deal with standard patent applications, not utility models). Both the standard and utility patents must be filed on the same date, and if the two applications are filed on different dates, the earlier application will destroy the novelty of the latter application.

For those Hong Kong technopreneurs who would venture into the Chinese market, it is important for them to take advantage of Mainland China's parallel rule of filing for both the invention and utility model patents at the same time. Mainland China's patent law allows patentees to apply for both an invention patent and a utility model[59] for the same subject matter on the same day.[60] The utility model patent ceases from the date of the announcement of the grant of the standard patent for invention.[61]

---

[59] The utility patent is widely and mostly available in non-English speaking countries. A utility patent is a short-term 'registered' right granted for invention 'that is fit for a particular use' that often lacks the same degree of inventive step that patent law requires the grant without a substantial examination.

[60] The second paragraph of Rule 41 of the Regulations of the Patent Law of The People's Republic of China stipulates that

> Where an applicant files on the same day (means the date of filing) applications for both a patent for utility model and a patent for invention for the identical invention-creation, he or it shall state respectively upon filing the application that another patent application for the identical invention-creation has been filed by him or it. If the applicant fails to do so, the issue shall be handled according to the provisions of Article 9, paragraph one of the Patent Law, only one patent right shall be granted for any identical invention-creation.

[61] The fourth paragraph of Rule 41 of the Regulations of the Patent Law of the People's Republic of China states that

> Where it is found after examination that there is no cause for rejection of the application for patent for invention, the patent administration department under the State Council shall notify the applicant to declare, within the specified time limit, the abandonment of his or its patent for utility model. If the applicant so declares, the patent administration department under the State Council shall make the decision to grant a patent for invention, and announce at the same time both the grant of the patent for invention and the declaration of the applicant to abandon his or its patent for utility model. If the applicant refuses to abandon his or its patent for utility model, the patent administration department under the State Council shall reject the application for patent for invention. If the applicant fails to respond within the time limit, the application for patent for invention shall be deemed to have been withdrawn.

Utility patents are a means to protect lesser inventions at lower costs but for a short period of time of 10 years instead of 20 years, as in the case of standard invention patent. Also, the grant of utility model patents may take three to six months as compared to two to three years for standard invention patents. A utility model patent would be a useful strategy, as the patentee could get the patent protection and start enforcing his rights in the market within six months. This would be especially useful if the perceived product life cycle of the new product is less than four or five years. Of course, if the standard invention patent is granted later, the patentee must abandon the utility patent and start enforcing his newly granted standard invention patent against infringers.

6.5 CONCLUSION

This chapter focuses on Hong Kong's innovative technology that deals with new knowledge for immediate commercial application and is ready for commercial exploitation rather than discussing about creative ideas with no immediate commercial value. It is clear that patents play a vital role in developing the innovative industry but patent protection in and by itself would not be sufficient to drive the Hong Kong innovative industry forward. There are other non-IP variables that affect the progress of economic development of skill-intensive, high value-added, capital and technology-intensive industries. Progress requires partnering with the government, academics, technopreneurs, and investors. It also involves the change of the investment culture and the mindsets of the Hong Kong government to formulate policies that address the economy, innovation and technology. This is a totally different approach from developing traditional industries.

All firms need to innovate to produce and sell new or improved products. Efficient processes and services are also required to compete in the global market given that the product life-cycle of technology products is relatively short because of fierce competition. Smartphones and smart TVs are good examples of products with short life cycles and today's new technology will become obsolete within a matter of years, if not months. Hong Kong only has limited manufacturing capacity and will not be able to generate high levels of technological advancement and upgrade the existing industries. It must move to a new specific industry where Hong Kong has a clear technological advantage. Nowadays, Hong Kong is mainly an importer and consumer of high-tech products and services. From a policy perspective, Hong Kong's drive to move on to the third phase of economic development presents a real challenge to the institutional requirements, the business environment, the investment culture, and the statutory regulatory framework that had become accustomed to dealing with services industry.

The low ratio of number of patent applications filed by Hong Kong residents (less than 2 per cent) to the total number of applications in Hong Kong indicates that Hong Kong has yet to establish a strong R&D base in the manufacturing sector. Until and unless Hong Kong is willing to spend more on R&D to upgrade its technology, the effort made by the government to drive Hong Kong industries into the third phase of economic development will be unlikely to succeed, as it requires industrial support to get there.

Hong Kong's innovation and technology policy should aim at encouraging the private sector to invest in R&D to build up its own technological base, which may lead to more standard patents being filed by Hong Kong residents. If Hong Kong has developed its innovative industry but the ratio of number of Hong Kong residents' patent application to total application remains below 2 per cent, this would suggest that Hong Kong has managed to build its innovative industry based on foreign patent licences or secure multinational corporations to establish R&D centres in Hong Kong. The percentage of GDP contributed by local R&D could be substantially increased in the former scenario but remain at the present low level in the latter case.

The Hong Kong government should understand the market situations before formulating any innovation and technology policies for Hong Kong's innovative industry. Filing invention and/or utility model patents in Mainland China is a good IP management strategy if the patentees intend to get into Mainland Chinese market. Patent protection is indispensable for innovation, and more patent applications coming from Hong Kong residents means more spending incurred in R&D. If Hong Kong has determined to build its own innovative industry, this increased expenditure could translate into a higher percentage of GDP for R&D comparable to percentages in South Korea, Singapore, and Mainland China.

7

An Overview of the Development of Hong Kong's Patent System

Leslie Shay

7.1 INTRODUCTION

Innovation is a key to the sustainable growth of a vivid knowledge-based economy. A patent system seeks to encourage innovation by granting the owner of an invention (e.g. an inventor) a monopoly right to exploit the invention for a definite term, usually 20 years. Hong Kong is a major international trading city and port where trading, imports and exports of numerous kinds of products and commodities frequently take place. For technical innovations that can be applied industrially for manufacturing products and commodities, it is of vital importance for the owners of these innovations to seek patent protection for acquiring an exclusive right to prevent others from manufacturing, using, selling or importing their patented inventions during the patent protection term.

In exchange for the monopoly for a limited term, the patent owner must fully disclose the invention to the public. Within this framework, the public interest lies in the full disclosure of the new technology upon which the scientific community can build. Apart from encouraging new technological innovations, the patent system in Hong Kong is also instrumental in facilitating the international exchange or joint exploitation of new technologies (such as by licensing), thereby fostering the development of Hong Kong as an innovation hub as well as an intellectual-property trading hub.

Hong Kong has always taken pride in its well-established rule of law, which provides a level playing field for businesses. Prior to China's resumption of sovereignty over Hong Kong, there was, however, a pressing need for Hong Kong to develop its own patent system, as it would be inappropriate for Hong Kong to continue to be dependent on UK patent law after the handover in 1997. Against the background of the changing sovereignty, Hong Kong also had to face challenges in the advance in information technology and the trend in harmonization of intellectual property law.

The Sino-British Joint Declaration and the Basic Law of the Hong Kong Special Administrative Region (HKSAR) adopted by the National People's Congress of the People's Republic of China (PRC) provide for a separate legal system in the HKSAR.[1] Hong Kong's constitution, the Basic Law, stipulates that all the laws previously in force in Hong Kong, which include the common law, shall be maintained.[2] Hence, Hong Kong courts may, in adjudicating cases before them, refer to patent cases decided in the UK and also the other common law jurisdictions, such as Australia, Canada and New Zealand. Article 139 of the Basic Law, a testament to the importance of patent laws in Hong Kong, specifically provides that the HKSAR government shall, on its own, formulate policies on science and technology, and protect by law achievements in scientific and technological research, patents, discoveries and inventions.

The Sino-British Joint Declaration contains provisions that allow for the continued application of international agreements to Hong Kong after 1997. The Paris Convention[3] and the Patent Cooperation Treaty[4] are the main treaties administered by the World Intellectual Property Organization (WIPO) in dealing with patents. Both China and the UK are parties to these treaties. The UK applied both the Paris Convention and the Patent Cooperation Treaty to Hong Kong in 1977 and 1981

---

[1] Constitutional and Mainland Affairs Bureau, The Government of the HKSAR, The Joint Declaration, 1 July 2007, available at www.cmab.gov.hk. Constitutional and Mainland Affairs Bureau, The Government of the HKSAR, The Basic Law, 1 July 2007, available at www.cmab .gov.hk.

[2] Article 8 of the Basic Law.

[3] 'Paris Convention' means the Paris Convention for the Protection of Industrial Property of 20 March 1883, as revised or amended from time to time, www.wipo.int. Pursuant to Article 4 of the Paris Convention, an applicant for a patent in one member country or economy has a period of 12 months within which to make patent applications for the same invention in other member countries or economies. The later applications are treated as having the same filing date as the first. Article 2 of the Paris Convention provides that each member country or economy must grant the same protection to nationals of other member countries or economies as it grants to its own nationals, and must grant to the nationals of all members the same privileges as are granted to the nationals of any member.

[4] 'Patent Cooperation Treaty' means the treaty of that name done at Washington on 19 June 1970, as revised or amended from time to time, available at www.wipo.int. Article 11 of the Patent Cooperation Treaty provides an applicant the procedural advantage of being able to file an international application designating any one or more signatory states in which he may wish to pursue a patent application. The UK Intellectual Property Office (UKIPO) was the receiving office for Hong Kong residents prior to the change of sovereignty in 1997, and thereafter, the State Intellectual Property Office (SIPO) in Mainland China has become the receiving office for Hong Kong residents since the application of PCT by China to the HKSAR upon the handover in 1997.

respectively.[5] China agreed that they would continue to apply to Hong Kong after July 1997.[6]

The growing importance of the intellectual property (IP) in international trading raised the concern of the protection of IP from developed economies and intense discussion took place between the late 1980s and early 1990s as part of the Uruguay Round of the General Agreement on Tariffs and Trade (GATT) negotiations with a view to creating broader international level of protection for patents and other IP rights (IPRs).[7] This eventually led to the signing of the agreement establishing the World Trade Organization (WTO) in 1994 under which Hong Kong is a founding member in its own right.

The Agreement on Trade Related Aspects of Intellectual Property (TRIPS) is administered by the WTO.[8] TRIPS, amongst others, sets the minimum requirements on patent protection concerning, *inter alia*, the availability, scope and use of IPRs with which all WTO member states will eventually have to comply.[9] There are also substantive provisions on national treatment and most favoured nation treatment.[10]

The local patent system has been subject to review and development from time to time, taking into account the changing social and economic needs, as well as the international development in patent practice. This chapter provides an overview of the development of Hong Kong's patent system from 1932 to present, and its future positioning.

---

[5]　The United Kingdom, by a notification dated 9 August 1977, informed the World Intellectual Property Organization that the Paris Convention would apply to Hong Kong: Paris Notification No. 91, www.wipo.int. The United Kingdom, by a notification dated 6 January 1981, informed the World Intellectual Property Organization that the Patent Cooperation Treaty would apply to Hong Kong: PCT Notification No. 34, www.wipo.int.

[6]　The People's Republic of China, by notification dated 6 June 1997, informed the World Intellectual Property Organization that the Paris Convention and the Patent Cooperation Treaty would apply to Hong Kong: Paris Notification No. 178 and PCT Notification No. 121, www.wipo.int.

[7]　The Uruguay Round of trade negotiations conducted under the aegis of GATT led to the creation of the WTO in 1995. The events leading to the creation of the WTO and the list of its founding members can be found at the website of the WTO, www.wto.org.

[8]　The TRIPS Agreement is Annex 1C of the Marrakesh Agreement Establishing the World Trade Organization, signed on 15 April 1994, www.wto.org.

[9]　Part II of the TRIPS Agreement sets standards concerning the availability, scope and use of intellectual property rights. Section 5 of Part II set out the provisions specifically relating to patents. In April 1996, the Intellectual Property (World Trade Organization Amendments) Ordinance was enacted to amend the then intellectual property laws to comply with the TRIPS Agreement.

[10]　Articles 3 and 4 of Part I of the TRIPS Agreement.

7.2 THE DEVELOPMENT OF THE EXISTING PATENT SYSTEM

7.2.1 *Pre-1997 Patent System (1932–1997)*

Prior to the enactment of the Patents Ordinance (Chapter 514) in 1997, protection for patents in Hong Kong was dependent on the UK patent law under the repealed Registration of Patents Ordinance (Chapter 42) as first enacted in 1932. In essence, patent protection was obtained by registering in Hong Kong with the Registrar of Patents a UK patent granted under the UK Patents Act 1949 or 1977 or a European patent granted under the European Patent Convention (EPC) designating the UK. The rights and privileges enjoyed by the patent owner in the UK were essentially extended to Hong Kong by simple registration.

The advantages of the pre-1997 patent system were that the system was inexpensive to administer and it was convenient for those who already had a UK patent or European patent (with a designation for the UK). This efficient patent system was, however, not without its drawbacks. As application for registration in Hong Kong could be made within five years of the grant of the patent by the UK Patent Office (UKPO),[11] no one could be sure, for as long as five years, as to whether protection of a patent granted in the UK would be sought in Hong Kong. There was no record kept by the Hong Kong registry of patents of the up-to-date status of a corresponding patent in the UK, including whether it had been renewed or revoked. Another major concern of the old system was that there was no power vested in the Hong Kong court to amend or revoke a patent.

7.2.2 *Localization of the Patent System (1986–1997)*

The resumption of sovereignty over Hong Kong by China in 1997 calling for the need of localizing the patent system of Hong Kong, and shortcomings in the pre-1997 patent system could be regarded as the major driving force for the review of the local patent system in 1980s and 1990s before the handover.

7.2.2.1 The Establishment of Patents Steering Committee and Various Options

During the 1980s, the Hong Kong government started considering the development of its then patent system. A Working Group on Patents chaired by the

---

[11] Section 3 of the Registration of Patents Ordinance.

secretary for economic services and comprising a number of experts from both the private and public sector was formed. On 23 December 1986 the attorney general invited a number of individuals to participate in a Patents Steering Committee (PSC) to advise the financial secretary and the attorney general on what patent system should be adopted in Hong Kong and, to draw up detailed proposals for the implementation of the system.[12]

The PSC recognized that one of the fundamental justifications for a patent system was to facilitate investment decisions. If the validity of patents granted in a country is ambiguous, or is difficult to ascertain, investment in technology is deterred. With this in mind, the PSC considered the advantages and disadvantages of the two major types of patent systems, namely non-examination system and pre-grant search and examination system.

NON-EXAMINATION SYSTEM. In a non-examination system, there is no search and examination, and the documents lodged are registered with only a check as to formalities. Issues of patentability and validity are left to be decided in the courts after grant. The major advantage of such a system is that obtaining a patent is simple and inexpensive. The drawback of a non-examination system, on the other hand, is its greater uncertainty without assessment of validity prior to grant. Although it is arguable that the validity of patent claims may be tested in court through litigation, it is considered to be not acceptable in the public interests. Litigation is by its very nature expensive, time-consuming and risky. Therefore, the validity of many patents is left uncontested and it also leads to possible abuse of such a system either intentionally or unintentionally. The grant of an invalid patent poses a considerable hindrance to other manufacturers and investors. Even though grounds for invalidity may be known, the expense of patent litigation is such that for many businesses it is prohibitive to challenge the patent and will often result in coerced settlement. Another objection to a grant of non-examined patent is that the definition of the monopoly set out in the claims may be unclear, because the patent office is bound to grant a patent for all patent applications even if they are imprecise. Such ambiguity in the patent claims may potentially deter some trade and investment.

PRE-GRANT SEARCH AND EXAMINATION SYSTEM. In a pre-grant search and examination system, the patent specification is searched and examined for validity before grant. The quality of a patent granted after such search and examination depends primarily on the competency of the patent examiner

---

[12]   The PSC completed its report in January 1993.

and the range of the technical information available in the patent office. The main advantage of this type of system is that strong patents, with clear claims, granted after search and examination by a well-respected patent office, provide a high degree of certainty for patent owners. This can prevent the abuses that are found in a non-examination patent system. It also assists the judicial process both at the interlocutory stage and at the full trial. The PSC recognized, however, that under such a system obtaining a patent would generally be an expensive and lengthy process.

The options for an examination system, as identified by the PSC, fell into the following categories:

1. Original grant of a patent after search and examination by the granting patent office;
2. Original grant of a patent after search and examination has been contracted out;
3. Original grant of a patent using the PCT;
4. Registration of a patent granted by another patent office; and
5. Issue or grant of a patent after registering a patent granted by another patent office.

(1) Original Grant of a Patent after Search/Examination by the Granting Patent Office The most common type of examination system is where the patent office, on receipt of a patent application, conducts its own search and examination before granting the patent, all under one roof. However, such a system is expensive and cannot be self-financing where there is a relatively small number of applications.

The PSC noted that an original grant system with full search and examination would require a substantial investment in accommodation, a comprehensive stock of published material, and a comprehensive programme to recruit and train the necessary teams of searchers and examiners. The cost of establishing the extensive technical information centre for a full search and examination system would be very expensive. In the light of the high costs and a realistic assessment of the likely number of applications, it was considered that a system of original grant after search and examination in Hong Kong would not be self-financing. It would take many years before a Hong Kong patent registry of original grant could develop the necessary expertise and experience to command the respect of the international community. Therefore, the PSC did not recommend a system of original grant with full search and examination for Hong Kong.

(2) Original Grant with Search and Examination Contracted Out Under this system, the patent office, on receipt of a patent application, checks for formalities before sending it to a contracted out patent office for search and examination. After receipt of the examination report, the original patent office would still require consideration as to whether to reject the application or grant the patent with or without amendment. A key advantage of this system is that it is not necessary to employ as many examiners as are required by other examination systems. The infrastructural requirements, such as the technical information centre, can also be less comprehensive.

The PSC recognized that this system, while superficially attractive, would still require the employment of a substantial number of staff including skilled examiners (after the search for novelty and inventiveness) to consider submissions and amendments and to assess whether the patent can be granted. Although the resource implications would be less than for an original grant after search and examination by the granting office, they would still be considerable particularly if the patents granted are to gain international respect. For these reasons the PSC did not recommend a system of original grant with search and examination contracted out.

(3) Original Grant Using the Patent Cooperation Treaty (PCT) The main aims of the PCT, which was concluded in 1970, were to provide procedures for obtaining legal protection for inventions and to provide for the dissemination of technical information. As discussed earlier, the PCT provides for the filing of an 'international' application as opposed to separate applications in a number of countries. It does not provide a system of international grant of patents, and each country can and does maintain its own system of grant.

The PSC considered whether the PCT could be an alternative mechanism for introducing a contracted out examination system. The advantages and disadvantages of any contracting out system as discussed above would apply equally to the use of the PCT for this purpose. In view of the requirement on skilled examiners with the consequential resource implications, it did not recommend a system of original grant using the PCT.

(4) Registration of a Patent Granted by Another Patent Office The pre-1997 patent system adopted the type of registration system where the patent remained dependent on the patent granted elsewhere – in Hong Kong's case, the United Kingdom. It was different from another type of registration system which involves both registering the patent granted by the other authority and then granting an independent patent. The advantages of any registration system are that it is not necessary to fund and develop the expertise to run

a search and examination system and that it is easier and quicker to implement than a system involving search and examination. It is also a system in which registering and consequently obtaining the patent is simple and inexpensive and should be acceptable to users. Furthermore, if the system from which the patents are registered has a strong search and examination system, the patents granted by registration are of good quality.

The biggest disadvantage of a registration from user's point of view is that he cannot seek patent protection in Hong Kong directly. Having considered all the circumstance, the PSC recommended adopting the option of granting of an independent patent after registering a patent granted by another patent office because the Hong Kong patent would have a separate life from its 'parent' and matters, such as validity and revocation could be dealt with locally.

(5) Grant of a Patent after Registering a Patent Granted by Another Patent Office The PSC considered that the requirements which should be taken into account for any registration system to be adopted in Hong Kong were

1. the country or the region must have a high level of trade and a strong market;
2. the patent office there must have a high number of applications for patents with an international spread of applicants;
3. the country or the region must apply the same standards and ambit of protection as under Hong Kong's system;
4. the patent office there must use English language; and
5. the country or the region must have a long-term financial and political future and that patents issued by its patent office are well respected internationally.

After assessment of which system or systems satisfied these requirements, it was concluded that whilst many systems satisfied some of these requirements, only the system of the European Patent Office (EPO) appeared to satisfy all of them.

In its report, the PSC recommended that

1. Hong Kong should have its own legislation and administrative system to provide for the grant and protection of patents in Hong Kong;
2. such legislation should provide for the grant of domestic patents after registering patents granted by the EPO under the provisions of the European Patent Convention (EPC); and

3. Hong Kong should have a Registrar of Patents who should continue to be the Director of Intellectual Property and that the new system should continue to be administered by the Hong Kong Patents Registry as part of the Intellectual Property Department.

The PSC also considered the special relationship between China and Hong Kong, and the developments of the China's patent laws at the time. Although the number of patent applications received by China patent office was relatively low at the time, China was about to become a party to the PCT in 1994 and China also adopted a first-to-file system that was similar to the EPO.

The PSC also recognized the difficulties that would arise if Hong Kong allowed the registration of patents from more than one system while introducing a new patent system at the same time. After carefully weighing all the options, the PSC recommended that after a period of one to two years from the introduction of the new system the Hong Kong legislation should provide for the grant of domestic patents after registering patents granted not only by the EPO but also by the Chinese patent office, the SIPO.

7.2.2.2 Petty Patents (Short-Term Patents)

Although the PSC was satisfied that under the new patent system Hong Kong patents would be of good quality, it was aware that this patent system would not benefit businesses which manufactured products of short commercial viability. Many of the short-term products made in Hong Kong were of significant economic value, such as watches, toys and consumer electronic products. The PSC, by a majority, considered that a petty patent (also known as short-term patent) system in Hong Kong would assist the protection of short-term products. It recommended a modified non-examination system in which application would be made to the Registrar, who would only ensure for the compliance of the formal requirements without any substantive examination. It recommended that a search report should be filed before grant and that the patentability of a petty patent be the same as those recommended for a standard Hong Kong patent. In terms of enforcement and prevention of abuse, they recommended that the onus should be on the proprietor of a petty patent to establish in any proceedings the validity of the petty patent to the satisfaction of the court, and where an interlocutory injunction was ordered, both parties should have a right to call for a speedy trial.

7.2.2.3 Technical Information Centre

The PSC recognized that technical information in patents could be useful to economic planners and investors for identification of trends in technology. Unfortunately, the Registry in Hong Kong lagged behind its counterparts in other developed economies at the time and did not provide any specialized technical information services, let alone electronic database of the information in patents registered in Hong Kong. Therefore, it further recommended the establishment in Hong Kong of a technical information centre providing services similar to those provided by the Search and Advisory Service of the UKPO and numerous other patent offices and technical information service organizations worldwide.

7.3 EXISTING PATENT SYSTEM (1997 ONWARDS)

The PSC submitted its report to the government in 1993. Many of the recommendations were accepted by the government leading to the eventual enactment of the Patents Ordinance (Chapter 514) in June 1997. The most notable change to the previous regime under the repealed Registration of Patents Ordinance by the Patents Ordinance was that, for the first time, patents in Hong Kong could be amended and revoked in Hong Kong. Under the Patents Ordinance, two types of patents are granted in Hong Kong, namely standard patents and short-term patents.

7.3.1 *Standard Patents*

A standard patent is granted in Hong Kong on the basis of a patent granted by one of three 'designated patent offices', namely SIPO, UKIPO and EPO for patents designating the UK. Hence, the current regime is also known as the 'reregistration' system. Under the current system, an applicant who wants to seek patent protection in Hong Kong alone cannot apply for a standard patent in Hong Kong directly. He must first file an application with one of the above three designated patent offices. The maximum term of protection for a standard patent is 20 years.

In 2016, out of the 14,092 applications for a standard patent filed in Hong Kong, 58.8 per cent, 38.0 per cent and 1.8 per cent were based on patent applications filed with SIPO, EPO and UKIPO, respectively. Amongst the 5,698 standard patents granted in Hong Kong in the same year, 68.1 per cent, 30.2 per cent and 1.7 per cent were based on patents granted by SIPO, EPO and UKPO, respectively. These percentages have remained relatively stable over the last five years.

An application for a standard patent is made in two stages: a request to record (filed within six months after the date of the publication of the corresponding patent application in a designated patent office); and subsequently a request for registration and grant (filed within six months after the date of grant of the patent by the designated patent office or publication of the request to record in Hong Kong, whichever is later).

The Hong Kong Patents Registry conducts a 'formality examination' of applications for a standard patent by verifying the documents and information submitted (including a copy of the specification of the patent as published by the designated patent office). The Registry does not conduct 'substantive examination', i.e. it does not assess whether the invention is novel, involves an inventive step and is susceptible of industrial application. Since the substantive examination is done by the designated patent office, it may be argued that the existing system does not encourage the development of the patent profession in Hong Kong, particularly the homegrown expertise necessary for drafting and prosecuting applications for patents. Second, a reregistration system may be perceived as a second-grade patent system given the international trend of adopting or moving towards original grant patent (OGP) systems, which allow application for patent protection to be filed direct with the patent office at home without first applying for a patent in another patent office. This perception does not facilitate Hong Kong in promoting innovation or developing itself into a premier intellectual property-trading hub.[13] Given competing choices of places to invest in research and development activities, some enterprises might not perceive Hong Kong, being outside the OGP mainstream, to be very attractive for setting up their businesses.

Although many practitioners in the patent field consider the current standard patent system user-friendly and cost effective, there are growing calls for Hong Kong to have its own independent OGP system which allows an inventor to apply for a standard patent direct in Hong Kong without first obtaining a patent in any patent office outside Hong Kong.

7.3.2 Short-Term Patents

The short-term patent system in Hong Kong is intended to supplement the standard patent system by offering protection to inventions with a shorter

---

[13] Information and services related to intellectual property trading for businesses and the general public are available at www.ip.gov.hk.

commercial life. Subject to renewal, the term of protection of a short-term patent is up to eight years. In 2016, the number of applications filed and the number of short-term patents granted were 762 and 485 respectively. An application for a short-term patent avoids the two-stage process and is made by filing a request for grant in Hong Kong direct without having to go through a designated patent office first. Applications are granted subject to a formality examination. China has applied the PCT to Hong Kong. Section 125 of the Patents Ordinance also gives an applicant who has made an international application for a utility model in China the right to make an application for a short-term patent within six months after the international application has entered the national phase in China.

Since the patentability of the invention is not subject to substantive examination before a short-term patent is granted, there is potentially more room for abuse. Some of the short-term patents granted may turn out to be invalid and unenforceable. For as long as these short-term patents remain on the register, third parties in Hong Kong may therefore be deterred from dealing with the technology covered by the inventions. The PSC once recognized the disadvantages with a non-examination short-term patent system but considered that with appropriate safeguards the advantages of offering protection for inventions with a shorter commercial life would outweigh the disadvantages.

7.3.3 Regulation of Patent Agency Services in Hong Kong

A patent agent or a patent attorney is a person who acts for his client in the patent-related matters. His scope of work normally includes providing advice on the patentability of inventions, drafting the specifications for patent applications and responding to objections raised by the patent offices in respect of the patent applications, and also advising on post-grant issues covering patent licensing; validity and enforcement.

Under the Patents Ordinance, for patent applications or proceedings before the Hong Kong Patents Registry, the Registrar of Patents can exercise some regulatory powers over patent agents to the extent that she shall refuse to recognize as an agent a person who neither resides nor has a place of business in Hong Kong.[14] In addition, the Registrar may refuse to recognize the capacity of a person to act as an agent in respect of business under the law in certain circumstances,[15] for example, where the person has been convicted of a criminal offence. Apart from the above, there is no other statutory requirement that has to be complied with in the provision of patent agency service.

---

[14] Section 140(4) of the Patents Ordinance.   [15] Section 85(7) of the Patents (General) Rules.

Any person may practise or act as a patent agent for others, although many patent agents who are in active practice in Hong Kong are in fact qualified patent practitioners in other jurisdictions, such as the UK, Europe, Mainland China, Australia, Canada and the US.

Without a regulatory regime, there is greater flexibility to users of the system. Any person may act as a patent agent in proceedings before the Registrar.[16] Clients have a free choice in hiring an agent, depending on the qualification, experience and reputation etc. of and the fees charged by the service providers. The fact that the provision of patent agency services is not regulated is seen by some to promote competition amongst service providers, with the fees for such services being kept low. With an unregulated profession, there is, however, less assurance of the quality of the services, and any person, with or without the relevant technical and legal skills, may claim to be a patent practitioner. Some people may also not know where to seek the appropriate services they require.

7.4 REVIEW OF THE EXISTING PATENT SYSTEM AND ITS FUTURE POSITIONING

To ensure that the local patent system would continue to meet present-day circumstances and that its further evolution would facilitate the development of Hong Kong into a regional innovation and technology hub, the government commenced a comprehensive review of the local patent system in October 2011 by launching a three-month public consultation vide a Consultation Paper entitled 'Review of the Patent System in Hong Kong'.[17] In the same month, the Secretary for Commerce and Economic Development appointed the Advisory Committee on Review of the Patent System in Hong Kong (Advisory Committee) to advise on

1. How the government should position Hong Kong's patent system, having regard to the public consultation paper of October 2011 and the responses received; and
2. How best to implement changes to the patent system, in the light of decisions made by the government on the way forward.

---

[16] Under the current standard patent and short-term patent systems, the Hong Kong Patents Registry conducts formality examination only without substantive examination. Hence, proceedings before the Registrar involve mainly documentary and procedural issues.

[17] The Consultation Paper on Review of the Patent System in Hong Kong is available at www.ipd.gov.hk.

7.4.1 *The Advisory Committee's Recommendations*

Having carefully examined the submissions of respondents to the public consultation and considered the relevant circumstances, including the patent systems in several advanced economies, the Advisory Committee submitted a report to the government in December 2012 with the following key recommendations on the future re-positioning of the local patent system:[18]

1. Introducing an original grant patent (OGP) system for grant of standard patents, with substantive examination outsourced to other patent office(s) as the starting point;
2. Retaining the current reregistration system for grant of standard patents;
3. Retaining the short-term patent system with suitable refinements; and
4. Developing a full-fledged regulatory regime on patent agency services in the long run, which has to be achieved in stages, with possible interim measures.

The above strategic recommendations were accepted by the government in February 2013.

7.4.1.1 Introducing an OGP Route for Granting Standard Patents

According to the analysis of the Advisory Committee, introducing an OGP system can demonstrate the government's commitment to intellectual property protection by developing a patent system on a par with those of advanced economies, thereby raising the international profile of Hong Kong on the world IP map. It would also allow Hong Kong to determine its own patentability criteria and procedures in a way that would best meet the economic needs of Hong Kong. With an OGP system, Hong Kong may explore further international cooperation opportunities, such as the Patent Prosecution Highway (PPH)[19] and PCT arrangements, in facilitating local patent applicants to obtain patent protection in other jurisdictions.

---

[18] The Report of the Advisory Committee on Review of the Patent System in Hong Kong is available at www.ipd.gov.hk.

[19] A PPH is a set of initiatives for promoting work-sharing between/amongst different patent offices and enabling patent applicants to request for accelerated processing of patent applications. Generally speaking, under a PPH agreement, a patent applicant can request an accelerated processing of a patent application at the patent office of second filing (OSF), when the patent office of first filing (OFF) has already found corresponding patent claims allowable. A PPH establishes a process whereby the OSF makes use of the work already carried out by the OFF in relation to the same invention. The OSF can process the patent application quicker because the examination process begins at a more informed level. However, the OSF is not compelled to follow the opinion of the OFF and may make its own decision on whether to grant a patent.

In the long run, an OGP system may facilitate Hong Kong to develop into an innovation and technology hub. It may attract and encourage local and foreign enterprises to make R&D investment and set up their operations in Hong Kong. The Advisory Committee also recognized that an OGP system may help nurture and attract talents, stimulate the growth of patent agency business and widen career paths for graduates with science and engineering degrees. From the users' perspective, the main difference between this new OGP system and the existing 'reregistration' system for standard patents (which will be retained) is that the OGP system would enable applicants to file standard patent applications directly in Hong Kong without first obtaining a patent in a designated patent office. On the other hand, the Advisory Committee noted the challenges in introducing an OGP system, such as the lack of local supply of technical examiners, and the costs associated with setting up and running an OGP system.

7.4.1.2 Retaining the Current Reregistration System

The general consensus from the consultation exercise was to retain the reregistration system if an OGP system was to be introduced. The Advisory Committee recommended that the reregistration system should run in parallel with the OGP system in view of the high quality of patents granted and its effective operation. In the meantime, the Advisory Committee also suggested not to expand the current reregistration system because it would entrench the reregistration system and go against the general direction of setting up an OGP system in Hong Kong.

7.4.1.3 Retaining the Short-Term Patent System with Suitable Refinements

The Advisory Committee agreed with the vast majority of respondents to the public consultation that the short-term patent system should be retained. To address users' concern that the current short-term patent system may be prone to abuse mainly due to the lack of substantive examination, the Advisory Committee recommended on refining the system in the following major areas:

1. Substantive examination of the invention underlying a short-term patent should be made a prerequisite to commencement of enforcement action;
2. The proprietor of a short-term patent or a third party having a legitimate concern or doubt about the validity of the patent should have the right to apply to the Registry for substantive examination of the patent; and

3. The proprietor of a short-term patent, when making a threat of infringement proceedings, should furnish with the person to whom the threat
   was made full particulars about the short-term patent in question, failing
   which the threat of proceedings may be deemed groundless thereby
   entitling a party aggrieved by the threat to seek relief.

Separately, the Advisory Committee also suggested of exploring the possibility
of relaxing the number of independent claims allowed for each short-term
patent. A claim, as far as a patent application is concerned, in essence
identifies the specific elements of the underlying invention to which the
patent applicant claims rights and seeks protection. An independent claim,
as opposed to a dependent claim, refers to a claim that does not rely upon or
refer to any other claims. Under section 113(1)(b)(ii) of the Patents Ordinance,
an applicant may apply for one or more claims but not exceeding one
independent claim in respect of a short-term patent.

7.4.1.4 Regulatory Regime on Patent Agency Services

The Advisory Committee anticipated that the introduction of a new patent
system with substantive examination would call for new sets of skills with
technical competence and expertise concerning patent prosecution which is
not required under the present system, thereby opening up a new demand for
patent agency service. It recommended to regulate local patent practitioners
by establishing a full-fledged regulatory system in the long run, under which
the specific professional requirements on examination, qualification, practice,
discipline and continuing development for patent practitioners are laid down,
as a complementary component of the OGP system.

7.4.2 *Major Tasks for Implementing the New Patent System*

The government supports the Advisory Committee's strategic recommendations on enhancing our local patent system and has initiated a series of efforts
to implement the new patent system.

7.4.2.1 Legislative Exercise and Other Major Tasks for Implementing the OGP System

In 2015, the government proposed legislative amendments to the Patents
Ordinance to implement the Advisory Committee's recommendations by
introducing the Patents (Amendment) Bill 2015 into the Legislative Council.

The bill was eventually passed by the Legislative Council in June 2016 leading to the enactment of the Patents (Amendment) Ordinance 2016.

The Patents (Amendment) Ordinance 2016 introduces new provisions into the Patents Ordinance under which an applicant may apply for a standard patent in Hong Kong under the OGP system. Under the new OGP system, if an OGP application fulfils the minimum filing requirements, the Registrar will accord the date of filing. Thereafter, the Registrar will then examine whether the application has also satisfied other formal requirements. Upon passing the formality examination, the application will generally be published after the date of filing (or if priority has been claimed, the date of priority) unless the applicant requests for an early publication. Following publication of the application, the Registrar, upon request by the applicant, will proceed with conducting substantive examination to determine whether the application has satisfied the patentability requirements for a patent grant. If a third party files observations with respect to an application within a prescribed period, such observations will also be considered by the Registrar during substantive examination.

The Registrar may raise objection where she is of the view that the application does not fulfil any prescribed patentability requirement. The Patents (Amendment) Ordinance 2016 incorporates provisions to allow the applicant to address the objection by filing submissions or proposing amendments to the specification. The applicant will also be given an opportunity to request the Registrar to review her decision on refusal of a patent application, and should such review turn out be unsuccessful, the applicant can still appeal to the Court of First Instance on the question of the law. On the other hand, if the application, upon substantive examination, is found to satisfy all the prescribed requirements, the Registrar will grant the standard patent and publish the grant accordingly. Apart from the above procedural framework, the Patents (Amendment) Ordinance 2016 introduces new provisions for post-grant matters such as amendments to specification of OGP patents.

Regarding the short-term patent system for products with a shorter commercial life, the Patents (Amendment) Ordinance 2016 introduces new provisions into the Patents Ordinance for implementing certain refinement measures. In particular, the new provisions lay down the procedural framework for substantive examination of short-term patents by the Registrar, such as who may apply for substantive examination, the legal and procedural requirements for making such applications and for conducting the substantive examination, and amendment of the short-term patent. The procedures for enforcement and related proceedings as well as the onus of proof of validity/invalidity of short-term patents have been addressed by the Patents

(Amendment) Ordinance 2016 in view of the inclusion of substantive examination as a new feature of the short-term patent system. Furthermore, having regard to the Advisory Committee's suggestion of exploring the possibility of relaxing the number of independent claims, the Patents (Amendment) Ordinance 2016 also relaxes the current restriction by allowing a maximum of two independent claims in a short-term patent application, which seeks to strike a reasonable balance between having a short-term patent system mainly to cater for relatively simple inventions with a limited commercial life span on the one hand, and enabling the grant of a short-term patent with more than one independent claim at a reduced costs on the other.

Another major area of change to be brought by the Patents (Amendment) Ordinance 2016 is to introduce an interim regulatory measure for patent practitioners in Hong Kong. Given that a full-fledged regulatory regime will likely be established sometime after the new patent system has been implemented, the interim regulatory measure under the new law is to make it an offence to use in connection with the provision of patent agency services of certain specific titles[20] as well as any other title or description which may reasonably cause anyone to believe that the person using or permitted to use the title or description holds a qualification that is specifically granted for approving that person to provide patent agency service in Hong Kong, and that is recognized by law or endorsed by the government. Appropriate exemption has been provided for to cater for the legitimate and reasonable use in Hong Kong of professional titles that have been lawfully acquired outside Hong Kong.

The interim regulatory measure will help reserve certain specific titles which may likely be used as formal patent professional titles under the future full-fledged regulatory regime, reduce public confusion as to the holders' professional qualification in patent practice in Hong Kong pending establishment of the full-fledged regulatory regime, while sending a clear message of the government's determination to formally regulate the patent profession in due course for building a strong local pool of patent profession in the longer run.

With the enactment of the Patents (Amendment) Ordinance 2016 which is yet to be brought into effect, further follow up tasks are being undertaken by the government for building the necessary hardware and software in support of the new patent system. These tasks include introducing appropriate legislative amendments to Patents (General) Rules (Chapter 514C), being the subsidiary

---

[20] These specific prohibited titles are 'certified patent agent', 'registered patent agent', 'certified patent attorney' and 'registered patent attorney'.

legislation to provide for the detailed application and examination procedures to be adopted by the Registry, drawing up examination guidelines, recruiting patent examiners with the necessary technical credentials, building a new electronic system for processing applications under the new patent system, and conducting publicity about the new system.

7.4.2.2 Co-operation Arrangement between IPD and SIPO

SIPO and the Hong Kong Intellectual Property Department (IPD) signed their first agreement in Hong Kong on 16 November 2011 to strengthen co-operation in the area of intellectual property by fostering exchange and deepening communication between the two places. On 6 December 2013, as part of the efforts to implement the OGP system in Hong Kong, IPD and SIPO signed the Co-operation Arrangement in the Area of Patent in Hong Kong. Under the arrangement, the SIPO will provide technical assistance and support to the IPD for substantive examination of patent applications and the training of staff.

The SIPO being one of the five largest intellectual property offices in the world[21] has extensive technical expertise and experience in substantive examination of patent applications and manpower training. Its pre-eminence has been demonstrated by its top position in the world for patent applications received. Therefore, the arrangement bears strategic significance in facilitating the development of Hong Kong into a regional innovation and technology hub, as well as a premier IP trading hub.

7.4.2.3 Further Potential Initiatives for Enhancing the Patent System in the Future

Under the current reregistration system, IPD only needs to conduct formality examination of applications for standard patents given that the corresponding patents have been published and granted by the three designated patent offices. Short-term patent applications under the existing regime are also subject to formality examination only.

The new OGP system will however call for both formality and substantive examinations under which IPD will need to receive and vet patent

---

[21] Also known as 'IP5' which 'together handle about 80 per cent of the world's patent applications, and 95 per cent of all work carried out under the Patent Cooperation Treaty', www .fiveipoffices.org/about.html. The other members of the IP5 are the European Patent Office, the Japan Patent Office, the Korean Intellectual Property Office and the United States Patent and Trademark Office.

applications, communicate with applicants on the applications, grant or reject applications and provide a review/appeal system. Although SIPO has agreed to provide technical assistance and support to IPD in conducting substantive examination of inventions and manpower training under the new patent system, it is the target for Hong Kong to develop in incremental stages its capacity in conducting indigenous substantive examination in the medium to long term, starting with the niche areas where Hong Kong has acquired considerable expertise or which Hong Kong is well placed to enhance its research and development capabilities. IPD will also help promote the sustainability of the OGP system through continuous enhancement of the system to ensure that it is on par with international standards, and potential cooperation with other patent authorities, such as by means of mutual facilitation of application procedures through PPH.

7.5 THE WAY FORWARD

The patent system in Hong Kong has come a long way in providing a more robust and sustainable conditions for innovation to flourish. While the enactment of the Patents (Amendment) Ordinance 2016 has established the basic legislative framework for the new OGP system and also for refining the short-term patent system, further efforts for attending to various critical implementation tasks are required to be expended for rolling out the new patent system as soon as practicable. The shift from a reregistration system to an OGP regime to be run in parallel with the reregistration system will help bring the Hong Kong patent system on par with those of other advanced economies.

The building of the new patent system in Hong Kong can be considered as one of the government's important initiatives for demonstrating its commitment to not only maintaining an effective and strong intellectual property protection in Hong Kong, but also creating an infrastructure for capacity building and fostering the development of Hong Kong as an innovation hub as well as an intellectual property trading hub.

8

Debates on the Role of the Original Grant Patent System in Hong Kong's Innovation

Jeffrey Mclean and Winnie Yue

8.1 BACKGROUND

As a Special Administrative Region (SAR) of the People's Republic of China, Hong Kong has a high degree of autonomy and will retain its own legal system until 2047. As such, under the Basic Law, for intellectual property purposes, Hong Kong remains a separate jurisdiction from the rest of China. Accordingly, the intellectual property laws and court decisions of China do not apply to Hong Kong, with intellectual property rights (IPRs) registered or protected in Hong Kong not extending to China and vice versa.

As a common law jurisdiction, the Hong Kong courts look to precedent (previous judgments) decided in respect of relevant cases within Hong Kong. They may also refer to other common law jurisdictions such as England, Australia and Canada. Although these decisions are not legally binding, they can be highly persuasive, particularly where the wording and overall approach of the laws are similar.

Before 1997, apart from the protection of trademarks, Hong Kong's intellectual property laws derived from United Kingdom (UK) legislation. The Registration of Patents Ordinance (1979) provided that a person who had obtained a patent in the UK, or a European Patent designating the UK, could have the patent registered in Hong Kong within five years of its grant. The patent would be effective in Hong Kong as long as the corresponding patent remained in force.[1]

This system was replaced by the Patents Ordinance (Cap.514), which came into force on 27 June 1997, in advance of the transfer of sovereignty over Hong Kong back to China. Although Hong Kong now has a substantive patent law, it still does not have a completely independent patent system.

---

[1] For the details about Hong Kong's patent system before 1997, see Chapter 7 of this book.

A Hong Kong patent is based on the re-registration of patents already granted in the UK, by the European Patent Office (EPO; designating the United Kingdom) and China. International applications under the Patent Cooperation Treaty (PCT) covering those countries will also qualify.[2]

The present re-registration system of Hong Kong for obtaining a standard patent offers the following advantages:

- It is a relatively quick, low cost and efficient mechanism by which a 20-year standard patent may be obtained in Hong Kong;
- Re-registration is based upon the progression of a corresponding designated application through rigorous substantive examination in the designated patent offices, which provides a high presumption of validity of granted patents;
- Determination of infringement and validity is conducted under established doctrine of precedent and statutory law in accordance with the rule of law.

Despite the above advantages, the Hong Kong SAR government amended the patent law to adopt an 'original grant patent' (OGP) system in June 2016. This chapter focuses on the debates concerning whether adopting such a new system is conducive to Hong Kong's innovation as some have claimed.

8.2 PATENT LAW REFORM

In 2011, more than a decade after the implementation of the Patent Ordinance (Cap.514), the government decided to conduct a comprehensive review of the patent system in Hong Kong, taking into account the latest international developments in patent protection. The intention was to ensure that the system would continue to meet the current needs of Hong Kong and to align the system with the government's vision to develop Hong Kong into a regional innovation and technology hub.

The initial consultation highlighted some diverging views in the patent community. Whilst it was generally accepted that the existing system is user-friendly and cost-effective, there were concerns that the current system may not continue to meet the needs of Hong Kong's changing economy. In particular:

- The requirement of first obtaining a patent in a Designated Patent Office is expensive and inconvenient for applicants with limited

---

[2]   See Section 7.3 of this book for the details of the application procedures of two types of patents: standard patents and short-term patents.

resources or those who only want a standard (20-year) patent in Hong Kong.

- The short-term patent system is potentially open to abuse due to the lack of substantive examination. It also creates uncertainty as to the validity of the patent.
- The lack of regulation of patent agents. Currently, any person who resides in or has a place of business in Hong Kong may carry on the business of a patent agent.

8.2.1 *Introduction of OGP System for Standard Patents*

The consultation paper 'Review of the Patent System in Hong Kong' was issued in October 2011, seeking views on the introduction of an OGP system in Hong Kong. This would allow an inventor to apply directly for a standard patent in Hong Kong without having to rely on a patent issued by another patent office. Substantive examination could be conducted locally or be outsourced to another designated patent office.

Following the issuance of the consultation paper, the government has been in discussions with stakeholders through different channels and forums, including targeted briefing sessions with R&D centres, small and medium-sized enterprises, industry associations, tertiary education institutes and chambers of commerce. The views of relevant advisory boards, including the Innovations and Technology Advisory Committee of the Hong Kong Trade Development Council and the Trade and Industry Advisory Boards, have also been sought.

After two years of consultation, the Report by the Advisory Committee on Review of the Patent System (hereafter, the Report) was published in 2013, with the recommendation to adopt the OGP system, but also in the meantime to retain the present standard patent re-registration system.[3]

8.2.2 *Reform of the Short-Term Patent System*

Short-term patents cover the same range of inventions that may be protected by standard patents and may be obtained after filing a search report from an international searching authority. However, there is no substantive examination of short-term patents prior to grant, which may provide the potential for abuse of the short-term patent system. We do not propose to discuss in detail

---

[3] For the details of the recommendation, see Section 7.4.1 of this book.

the pros and cons of the short-term patent system here to the extent that these are not directly related to the advantages and disadvantages of an OGP system itself. However, the proposals to reform short-term patents in Hong Kong are part of the current reform package.

Supporters of the existing short-term patent system feel that it offers a fast and inexpensive way of protecting simple inventions with a limited commercial lifespan. Many regard it as a benefit that the Hong Kong system covers a relatively wider range of inventions as compared with 'petty patent' systems in other jurisdictions. As discussed below, the system also has certain strategic uses for many patent owners. Critics argue that short-term patents are not substantively examined, leading to the grant of patents that may actually be invalid and unenforceable, and which may remain on the register and deter others from using the technology covered by the patents.

To address this issue, the Report proposes retaining the short-term patent system but including substantive examination as a precondition to the commencement of infringement proceedings. The drawback of requiring such pre-commencement substantive examination is increased costs and longer processing time, which could reduce the overall attractiveness of the short-term patent system. However, most commentators regard the short-term patent as playing an important role in the patent system in Hong Kong. In particular, some feel that in the absence of an OGP, the short-term patent system provides an effective 'second tier' of patent protection for both domestic and foreign applicants.

8.2.3 *Regulation of the Patent Profession*

Some argue that lack of regulation for the patent profession does not encourage the development of patent agency business in Hong Kong or the development of local expertise in the drafting and prosecution of patents. It has been suggested that a regulatory regime would enhance the credibility of the patent agency profession and offer career opportunities to local graduates with a scientific or technical background. There appears to be widespread support for some form of regulation of the profession, but there are differing views as to the finer details. Many feel that the introduction of a regulatory regime for patent practitioners should not be considered dependent upon the introduction of an OGP system in Hong Kong. Others see a need for a regulatory regime only if an OGP system is to be introduced in Hong Kong.

Amongst those who favour a regulatory regime, there are different views as to whether Hong Kong should regulate the provision of some or all patent-related services, the titles that should be regulated and the type of qualifications that would be required. It has been suggested that a regulatory regime would help to build a local patent profession, which is one of the purported advantages of OGP discussed below. However, it is also one of the preconditions for an OGP system that it can provide substantive examination in Hong Kong and is arguably dependent on many other factors beyond the mere introduction of OGP.

8.3 THE ADVANTAGES OF INTRODUCING OGP IN HONG KONG

It is clear from the consultation process that the views on whether Hong Kong should have an OGP system are diverse. The Report sets out quite succinctly the potential benefits of an OGP system, including the following:

- Encouraging local innovation and attracting enterprises to set up their R&D operations in Hong Kong, thereby promoting Hong Kong as a regional innovation and technology hub.
- Promoting Hong Kong as the place of 'first filing' for patents.
- Allowing applicants to obtain patent protection in Hong Kong at a lower cost.
- Facilitating more flexible and expedient examination procedures.
- Promoting direct communication between local enterprises and Hong Kong patent practitioners without language barrier, resulting in higher patent quality.
- Stimulating the growth of patent agency business and helping to build up local patent professionals.
- Creating added career opportunities for graduates with science and engineering backgrounds.

8.3.1 *Promoting Hong Kong's Innovation*

Advocates of the OGP system point out that Hong Kong is a global finance and commercial centre with a legal regime that meets and in many cases exceeds international standards. Hong Kong has had an independent trademark system since 1873 and an original grant system for designs since 1997. However, its intellectual property regime still lacks a full-fledged patent system. Although the re-registration system has served Hong Kong's needs up until now, Hong Kong's economic structure continues to rapidly evolve.

It is argued that a re-registration system may be perceived as a second-grade patent system, given the international trend of adopting or moving towards OGP regimes. Other comparable jurisdictions, whose economic development have followed a similar course as Hong Kong, such as Taiwan, Singapore and Korea, already have implemented independent patent systems. Macau, the other Special Administrative Region of China, also has an extension as well as capacity for an independent patent system.

With the development of ever-complex technologies, ownership of intellectual property rights has become central to the business strategies of many innovative companies around the world. Introduction of the OGP would be in keeping with Hong Kong's status as an advanced economy. By contrast, continuing with a re-registration system would leave Hong Kong in the company of developing economies such as Fiji, the Solomon Islands and the Seychelles. Advocates of an OGP system therefore indicate that an independent patent system is crucial to facilitate the government's ambitions to develop Hong Kong into a regional innovation and technology hub. A well-functioning patent institution is a cornerstone of successful innovation systems. It is argued that an effective local patent regime will also help to attract and encourage foreign enterprises to make R&D and other investments in Hong Kong.

It appears to be the government's hope that the development of an independent patent regime will lead to an increase in domestic innovation and invention, which is essential for maintaining competitiveness and economic growth. Raising awareness of patents and the international patent profile of Hong Kong by introducing an OGP system may also help to promote Hong Kong as a jurisdiction for the first-filing of patent applications.

Following the significant investment by the Singaporean government in the development of the intellectual property ecosystem, various reports highlight the significantly increased royalty fees payable to Singapore as an indication of the economic success arising from the investment in IP. For example, between 2009 and 2012, payments to Singapore for royalty and licence fees increased from USD 842 million (2009) to USD 1.65 billion (2012) as noted in balance of payment figures.[4] Although this is only one metric, it does offer a useful indication as to how IP-driven growth contributed to national GDP in that case.

---

[4] A. Gill, Z. Vari Kovacs and A. Lall, The Development of Singapore's Intellectual Property Regime, Lee Kuan Yew School of Public Policy: Microsoft Case Studies Series, available at http://lkyspp.nus.edu.sg/wp-content/uploads/2014/11/LKWMS_Series01_SG_IP.pdf.

8.3.2 *Promoting Innovation and Job Opportunities*

The combination of Hong Kong's strong financial and legal systems, a low-tax regime and well-trained business professionals provides a solid foundation for the government's plans for Hong Kong to develop into a regional marketplace for providing professional services in licensing, franchising and registration of IP.

Certainly, since 1999, the government has been making significant investments in support of its long-term goal to turn Hong Kong into an innovation and technology hub including the following:

- Setting up the Innovation and Technology Fund with an investment of HKD 5 billion.
- Establishing the Innovation and Technology Commission and the Hong Kong Applied Science and Technology Research Institute.
- Developing essential infrastructure such as the Hong Kong Science Park, Industrial Estates and Cyberport.
- Setting up five R&D centres to drive and coordinate applied R&D in five focus areas:
  - automotive parts and accessory systems;
  - information and communications technologies;
  - logistics and supply chain management enabling technologies;
  - nanotechnology and advanced materials; and
  - textiles and clothing.
- Establishing the R&D Cash Rebate Scheme to encourage more private sector investment in R&D and collaboration with public research institutions.

A key additional factor is the need to increase talent and expertise in the IP field. Proponents of an OGP system argue that it will create more career and job opportunities for Hong Kong in terms of nurturing and attracting talented professionals, stimulating the growth of patent agency business, which in turn will lead to opportunities for more local patent professionals and additional career opportunities for graduates with science and engineering backgrounds.

8.3.3 *More Efficient and User-Friendly*

It is argued that an OGP system will be more efficient and user-friendly for those applicants who only want to obtain a patent in Hong Kong. It will be possible for such applicants to apply for patent protection in Hong Kong directly, without first going through another designated office. This may be at a lower cost and could potentially be more convenient. This should encourage local applicants who otherwise may be discouraged by the need to file first overseas. Such applicants will also be able to communicate directly with the local professionals and Patents Registry without the need to engage foreign patent agents to handle the application at the designated overseas patent office.

Advocates of OGP also highlight the capacity of skilled professionals to provide direct advice on strategy and commercialization in the Chinese language for local patent owners and may facilitate higher patent quality. Many commentators highlight the development of another city-state, Singapore, which has been making significant strides in providing applicants with a number of choices for obtaining patent protection, including examination based upon the grant of an existing application in another substantive examining jurisdiction, or substantive examination carried out by or under the supervision of the Singaporean Patent Office. Singapore has also been quite active in engaging in treaties and agreements with a number of different patent offices for facilitating quicker and more efficient patent examination. For example, Singapore has commenced Patent Prosecution Highway (PPH) programmes with the German Patent Office and has joined the Global Patent Prosecution Highway Network.

Proponents of OGP also state that having accredited local examination can provide applicants with expedited grant of corresponding applications in overseas jurisdictions via entry into such agreements.

8.3.4 Tailored to Hong Kong's Needs

The current re-registration system arguably means that Hong Kong is subject to the laws and practices of the designated patent offices. An OGP system where examination and grant is truly based on Hong Kong law could allow Hong Kong to determine patentability criteria and standards, procedures, practices and other matters, in accordance with Hong Kong's own requirements, provided such requirements meet minimum internationally accepted norms. This will mean that Hong Kong could build up its own implementation of laws that may be more reflective of Hong Kong's specific needs, culture and environment. It could also facilitate more flexible and expedient examination procedures. Accordingly, in keeping with the desire to have a mature and independent patent system, the long-term goal of the government is for Hong Kong to develop its own patent examination capacity.

8.3.5 *International Cooperation/Better Cooperation with China*

Arguably, if the new OGP system provides for the outsourcing of examination to the Chinese State Intellectual Property Office (SIPO), which currently seems to be the most likely possibility, then this may provide a potential basis for mutual recognition of patents between Hong Kong and Mainland China. It may also have the benefit of expediting the processing of any subsequent corresponding applications with the SIPO, since it will already have conducted the substantive examination depending on the negotiated processing times and service times agreed.

8.4 DISADVANTAGES OF INTRODUCING OGP TO HONG KONG

On the other hand, critics have questioned the relative strength of the business case for adopting an OGP system in Hong Kong. Arguments against OGP set out in the Report include the following:

- The availability of an OGP system is not a significant factor for deciding where to file a patent application.
- There is no credible empirical evidence to support the idea that adopting an OGP system would stimulate local innovation.
- There is unlikely to be sufficient demand to support a cost-effective OGP system in Hong Kong.
- The cost of obtaining an OGP (particularly if the system is not supported by a sufficient critical mass) could be much higher than that of obtaining a patent under the current re-registration system, which raises questions of whether public funds should be spent in subsidizing the patent system.
- The current re-registration system is efficient and inexpensive; having an OGP system would complicate rather than streamline patent grant procedures at a time when the international trend is moving away from duplicate patent examination.
- Introduction of an OGP system would not enhance the quality of standard patents granted, which is already very high.
- It is doubtful as to whether an OGP system with outsourced substantive examination would help develop and train patent professionals.
- It is doubtful as to whether the number of added jobs created for technical graduates would justify the substantial resources and investment required for implementing and maintaining an OGP system.

8.4.1 Insufficient Demand

Critics of OGP believe it is simplistic to assume that introduction of local examination will necessarily increase the proportion of Hong Kong local applicants filing patents/applications. It is argued that, in fact, motivation for local and multinational entities to pursue a Hong Kong patent through the OGP is likely to be relatively low in view of the considerations set out below. In particular, in a global context, Hong Kong is not an important or major territory for securing patent protection. However, the relatively inexpensive cost of securing patent grant by the current two-step recordal process assists in maintaining a reasonable level of registrations. Advocates of OGP argue OGP would encourage applicants to 'first file' an originating 'standard' patent application in Hong Kong so as to (a) establish convention priority and (b) have full 20-year patent rights in Hong Kong.

However, critics of OGP suggest that such a 'first-filing' system would generally only be utilized by Hong Kong applicants and may be of limited commercial relevance to Hong Kong entities. If other jurisdictions are of higher strategic/commercial importance, then it may be advantageous simply to pursue a first filing elsewhere, rather than first filing in Hong Kong and later pursuing additional filings in the other country/countries of interest.

8.4.2 OGP Not a Significant Factor in Filing Decision

Some commentators suggest that multinational entities are also unlikely to pursue the OGP. For example, foreign applicants are unlikely to experience significant legal or commercial advantage from establishing priority in Hong Kong. A priority date (the date on which the invention is assessed for novelty/inventive step) may be established by first filing in a country party to the Paris Convention (e.g. in the United States or China), thereby allowing a 12-month 'Convention Period' in which further applications must be filed. Having established priority in their (home/head office) jurisdiction, foreign applicants will usually only pursue substantive protection in jurisdictions of relevance to their business. Filings in other countries are determined on a technology-by-technology, country-by-country basis. Importantly, the presence or (current) absence of an OGP system in Hong Kong does NOT affect the right of any applicant (in Hong Kong or elsewhere) to establish a priority date in a desired jurisdiction.

8.4.3 *Priority Concerns*

Although the current system in Hong Kong does not offer a 'first-to-file' application which it can grant as a standard 20-year patent, a 'first-to-file' patent application that allows an applicant to establish priority in Hong Kong by filing a Hong Kong short-term patent does exist. Although the short-term patent only has a maximum term of eight years, the Hong Kong application can serve as the basis for filing either foreign applications or a PCT international type application. Accordingly, the short-term patent application allows Hong Kong patentees to establish priority in their own jurisdiction quickly and cheaply, as well as providing intermediate protection for patentees between the time of filing the Hong Kong short-term patent up until when a full-term standard patent of the same patent family may ultimately be pursued.

If the subsequent applications are filed in the United Kingdom, Europe (designating United Kingdom) or China, either as direct filing or as PCT National Phase applications claiming priority to the initial Hong Kong short-term patent filing, then it is possible to also pursue a standard patent in Hong Kong as discussed previously. Accordingly, the short-term patent system is a mechanism by which priority may be established, and to which further successive applications claiming this priority may be filed in jurisdictions of interest. In this way, the short-term patent application may be utilized in a manner similar to 'provisional' patent applications.

Typically, provisional patent applications may be used to establish priority in Australia, the United States, and Canada. One or more provisional patent applications may be lodged within a 12- month period from the earliest provisional filing, with an overall filing combining initial developments with any additional developments in provisional patent applications. Thus the short-term patent system allows for further development from the initial filing date to be undertaken, but also provides the capacity for protection of the initial inventive concept from the earliest priority date.

Under the Hong Kong system, a short-term patent can progress to grant, upon submission of a search report from a patent office. Critics of the current form of the short-term patent system highlight that because there is no requirement for the contents of this search report to be addressed by the patentee, this may permit potentially invalid patents to be retained on the register.

Finally, the short-term patent system allows applicants to gain an indication of potential patentability of their invention, by obtaining an international type search from an examining authority, without needing to undergo substantive examination.

8.4.4 *Absence of Motivational Factors*

Pursuit of patent rights can be an expensive, time-consuming and difficult process, as patents are only granted by countries to inventions that are novel, inventive and industrially applicable. Due to the high costs of filing, examination, prosecution and maintenance, patent owners rarely file for protection in every jurisdiction.

Patents are primarily pursued in jurisdictions where intellectual property rights are developed, manufactured and sold, or where there are commercial or strategic reasons for filing a patent application, e.g. there is ongoing infringement or to prevent a competitor from entering the market. Accordingly, the availability of an OGP system (or indeed the absence of an OGP system) will not be decisive as to where to first file a patent application. It is important to consider factors influencing an applicant's selection of jurisdictions in which to file, either as the first filing (to which subsequent filings claim priority), or as a subsequent application (either as a PCT application or as a Convention Application).

Bearing these in mind, even if an invention is developed in Hong Kong, an applicant may not choose to first file in Hong Kong. This is because the invention is likely to have been developed for the US, European or Chinese markets, rather than solely for the local market.

In the last few decades, Hong Kong has also moved away from being an original equipment manufacturer (OEM) centre, so very little manufacturing takes place here. In addition, there is less trans-shipment than previously. Accordingly, patent infringement cases are rarely pursued in Hong Kong.

8.4.5 *First-Filing Requirements*

In some situations, applicants may not have a choice to first file in Hong Kong. Some countries have national 'first-filing' requirements (usually under their national security laws) which compel the filing of patent applications for inventions developed/completed within that jurisdiction to be first filed *in that jurisdiction*.

In practice, arguably, therefore only Hong Kong inventions that have not received any input from such jurisdictions may use the OGP system for 'first filing'. Practitioners emphasize that Hong Kong applicants who may fall into this category can already utilize the Hong Kong short-term patent for establishing priority anyway, and they therefore doubt the OGP system would be used by these applicants.

8.4.6 Relationship with China

Hong Kong's geographical and strategic relationship with China creates additional factors that may lead local businesses to file in China rather than Hong Kong. For most Hong Kong companies, their R&D and manufacturing are in China, and any counterfeits are also likely to be originating from China. Accordingly, even for Hong Kong applicants, China is also likely to be a more important jurisdiction for obtaining patent protection than Hong Kong itself.

Many businesses would need to include China in their patent portfolio anyway to protect their ability to manufacture and to provide a basis for preventing competitors from manufacturing in China. Some commentators point out that, since the current re-registration system already allows an owner/inventor to pursue a Chinese patent as the basis for an inexpensive patent re-registration in Hong Kong, an OGP system would not provide any additional strategic advantage to such businesses.

8.4.7 European Patent Office

Critics of OGP argue that introduction of an OGP system in Hong Kong would not increase the quality of Hong Kong patents. As territorial rights, patents are issued under specific national laws, in accordance with overarching minimum requirements of relevant international treaties, such as the Paris Convention and PCT.

Currently Hong Kong patents are granted based upon grant by three internationally respectable patent offices: EPO, the UK Patent Office and, in more recent times, SIPO. In Hong Kong's case, the relevant judicial approaches in interpretation of the Patents Ordinance, particularly in relation to the determination of interpretation and validity, are the decisions of United Kingdom and Commonwealth common law courts.

As the relevant precedent and legislation draw heavily upon Commonwealth common law tradition, patents issued by the internationally recognized United Kingdom and European patent offices are of a relatively high standard. Highly trained and experienced examiners conduct relatively thorough examination across a wide range of technologies, resulting in patents in these jurisdictions which have a strong presumption of validity. Furthermore, the Hong Kong legal system, common law, in conjunction with the sophistication of the relevant body, affords patentees with confidence should validity and/or enforcement issues arise.

Under an OGP system, a Hong Kong patent would need to undergo substantive examination (i.e. examination for novelty and inventiveness), to progress to grant. However, it would be extremely important to maintain the high presumption of validity as currently offered by the existing Hong Kong re-registration system.

Some practitioners argue that the standard patent system presently in place is, in fact, already similar to outsourced substantive examination, relying as it does, upon the progression of corresponding designated patents through substantive examination by credible patent offices. Upon publication and grant of the outsourced examination, a patent application can be pursued in Hong Kong. Therefore, the introduction of an OGP system that relies on outsourced examination will bring little additional benefit.

The current proposal is for an OGP system with examination outsourced to another patent office. However, such an arrangement itself is not straightforward, as there will need to be negotiations with the potential outsourcing patent offices on the implementation of substantive examination, including such issues as the examination standards, the procedure and interface for document transfer, and the review mechanism.

It seems likely that the examination will initially be outsourced to SIPO. Bearing in mind the issues highlighted above, it is not clear how this will work in practice. Hong Kong's Patent Ordinance (Cap.514) is principally based on the content and style of the United Kingdom Patents Act 1997. Historically, Hong Kong's patent law and experience is similar in approach to established United Kingdom and Commonwealth precedents. The Chinese legal and patent system is very different, and it is not clear how easy it will be to reconcile the significant differences in the legal systems and patent law and practice of Hong Kong and China.

Whilst using SIPO as an office for substantive examination may have its advantages if a Chinese language patent is involved, it does create some difficulty in determining how the validity of a patent in dispute will be assessed in Hong Kong.

As patent offices around the world struggle with ever-increasing pendency of applications, additional processing time/resources may need to be allocated by SIPO, depending upon the extent of use of the OGP System. If the allocation of resources does not match the requests, then this may lead to unacceptable delay being experienced by applicants from HK using the OGP system.

8.4.8 *Lack of Technical Expertise*

The establishment of a patent office which conducts substantive examination is a significant task. Typically, patent offices which conduct substantive examination have numerous examiners who undergo detailed training to develop expertise. Furthermore, jurisdictions having substantive examination generally have a relatively large population and large customer base for their patent system.

For an OGP system to work, numerous technical staff would need to be identified and trained. The Report has already acknowledged the current problem of a lack of local technical expertise. Based on overseas experience, it was recognized that a large number of technical experts would be required for developing an OGP system with search and examination capabilities. However, supply of local talent is unlikely to be sufficient in the short to medium term.

Critics argue that patent review may be even more difficult to handle than the review of trademarks. Accordingly, the introduction of OGP may decrease patent quality unless a substantial investment of time and resources is made in administering outsourced local examination and/or conducting local examination by government. Accordingly, it is not clear when substantive examination will become a reality in Hong Kong.

In recent times, Singapore, after establishing 'substantive examination' almost 10 years ago has now developed its own substantive examining capacity. Singapore has also recently been appointed as an ASEAN International Search Authority (early 2015). Up until this change, in practice, examination in Singapore had been either based upon the examination report of an international PCT application or substantive examination (if local examination is in fact requested by applicant). This previous approach has meant that most of the substantive examination for Singapore patents was largely outsourced.

Other jurisdictions in Asia which purport to conduct 'substantive examination' can be persuaded quite readily by the grant of a patent in a jurisdiction in which substantive examination has been conducted and sufficient experience exists. In fact, several patent offices which hold out to conduct substantive examination, particularly those in the Asia region, will not conduct examinations until they see progression of an application in another jurisdiction and simply base the examination report on that of the European, UK or US Patent Office.

This approach is akin to a form of de facto 'modified examination' in the sense that the grant of a patent in a first substantive examining jurisdiction is used as the basis for grant of another patent in a second (often smaller) jurisdiction. Validity and infringement is determined according to the law of the second jurisdiction, although there is a presumption of validity based upon grant in the first substantively examining jurisdiction. This approach inherently creates tension as the laws of the first substantive examining jurisdiction and second jurisdiction may differ. In this scenario, validity and infringement may be determined according to potentially different (and conflicting) approaches.

8.4.9 Cost to the Public

The Report acknowledged that considerable costs would inevitably be incurred in setting up and running an OGP system. As well as hiring and training technically skilled staff, the Patents Registry does not currently have a comprehensive library or reference materials relating to scientific and engineering aspects required for substantive examination. Considerable resources would also be needed to build the necessary IT infrastructure for OGP and substantive examination.

Currently, fees charged by the Patents Registry are set at a cost-recovery level in accordance with the Patent Ordinance. There are concerns about whether there will be sufficient market demand to make a business case for the OGP system. In any case, substantial costs associated with setting up OGP may result in increased official fees and increased costs to all applicants (whether from Hong Kong or elsewhere), as fees charged by the Patent Registry to offset wages and associated overheads for conducting examination are likely to be passed on to the applicant.

The Report also noted that some would regard any government subsidy of the OGP system as unfair. Critics of the systems argue that one of Hong Kong's many strengths is that, in as far as public finance is concerned, it has adopted 'a user pays system'. However, if the user does not pay for resources and services, then the taxpayers and the general public will have to pay. The substantial cost associated with setting up an OGP system in Hong Kong begs the question of whether Hong Kong people (the overwhelming majority who are not inventors) would wish to subsidize a patent system and a limited number of inventors and commercial entities who may wish to file patents?

8.4.10 Cost to the Applicant

In addition to any increase in official fees that may be passed onto an applicant, the drafting and preparation of a patent application by a competent attorney requires detailed consideration, analysis and often many rounds of discussion between the inventor and Patent Attorney.

Conducting substantive examination of patent applications is a time-consuming, expensive and complex process. The current cost for applying for and securing patents in Hong Kong is relatively modest. In fact, it is very cheap compared to the extremely high costs involved in countries where an 'original grant' system is in place. The re-registration system from an existing application potentially allows patent owners and inventors to extend their rights more widely than if they were compelled to pay for a separate originating patent in Hong Kong.

8.4.11 *Time Concerns*

Another drawback of the proposals acknowledged by the Report is that a long timeframe would be needed to set up an OGP system with substantive examination capability. Building the necessary technical expertise, comprehensive databases and infrastructure, drafting of procedures and manuals for examination, and setting up of a review mechanism, as well as necessary amendments to legislation, will all take a significant amount of time. It cites the example of Singapore, which took more than 17 years after adopting an OGP system before its own substantive examination was undertaken. Those impatient for rapid change or improvement to Hong Kong's patent system may find such a timeframe unpalatable.

8.4.12 *International Trends*

Critics argue that introduction of OGP would actually be in direct contravention of general international trend of mutual recognition of the work between various patent offices. There is an increasing reliance on international cooperation such as filing through the PCT where a national or resident of a PCT contracting state may file one 'international application' with a single patent office or with the International Bureau of World Intellectual Property Organization in Geneva, in one language and with a single set of forms (and fees) instead of filing numerous separate national and/or regional patent applications.

The increasing backlog at most of the major examining offices has led to a number of international agreements between some of the major patent offices that carry out substantive examination. For example the US Patent and Trademark Office, Korean Intellectual Property Office, Japanese Patent Office, Australian Patent Office, EPO and SIPO have begun to enter into bilateral PPH arrangements to expedite the examination process through mutual recognitions of certain examination reports, which facilitate applicants to file patent applications in other jurisdictions. Critics argue that it is a retrograde step to implement substantive examination in Hong Kong when, on an international level, there is an emphasis on reducing local examination.

8.5 THE WAY FORWARD

Hong Kong's development from a virtually unpopulated backwater to one of the most important international financial centres in the world is a well-known success story. The reform of its patent system is seen as one of the key components of the next stage of Hong Kong's political and economic development.

It is clear that there are divergent views as to the merits of an OGP system in Hong Kong. Having discussed at length the advantages and disadvantages of OGP, it is important to note that the proposal is to retain the present standard patent re-registration system. Some have expressed concern that operating a parallel system will increase administrative and substantive workloads. This will obviously entail extra cost that will inevitably be passed on to users of the system. It is too early to accurately assess the financial and practical impact of the proposals.

The retention of the old system would allow applicants the choice of applying directly in Hong Kong for an originating patent, or to protect their rights through 're-registration' as before. Accordingly, the new law should provide patent owners with more options for protecting their rights. Patent owners will need to plan their filing strategy carefully depending on market and operational needs.

It remains to be seen whether an OGP regime will be embraced by the patent community given the retention of the re-registration option and the short-term patent system.

9

Patent Law Reform in Hong Kong
Lessons from Singapore

Ronald Yu

9.1 INTRODUCTION

Hong Kong and Singapore both have been trying hard to become international centers of innovation and intellectual property (IP), and their respective governments have invested heavily in local research and development (R&D) to boost innovation. Both agree that a robust IP protection regime is important complement to their innovation and IP ambitions; and both see value in having original grant patent (OGP) system. But Singapore has had a head start in building and reforming its patent system. The nation amended its patent law and introduced its "positive grant patent" (PGP) system, a Singapore version of OGP system, as well as the Search and Examination (S&E) Unit of Intellectual Property Office of Singapore (IPOS) well before Hong Kong adopted its OGP system.[1]

Is being the second in the race a bad thing for Hong Kong which appears to be playing catch-up, but will have the opportunity to observe and learn from its economic rival? More importantly, are the massive government investments Singapore and Hong Kong are making in building local innovation capacity, including investments in improving the local patent regime, really what is needed for them to become leading centers of innovation? This chapter answers these two questions by examining Singapore's efforts to improve its

---

[1] About nine months after Singapore announced its positive grant system (in May 2012) Hong Kong announced it would introduce an OGP scheme with substantive examination outsourced to other patent office(s) while retaining its re-registration system. As of the writing of this chapter, Hong Kong had not yet passed its Patents (Amendment) Bill. Lionel Ser, "Singapore – Moving To A Positive Grant Patent System," *Conventus Law*, May 31, 2012, www .conventuslaw.com/singapore-moving-to-a-positive-grant-patent-system/. The Hong Kong government also announced it would be retaining the short-term patent system with suitable refinements. See Hong Kong Government Press Release, "Way Forward for Hong Kong Patent System Announced," February 7, 2013, www.info.gov.hk/gia/general/201302/07/P201302070436 .htm.

IP regime, notably its patent system, and exploring whether Singapore's example holds any lesson for Hong Kong's patent system reform. But before tackling these questions, this chapter starts with a brief assessment of the role patents play in the innovation space.

9.2 THE ROLE OF PATENT IN INNOVATION

9.2.1 *The Value of Patents*

Today, there is a great deal of focus on patents. An estimated 10,000-plus transactions involving the sale and purchase of patents have taken place since 2010, including:

- Nortel's sale of its patents for USD 4.5 billion to Rockstar, a consortium comprising of Apple, EMC, Ericsson, Microsoft, RIM and Sony in July 2011
- AOL's sale and license of patents to Microsoft for USD 1.1 billion in April 2012
- Eastman Kodak's sale of its digital imaging patents for USD 525 million to a consortium led by Intellectual Ventures and RPX in December 2012
- MIPS sale of its patents to a consortium managed by Allied Security Trust for USD 350 million in December 2013
- Google's purchase of Motorola Mobility for USD 12.5 billion in 2011, and its subsequent sale of the business to Lenovo without the patents in June 2014 for USD 2.91 billion.[2]

Underlying this newfound fixation (with patents) is competitive pressure that, in turn, is driven by a desire or perceived need to innovate?

9.2.2 *The Innovation Imperative*

Companies today innovate both for competitive reasons and financial rewards. The average time it takes a company's competitors to copy its new products and services has dropped from 369 to 266 days over the last decade,[3] and this is driving companies to innovate and continually launch new products and

---

[2] Jeremy Philips, "The Trillion Dollar Tipping Point: Exploiting the Untapped Value in Patents," 2014, http://aistemos.com/wp-content/uploads/2014/09/The-Trillion-Dollar-Tipping -Point_Aistemos-Report.pdf.

[3] Evan F. Sinar, Richard S. Wellins and Chris Pacione, "Creating the Conditions for Sustainable Innovation," www.ddiworld.com/ddi/media/trend-research/creatingtheconditions forsustainableinnovation_tr_ddi.pdf.

services. Yet, innovative companies also enjoy better sales, profits and stock returns than less innovative ones.[4]

Moreover, innovation has become a national imperative – in his 2010 State of the Union Address, US President Obama mentioned the word "innovation" 11 times,[5] while Hong Kong Chief Executive C. Y. Leung announced that the Hong Kong government will inject HKD 5 billion into the Innovation and Technology Fund and establish an Innovation and Technology Bureau to boost development in innovation in his 2015 Policy Address.[6] Consequently, nations are looking more closely at their patent systems, patent-related developments and the impact of patents and patent policy on current and future innovation.

9.2.3 *Patents and Innovation in History*

Patents serve to promote innovation by permitting inventors to enjoy appropriate returns from their research and development efforts, through temporary monopoly-like rights, and to diffuse the knowledge that results by requiring the inventor to publicize the technical ideas as a patent in sufficient detail to allow a skilled person to reproduce the invention.[7]

But patents also offer positive incentives by giving inventors hope for success[8] and stimulating technological knowledge sharing,[9] though *how* this encouragement and sharing is done makes a huge difference in the ability of the patent system to promote national development.

---

[4]   Ibid.
[5]   Fareed Zakaria, "The Future of Innovation: Can America Keep Pace?," *Time*, June 5, 2011, http://content.time.com/time/nation/article/0,8599,2075226,00.html.
[6]   Hong Kong Government, "$5b earmarked to boost innovation, HK Government Press Release," January 14, 2015, www.news.gov.hk/en/categories/finance/html/2015/01/20150114_104 945.shtml.
[7]   Tom Nicholas, "Are Patents Creative or Destructive?," *Harvard Business Review* Working Paper 14–036 November 12, 2013, www.hbs.edu/faculty/Publication%20Files /14–036_88022f59-a293-4a6f-b643-b205304bce91.pdf.
[8]   Joel Mokyr noted that in the eighteenth century, the type of encouragement given to inventors in Britain differed from that in France and was one reason for the difference in the relative economic progress and success of the two countries. Joel Mokyr, *The Enlightened Economy: An Economic History of Britain, 1700–1850* (New Haven: Yale University Press, 2009), p. 406.
[9]   In their paper "Patents and Innovation: Friends or Foes?," Leveque and Ménière noted that in "American, European and Japanese firms, 88 percent of respondents report that the information disclosed in patents is useful for designing and implementing their own R&D strategy and that patents are a key source of information on competitors." Francois Leveque and Yann Ménière, "Patents and Innovation: Friends or Foes?" December 2006, Cerna, Centre d'économie industrielle Ecole Nationale Supérieure des Mines de Paris, http://ssrn.com/abst ract=958830 or http://dx.doi.org/10.2139/ssrn.958830.

In the nineteenth century, the US patent system systematically attempted to spread new technology throughout society, thereby creating a virtuous circle of innovation begetting more innovation. In contrast Britain, for example, did not officially print patents until 1852, and patents were only open to public inspection upon payment of a fee.

Moreover, as American inventors could submit patent applications by mail, inventions were widely distributed throughout the country both in urban and rural areas unlike, for instance, Britain where most industrial breakthroughs were confined to London or other major cities. The result was broad-based economic growth and less income inequality in the US than Europe[10] and by 1865, the US per capita patenting rate was more than triple that of Britain's and by 1995, it was more than quadruple.[11]

9.2.4 *Patent Examination and Licensing*

The competence of a country's overall business, legal and technological ecosystem[12] is also important to national innovation and a nation's patent regime plays a role in the development of this environment. For instance, the introduction of an examination system in the United States in the eighteenth century reduced uncertainty about the validity of patents and thereby facilitated the growth of a market in the sale and licensing of patent rights.[13]

It was this market in America for patented technologies over the late nineteenth and early twentieth centuries that facilitated the emergence of a group of highly specialized and productive inventors by making it possible for them to transfer responsibility for developing and commercializing their inventions to others.

---

[10]   David Kline, *The Intangible Advantage: Understanding Intellectual Property in the New Economy* (Los Angeles: The Michaelson 20MM Foundation, 2016), p. 74.

[11]   Ibid., p. 80.

[12]   Part of eighteenth-century Britain's technological and competitive advantage over its contemporary European rivals came about as a result of its greater relative population of competent artisans and craftsmen. Morgan Kelly, Cormac Ó Gráda and Joel Mokyr, Precocious Albion: a New Interpretation of the British Industrial Revolution, WP13/11 September 2013, CD Centre For Economic Research Working Paper Series 2013, http://researchrepository.ucd .ie/bitstream/handle/10197/4796/WP13_11.pdf?sequence=1.

[13]   This was in contrast to European regimes. For example, in France, the following caveat was printed on each patent: "The government, in granting a patent without prior examination, does not in any manner guarantee either the priority, merit or success of an invention" while in Britain the lack of any examination of patent validity made the purchase of a patent right highly speculative and costly, thereby limiting investment in new technology. David Kline, *The Intangible Advantage*, pp. 77–78.

The expanded opportunities to trade in the rights to patented technologies enabled independent inventors of this age to flourish, in turn stimulating the growth of inventive activity more generally.[14] Furthermore, this growth was also accompanied by the emergence and increased importance of intermediaries – lawyers, patent licensing agents, venture financiers[15] – who were specialized at working in that market.[16]

9.3 SINGAPORE AS AN IP HUB

Singapore views a robust IP rights regime as essential to encourage innovation, creativity and the growth of industry and commerce and is committed to deepening manpower expertise across the local IP value chain. Thus Singapore's efforts to upgrade its patent system ought to be examined holistically, i.e. as part of a greater overall effort to make Singapore a global IP hub for examination, service and IP finance, which in turn complements greater national policy objectives (i.e. to encourage innovation, economic and manpower development).

To achieve these goals, the country changed its laws: IPOS has established in-country patent S&E capabilities in key technological areas,[17] and to encourage local innovation, Singapore provides funding for R&D and for patent filing, and even offers tax benefits to companies of Singaporean origin actively filing patents.[18]

9.3.1 *Background of the Changes to the Singapore Patents Act*

Singapore, which once had a reregistration scheme,[19] started its own patent system in 1995, initially with a self-assessment system. In May 2012, Singapore's

---

[14]   Naomi R. Lamoreaux and Kenneth L. Sokoloff, "Inventive Activity and the Market for Technology in the United States, 1840–1920," www.nber.org/papers/w7107.pdf.
[15]   David Kline, *The Intangible Advantage*, p. 85.
[16]   Naomi R. Lamoreaux and Kenneth L. Sokoloff, "Intermediaries in the US Market for Technology, 1870-1920," Working Paper 90, www.nber.org/papers/w9017.
[17]   Singapore Ministry of Law. Intellectual Property Policy, August 28, 2014, www.mlaw.gov.sg/our -work/intellectual-property-policy.html.
[18]   Grey B., "The Race of Singapore to Become the Next IP Hub of Asia," *IP Analytics*, August 27, 2015, www.greyb.com/case-study-singapore-the-upcoming-ip-intellectual-property-hub/.
[19]   Whereby the only way to obtain patent protection in Singapore was through the Registration of UK Patents Act 1937, which required an applicant to first obtain a patent in the UK before re-registering the patent in Singapore with the Registry of Trademarks and Patents (Registry). See Lee Kuan Yew School of Public Policy, "The Development of Singapore's Intellectual Property Rights Regime," 2014, http://lkyspp.nus.edu.sg/wp-content/uploads/2014/11/LKWM S_Series01_SG_IP.pdf.

Ministry of Law and IPOS proposed several amendments to Singapore's Patents Act as well as other IP-related initiatives to both enhance Singapore's IP infrastructure and position Singapore to become a key node for patent agency work.[20]

One of the key amendments to the Patents Act was a change from a "self-assessment" scheme which, in the past, had allowed patent applications to be granted regardless of the outcome of their examination reports meaning that patent applications might be granted without fully complying with patent-ability criteria,[21] to a "positive grant" patent system, whereby only patent applications that fully met patentability criteria would be granted.[22] Under the new "positive grant system," search and examination would be done in Singapore via partnering patent offices (Austria, Denmark, Hungary) according to Singapore laws and requirements.[23]

This change aimed to raise the overall quality of patents granted in Singapore, align Singaporean practices with that of other established regimes (e.g. the European Patent Office, the patent offices of the US, UK and Japan) and strengthen business and investor confidence in Singapore's IP regime.

9.3.2 *In-House Examination*

Prior to the introduction of the positive grant system, Singapore had out-sourced patent S&E work to patent offices in other countries. This changed in 2013 when IPOS established its patent S&E unit, initially with a group of 18 examiners[24] (the IPOS S&E unit presently has 103 examiners[25]), with a mandate to create world-class search and examination capabilities in specific technology classes aligned with Singapore's main R&D thrusts.

---

[20] The legislative amendments were passed by Singapore's Parliament on July 10, 2012. The provisions of the amended Singapore Patents Act came into force on February 14, 2014, together with amended Singapore Patent Rules.

[21] Intellectual Property Office of Singapore. Proposed Amendments to the Patents Act and Other Intellectual Property Related Acts.

[22] IPOS, "Amendments to the Patents Act and Other Intellectual Property Related Acts Passed in Parliament," www.ipos.gov.sg/ipcf/News/AmendmentstothePatentsActandOtherIntellectu .aspx.

[23] Sharmaine Wu, "Singapore Patent Search & Examination Presentation for KL Workshop," November 29, 2011, www.wipo.int/edocs/mdocs/aspac/en/wipo_ip_kul_11/wipo_ip_kul_11 _ref_t11.pdf.

[24] Leck Kwong Joo, "Challenges in Examination," November 26, 2013, www.wipo.int/edocs/m docs/aspac/en/wipo_reg_pct_tyo_13/wipo_reg_pct_tyo_13_t2i.pdf.

[25] "How Many of These IPOS Patent Examiners Do You Know?," IPOS Facebook page, August 6, 2015 www.facebook.com/IPOSG/posts/790163707749707.

Having an in-country S&E unit is important as Singapore sees this as enlarging the suite of patent-related capabilities available locally thus strengthening the nation's credentials as an IP hub.[26]

9.3.3 Development of Human Capital

Singapore also introduced other initiatives geared toward developing local human capital in the IP space. Another amendment[27] to the Patents Act liberalized the local patent agent regime to allow foreign-qualified patent agents to register in Singapore to undertake offshore patent agency work (e.g. applying for patents for other jurisdictions), thereby providing users with easier access to a wider range of patent agency services in Singapore.

To complement the changes in its patent law Singapore also launched a professional conversion program to place mid-career workers in relevant companies that will train them to become registered patent agents.[28]

Singapore also introduced its Intellectual Property Competency Framework, which defines the competencies required for key IP job roles in the industry, accredits training providers and their programs, and certifies the competencies attained as industry recognized qualifications. Under agreements with IPOS, The Law Society of Singapore, the Association of Singapore Patent Agents, and the Institution of Engineers Singapore will work with IPOS to professionally certify new and existing IP lawyers, patent agents, researchers, scientists and engineers specializing in IP.[29]

---

[26] Singapore Ministry of Law, "Proposed Amendments to the Patents Act and Other Intellectual Property Related Acts," May 14, 2012, www.mlaw.gov.sg/news/press-releases/proposed -amendments-to-the-patents-act-and-other-intellectual-property-related-acts.html.

[27] Other changes involved the introduction of a new Integrated Registries IT system at IPOS, making it easier and more convenient for customers to execute transactions and access information related to the different types of IP, abolition of the "slow track" in favor of a single track and removal of any provision for requesting a block extension of time. Intellectual Property Office of Singapore, "Amendments to the Patents Act and Other Intellectual Property Related Acts Passed in Parliament," www.ipos.gov.sg/ipcf/News/Amen dmentstothePatentsActandOtherIntellectu.aspx Cantab-ip, "Guide to the Singapore Patents Act Amendments," https://guides.cantab-ip.com/singapore-patent-amendments.

[28] Joanna Seow, "New Programme to Train More Registered Patent Agents for Singapore's Growing IP Scene," *Straits Times*, April 7, 2015, www.straitstimes.com/singapore/new -programme-to-train-moreregistered-patent-agents-for-singapores-growing-ip-scene.

[29] Kristian Robinson, "IPOS' IP Competency Framework to Be Adopted by LAWSOC, ASPA & IES, Spruson & Ferguson Intellectual Property," April 8, 2014, www.spruson.com/ipos-ip -competency-framework/.

To date Singapore has achieved some degree of success in the development of a thriving local IP landscape.[30] According to a recent manpower survey of 10,000 companies, are were over 100,000 full-time equivalent (FTE) employees involved in IP and IP-related activities including over 10,000 FTE employees directly involved in IP prosecution, IP strategy and IP portfolio management work such as patent attorneys, licensing managers, ip lawyers, trade mark agents, research and development managers, business consultants and chief technology officers and some 90,000 FTE employees whose work involved some form of engagement with IP-related activities, including legal counsels, business associates, technical associates and information analysts.[31]

IPOS even has a website featuring an "interactive IP Career Planner" that covers legal advisory, prosecution, strategic consulting, IP valuation and financial positions, to help people find their ideal IP-related job.[32]

9.3.4 The Impact in the Region

So far, the country has already realized some short-term success with its recent patent-related endeavors. In September 2015, Singapore was appointed ASEAN's first International Patent Search and Examination Authority under the Patent Cooperation Treaty (PCT), joining China, India, Japan and Korea as an international patent authority recognized by the World Intellectual Property Organization (WIPO). This allowed local and global businesses and inventors to fast-track their applications for patent protection in multiple markets via Singapore.[33] Later, in January 2016, IPOS announced a cooperative program with Cambodia to issue first-office-action S&E reports for patent applications filed in Cambodia.[34] Under the cooperation agreement between IPOS and the Cambodian Ministry of Industry and Handicraft (MIH), Singapore patent owners can reregister their Singapore patents at

---

[30] IPOS, "Intellectual Property Hub Master Plan: Developing Singapore as a Global IP Hub in Asia," March 1, 2013, www.ipos.gov.sg/Portals/0/Press%20Release/IP%20HUB%20MASTER %20PLAN%20REPORT%202%20APR%202013.pdf.

[31] IPOS, "Intellectual Property Sector Boosts High Valued Jobs in Singapore," 2014 www.ipos.gov .sg/Portals/0/Press%20Release/Factsheet%20%202014%20IP%20Manpower%20Survey.pdf.

[32] See www.ipos.gov.sg/ipcf/TheIPCareerPlanner.aspx.

[33] "Singapore Appointed ASEAN's First International Patent Authority, Singapore has joined China, India, Japan and Korea as an international patent authority recognized by the World Intellectual Property Organization," *Asian Scientist Newsroom*, September 14, 2015, www .asianscientist.com/2015/09/topnews/ipos-asean-wipo-pct/.

[34] IPOS, "Singapore Furthers IP Cooperation with Cambodia to Expedite Quality Patent Grants," Press Release, January 19, 2016, www.ipos.gov.sg/MediaEvents/Readnews/TabID/873/articleid /330/Default.aspx.

the MIH and submit an IPOS-issued Search and Examination report to the MIH for the grant of a Cambodia related patent application.[35]

While it is too early to determine how these changes and announcements have impacted Singapore's IP regime – which has been consistently ranked among the top five in the world by the World Economic Forum, and top 10 by the Institute for Management Development according to the Global Innovation Index 2013 compiled by the INSEAD Business School in collaboration with WIPO[36] – it is nevertheless probably safe to assume they have had a positive effect on Singapore's IP reputation.

9.3.5 *Patenting Trend*

However, this has thus far not translated into any substantial, tangible uptick in the number of patent filings and most Singapore patents are still being filed by outside, not local, companies. Though overall patent filings in Singapore have risen by more than 30 per cent over the past decade from 7,908 in 2003 to 10,312 in 2014[37] (rising from 9,722 in 2013 to 10,312 in 2014[38]), the total number of applications and grants between 2009 and 2014 fluctuated between a low of 14,623 patent applications and grants in 2010 to 16,425 in 2011. In fact, there were fewer patent applications and grants in 2013 than 2009, 2011 or 2012.[39]

---

[35] IPOS, "Patent Cooperation with Cambodia," May 24, 2016, www.ipos.gov.sg/AboutIP/Types ofIPWhatisIntellectualProperty/Whatisapatent/Applyingforapatent/PatentCooperationwithC ambodia.aspx.

[36] Singapore was also ranked in ninth place in the Taylor Wessing's fifth Global Intellectual Property Index. Conventus Law. "Singapore Highly Ranked In Latest Global Intellectual Property Index, Legal News & Analysis – Asia Pacific – Singapore – Intellectual Property," June 16, 2016, www.conventuslaw.com/report/singapore-highly-ranked-in-latest-global/.

[37] Joanna Seow, "New Programme to Train More Registered Patent Agents."

[38] Intellectual Property Office of Singapore. Singapore Patent Statistics 2014, www.ipos.gov.sg /Portals/0/resources/Patent%20Statistics%202014_final.pdf.

[39] According to statistics from IPOS,
Total number of patent applications and grants

Year	Number
2009	15405
2010	14623
2011	16245
2012	15991
2013	15132

26,317 patents were granted during the period of 2009–2014, the average grant rate of the patents published during 2009–2014 was 3.6 years and the average time between a request for

A breakdown of patent applicants reveals that most Singapore patent filings are done by outsiders (i.e. non-locals) with the bulk of all patent applications – nearly 60 percent – being filed by American or Japanese entities.[40] Only about 5 percent of the total number of all local patent applications in Singapore are currently filed by Singapore-based organizations and most of these come from two entities; the Agency for Science, Technology and Research, and Nanyang Technological University, which respectively filed 335 and 127 patents in 2014,[41] accounting for 4.5 percent of all local patent filings that year.[42] By comparison there were more patent filings in Denmark, a country roughly equivalent to Singapore in population size, than in Singapore in 2014, and local entities filed 26 percent of all Danish patent applications that year.[43]

9.4 PATENT AND INNOVATION IN HONG KONG

Given the concerns that Hong Kong's role as the main thoroughfare between the Mainland and the rest of the world – a key element of its past success – is fast becoming obsolete[44] and that Hong Kong's may be unable to retain its position as a "super connector" for China sparking calls for Hong Kong to find other roles for itself,[45] the territory's need to transform itself was all too clear.

Consequently, Hong Kong began looking to innovate and diversify its economy. Over the past half century, Hong Kong experienced two major economic transformations – first in the 1950s and 1960s when Hong Kong shifted from an economy based around international trade to one focused on

---

search and examination to the issue of a first office action was 57 days for first filings in 2014. Grey B. "The Race Of Singapore."

[40] The top patent filers between 2008 and 2014 included Qualcomm, Intel, Exxonmobil, 3M, Microsoft, Interdigital and Micron Technology. Grey B. "The Race Of Singapore."

[41] Intellectual Property Office of Singapore. Singapore Patent Statistics 2014.

[42] Jacqueline Yuen, "Hong Kong: Asia's Hub for IP trading," *HKTDC Research*, March 12, 2013, http://economists-pick-research.hktdc.com/business-news/article/Research-Articles/Hong-Kong-Asia-s-hub-for-IP-trading/rp/en/1/1X000000/1X09S9WD.htm.

[43] WIPO, "Statistical Country Profiles: Denmark," www.wipo.int/ipstats/en/statistics/country_profile/profile.jsp?code=DK.

[44] Alexa Lam, "Looking Ahead as China Opens Its Capital Account," HKSI Institute SFC Executive Director Series, February 10, 2015, www.sfc.hk/web/EN/files/ER/PDF/Speeches/Alexa_20150210.pdf.

[45] Leigh Powell, "It's Time for Hong Kong to Reinvent Itself Says Alexa Lam," *Asia Investor*, May 28, 2015, www.asianinvestor.net/News/397888,it8217s-time-for-hk-to-reinvent-itself-says-alexa-lam.aspx?eid=13&edate=20150528&utm_source=20150528&utm_medium=newsletter&utm_campaign=daily_newsletter.

manufacturing and processing industries; and then in the late 1970s and 1980s when its service industry expanded to become the main part of its economy, thereby further enhancing Hong Kong's position as a financial, trading and transportation center in the Asia Pacific region.[46] Hong Kong is hoping that the development of innovation- and technology-based high value-added industries will serve as the catalyst for its next economic transformation.

9.4.1 *The Hong Kong SAR as an IP Trading Hub*

In contrast to Singapore, which seeks to position itself as a "Global IP Hub in Asia,"[47] Hong Kong has declared its ambition to be an IP *trading* hub.[48] Despite the different name, Hong Kong's stated ambitions – to become a center of innovation, build local IP awareness and expertise, enhance the role of IP in finance, etc. – mirror those of Singapore though, unlike Singapore, Hong Kong has introduced an online IP Trading platform (AsiaIPEX).[49]

Hong Kong believes it is well positioned to be an IP trading hub, given its legal system and financial resources, robust IP protection, and presence of a pool of IP specialists able to provide comprehensive services to IP related industries. The SAR also believes that IP trading can enhance local R&D capacity and facilitate technology transfer, complement its efforts to become an innovation and technology hub, provide companies with opportunities (presented by IP trading) to increase their competitiveness by branding and upgrading, create demand for IP-related services and provide potential career opportunities for the younger generation.[50]

According to research done by the Hong Kong Trade Development Council (HKTDC), more businessmen put Hong Kong ahead of Singapore or Shanghai as the IP management hub serving Asia, and the views were reinforced if Greater China was the underlying market.[51] There were even more patent applications in Hong Kong from 2012 to 2014 than in Singapore

---

[46] "Hong Kong's Third Economic Transformation and the Development of Innovation and Technology," Working Paper No. 1, www.pland.gov.hk/pland_en/p_study/comp_s/hk2030/eng /wpapers/pdf/workingPaper_01.pdf.
[47] IPOS, "Intellectual Property (IP) Hub Master Plan."
[48] "HK Aims to Be IP Trading Hub," *Asia Weekly, China Daily Asia,* March 28, 2014, http:// epaper.chinadailyasia.com/asia-weekly/article-2192.html.
[49] AsiaIPEX, was launched by the HKTDC in December 2013. See Hong Kong, Report of the Working Group on Intellectual Property Trading, 2015, www.ip.gov.hk/materials/news/20150 320162103.19.pdf.
[50] Ibid.   [51] Jacqueline Yuen, "Hong Kong."

over the same period, though it should also be noted that the number of patent applications in Hong Kong for 2014 was down from 2012 and 2013, while the number of applications from 2012 to 2014 in Singapore shows a steady upward trend.[52]

That same HKTDC research report, however, also revealed that less than 1.5 percent of patent applications in Hong Kong were done by local entities and acknowledged Singapore's superiority in IP-related services and that Singapore is perceived to have a better legal environment and to have the presence of industry clusters than Hong Kong.[53]

9.4.2 *Hong Kong's IP Ambitions*

Nevertheless, toward furthering its goal of establishing Hong Kong as an IP trading hub, the SAR launched a free online platform and database to facilitate international IP trading (Asia IP Exchange or AsiaIPEX) in December 2013[54] and established a Working Group on Intellectual Property Trading.[55] The latter set forth several recommendations to facilitate the development of Hong Kong into a regional innovation and technology hub as well as a premier IP trading hub including the introduction of IP Manager and other training programs to promote IP awareness and build local IP-related skills.[56]

The Hong Kong government also endorsed the recommendations made by the Advisory Committee on Review of the Patent System in Hong Kong (Advisory Committee)[57] and, in February 2013, announced its decision to introduce of an OGP system with substantive examination conducted by other patent office(s), while retaining the current reregistration system for grant of standard patents despite concerns expressed by local professional

---

[52] There were 12,542, 13,916 and 12,988 patent applications filed in Hong Kong in 2014, 2013 and 2012 respectively. There were 10,312, 9,722 and 9,685 patent applications filed in Singapore in 2014, 2013 and 2012 respectively. Hong Kong Legislative Council. Bills Committee on the Patents (Amendment) Bill 2015 Patent application statistics in selected economies LC Paper, No. CB(1) 334/15-16(01), December 2015, www.legco.gov.hk/yr15-16/english/bc/bc02/papers/bc0220151222cb1 -334-1-e.pdf.

[53] Jacqueline Yuen, "Hong Kong."

[54] Sec. 6.3, Hong Kong, Report of the Working Group on Intellectual Property Trading.

[55] Hong Kong Intellectual Property Department, Intellectual Property Trading, http:/www.ipd .gov.hk/eng/IP_trading.htm.

[56] The Working Group also advocated a government-supported standard for IP valuation. Hong Kong, Report of the Working Group on Intellectual Property Trading.

[57] Notably the recommendation to introduce an OGP system. Hong Kong Intellectual Property Department, Report of the Advisory Committee on Review of the Patent System in Hong Kong, p. ii, www.ipd.gov.hk/eng/intellectual_property/patents/review_report.pdf.

bodies including the Law Society, the Asian Patent Attorney Association (Hong Kong Group), and the Hong Kong Institute of Trademark Practitioners regarding the demand for and the cost effectiveness of an OGP scheme,[58] though it could be noted that these negative arguments overlooked the fact that Denmark, a country with a population of 5.7 million,[59] has had substantive patent examination in place for some time[60] and has seen its number of patent filings grow from 5,496 in 2000 to 12,547 patents in 2014.[61] Moreover, some have noted weaknesses in Hong Kong's IP ecosystem, pointing out, for example, Hong Kong's lack of local patent experts capable of drafting patent specifications for enterprises in Hong Kong for use and protection in Hong Kong – blaming this on the territory's reregistration system.[62]

Later that same year, the Hong Kong Intellectual Property Department (HKIPD) announced a cooperative arrangement with China's State Intellectual Property Office (SIPO) whereby SIPO will provide technical assistance and support for substantive examination of patent applications as well as staff training.[63] Hong Kong also announced its intention to introduce a regulatory scheme for local patent agency services, based on the recommendation of the Report of the Advisory Committee on the Review of the Patent System, to complement the OGP scheme.[64] In addition, Hong Kong continues to invest in making the SAR a leading IP trading hub. For example, the HKIPD announced that it would spend HKD 2.55 million (approximately USD 327,000) in 2015–2106, on promotion and education efforts targeted at the business sector and HKD 1.85 million (approximately USD 237,000) on young people.[65]

[58]   Kenny Wong. An Original Grant Patent System and Other Changes Recommended, Mayer Brown JSM Legal Update, February 18, 2013.
[59]   Wikipedia. Denmark, https://en.wikipedia.org/wiki/Denmark.
[60]   Patent Registration in Denmark (Non-PCT), www.ip-coster.com/IPGuides/patent-denmark.
[61]   WIPO, "Statistical Country Profiles: Denmark," www.wipo.int/ipstats/en/statistics/country _profile/profile.jsp?code=DK.
[62]   Kenny Wong, "Is Patent Reform in Hong Kong on the Horizon?," *Intellectual Property*, June 2012, p. 62.
[63]   Hong Kong Government, "Co-operation Arrangement on Patent Signed between Mainland and Hong Kong," Press Release, December 6, 2013, www.info.gov.hk/gia/general/201312/06 /P201312060394.htm.
[64]   Hong Kong, Report of the Working Group on Intellectual Property Trading, 2015. See also Hong Kong Intellectual Property Department, Report of the Advisory Committee on Review of the Patent System in Hong Kong, p. iv.
[65]   Hong Kong Intellectual Property Department, "Examination of Estimates of Expenditure," 2015–2016, Controlling Officer's Reply (Reply Serial. No. CEDB(CIT)250)), www.ipd.gov.hk /eng/about_us/CITB_E.pdf.

Hong Kong SAR government hopes that the introduction of the OGP will foster development of a richer IP ecosystem[66] by helping to build up local expertise in drafting and patent prosecution as well as support a system of patent professionals,[67] IP-related jobs and offer added career opportunities for graduates with science and engineering backgrounds as well as professionals with technical and legal backgrounds.[68]

The idea is that an environment filled with professionals and service providers able to manage the legal, technical, licensing, strategy, finance, valuation, management, dispute and prosecution-related aspects of patents and other IP assets, would complement developers, inventors and innovators by helping them protect, monetize, commercialize and financially benefit from their IP. Whether this ultimately comes to fruition remains to be seen.

9.4.3 *Singapore and Hong Kong Compared*

So while Singapore and Hong Kong both see IP, in particular patents and improvements to their respective patent regimes, as beneficial to their overall efforts to boost local innovation, they each have taken different approaches to implement patent examination schemes.

Singapore has actually invested in and established an in-country patent S&E infrastructure while Hong Kong, in spite of the potential benefits of introducing an OGP and a locally based examination unit[69] and the

---

[66] As noted by S. K. Lee, Deputy Director Hong Kong Intellectual Property Dept. during the HKU-HKIPD IP Forum 2015 "Patent and Innovation: Worldwide Patent Law Reform and Hong Kong's Response" (January 16, 2015).

[67] Submission by Dr. Kam Wah Law for the Consultation on Review of the Patent System in Hong Kong (October 4, 2011 to December 31, 2011), www.ipd.gov.hk/eng/intellectual_prop erty/patents/submissions/062.pdf.

[68] Submission by HKUST Biochemistry Alumni Association for the Consultation on Review of the Patent System in Hong Kong (October 4, 2011 to December 31, 2011), www.ipd.gov.hk/eng /intellectual_property/patents/submissions/056.pdf.

[69] For example: promoting R&D and local innovation – encouraging local innovation and attracting enterprises to set up R&D operations in Hong Kong, local autonomy, facilitating more flexible and expedient examination procedures, providing a better basis for the mutual recognition of patents granted by Mainland China and Hong Kong, promoting direct communications between local enterprises and Hong Kong patent practitioners without language barrier resulting in higher patent quality, development of patent examination capacity, creating career opportunities for science and engineering graduates, and that advanced (e.g. the US, Germany, Japan, UK) and innovative economies (such as Israel, Taiwan and Korea) have OGP systems in place. Report of the Advisory Committee on Review of the Patent System in Hong Kong, www.ipd.gov.hk/eng/intellectual_property/patents/review_report.pdf.

acknowledged weaknesses of the current reregistration scheme,[70] chose to effectively outsource patent examination to SIPO, at least for now.[71]

This means, at least in the short term, that Hong Kong will not be able to build up indigenous examination expertise in the same way Singapore can. Thus it cannot reap the benefits from such local capability, including offering a new patent examiner career path for local science and engineering graduates, providing patent S&E services to other countries, enabling direct communications with local inventors, and having local control of patent prosecution, the way Singapore already has – and may be able further exploit in the future.

Yet, as noted before, while Singapore's new patent S&E capability has won it some plaudits, it is too early to assess its full impact on the country's overall IP ecosystem in terms of new job creation, additional numbers of patents, more patent filings by local entities, or other indicators of increased innovative activity. Similarly, as Hong Kong's OGP system has yet to be implemented (as of the writing of this piece) it is far too early to tell what impact, if any, it will have on the local IP ecosystem or local innovation.

We should also not forget that given Singapore's greater emphasis on and investment in the biomedical area,[72] which are heavily reliant on patent work,

[70] For example, the lack of local control over the prosecution, inconvenience to local entities and the perception that a re-registration system is second-rate, given international trends toward adopting or moving toward an OGP system. Report of the Advisory Committee on Review of the Patent System in Hong Kong, available at www.ipd.gov.hk/eng/intellectual _property/patents/review_report.pdf.

[71] Though it should be noted the Advisory Committee did recommend the government consider introducing in-house substantive examination capability in incremental stages, at least focusing on specific technological areas where Hong Kong has acquired considerable expertise. This point was also echoed by the Working Group on Intellectual Property Trading, Report of the Advisory Committee on Review of the Patent System in Hong Kong, www.ipd.gov.hk/eng /intellectual_property/patents/review_report.pdf. Hong Kong, Report of the Working Group on Intellectual Property Trading, 2015.

[72] The biomedical industry is the fourth pillar of Singapore's economy. Since 2000, the sector's manufacturing output has increased by nearly five-fold from USD 6 billion in 2000 to 29.4 billion in 2012 while employment in the manufacturing industry, from 6,000 to 15,700 in the same period. The biomedical sector is now the largest value added contributor to the manufacturing sector in Singapore. In contrast, the Hong Kong government's Innovation and Technology Fund (ITF), which was set up in 1999 to encourage the development of innovative ideas and technology businesses, approved 5,088 projects with a total ITF funding of HKD 11 billion (approximately USD 1.375 billion) were approved as of March 2016, yet only 10 percent of these were in biotechnology. While the 22-hectare Hong Kong Science Park is an important part of Hong Kong's infrastructure in support of the government's mission to turn Hong Kong into a regional hub for innovation and technology, biotechnology is only one of the Science Park's five target sectors (the others being electronics, green technology, information and communications technology, and material and precision engineering). Agency for Science, Technology and Research (A*STAR), "Singapore's Biopolis: A Success Story," Press release, October 16, 2013, www.a-star.edu.sg/Media/News/Press-Releases/ID/1893/Singapores

patents are of greater relevance to Singapore than Hong Kong, which has, more recently, emphasized development in information and communications technology – in particular the Internet of Things or IOT[73] and financial technology[74] (Fintech), both of which are heavily software based and, as a consequence, place considerable, if not more emphasis on copyright than patent protection.

9.4.4 *Something to Ponder*

Apart from IP and IP-related services, both Singapore and Hong Kong have made substantial investments to turn their respective locations into innovation hubs: Hong Kong set up its Innovation and Technology Fund, developed the Hong Kong Science Park, established the Applied Science and Technology Research Institute and five R&D centers to conduct industry-oriented applied R&D centers in five focus areas,[75] and launched other initiatives such as the Digital 21 Strategy[76] and Science Park. Singapore has made substantial investments in technology as part of its national development injecting millions of dollars to fund new start-ups[77] and investing heavily in national research infrastructure in the form of the Singapore Science Park, Fusionopolis,[78] Biopolis,[79] the Diagnostics Development Hub[80], and the

-Biopolis-A-Success-Story.aspx. "Bioentrepreneurship – What can Singapore learn from other Asia Pacific countries?" Asia Pacific Biotech News, available at www.asiabiotech.com/17/1707/17070033x.html. Hong Kong: The Facts, Innovation and Technology, www.gov.hk/en/about/abouthk/factsheets/docs/technology.pdf.

[73] Allen Ma, "Why the Internet of Things Represents a Golden Opportunity for Hong Kong," *South China Morning Post*, June 16, 2015, www.scmp.com.

[74] Hong Kong Government, "Enhancing Hong Kong's Competitiveness," Press release, January 20, 2016, www.info.gov.hk/gia/general/201601/20/P201601200324.htm.

[75] Information and communications technologies, logistics and supply chain management, nanotechnology and advanced materials, textiles and clothing, automotive parts and accessory systems. Report of the Advisory Committee on Review of the Patent System in Hong Kong, www.ipd.gov.hk/eng/intellectual_property/patents/review_report.pdf.

[76] Hong Kong launched the first Digital 21 Strategy in 1998 setting out the blueprint for Information and communications technology (ICT) development in Hong Kong. See www.digital21.gov.hk/eng/.

[77] Newell Purnell, "Singapore Aims to Become Southeast Asia's Silicon Valley Venture-Capital Investments in Tech Outstrip Many Asian Neighbors," *Asian Wall Street Journal*, February 26, 2014, www.wsj.com/articles/SB10001424052702304071004579406393779804868.

[78] Wikipedia. Fusionopolis, http://en.wikipedia.org/wiki/Fusionopolis.

[79] Wikipedia. Biopolis, http://en.wikipedia.org/wiki/Biopolis.

[80] "Singapore Aims to Become 'Investment Hub for Global Diagnostics Industry'", December 2, 2014, www.out-law.com/en/articles/2014/december/singapore-aims-to-become-investment-hub-for-global-diagnostics-industry-/.

Tuas Biomedical Park.[81] From 2011 to 2015, the Singapore Government committed to spending SGD 16 billion (approximately USD 11.9 billion) in research, innovation and enterprise to establish Singapore as a world-class R&D hub through the development of human, intellectual and industrial capital.[82]

In the meanwhile, Hong Kong, so far, has seen some successes in its efforts in innovation such as GoGoVan, which has harnessed the power of mobile technology to establish a successful logistics business; Dragon Law, which offers Internet-based basic legal support for small and mid-sized business; and Air Button, whose wireless RFID[83] button allows users access to their devices with one touch.[84] Hong Kong wants more such successes and is, among other things, hoping its revamped patent system – along with other government backed initiatives – will help kick its transformation into a high tech hub into high gear.

But is such massive investment in infrastructure and IP capability really necessary to turn a city into an innovation hub? Consider that Shenzhen, China, a city with a population close to that of Hong Kong and Singapore combined,[85] has managed to become one of the top innovation hubs in the world without the same level of concerted government support[86] and investment (to turn it into a global innovation hub) as Hong Kong or Singapore. Shenzhen-based companies filed 13,308 PCT patent applications

[81]   Singapore MedTech Infrastructure for the Biomedical Sciences Industries, available at www.medtech.sg/infrastructure-for-the-biomedical-sciences-industry/.
[82]   Under the sixth science and technology plan for Singapore – the RIE2020 Plan – the government has committed SGD 19 billion (around USD 14.1 billion) over 2016 to 2020 to research, innovation and enterprise to take Singapore to the next stage of development. This is 18 percent more than the previous plan, with spending close to one per cent of the nation's gross domestic product (GDP). Singapore National Research Fund, R&D Development, www.nrf.gov.sg/research/overview#sthash.WKB4YyLN.dpuf.
[83]   Radio frequency identification.
[84]   Herman Lam, "Supporting Start-Ups to Transform Hong Kong into a Hub for Innovation and Technology," Hong Kong Business, February 13, 2015, http://hongkongbusiness.hk/economy/commentary/supporting-start-ups-transform-hong-kong-hub-innovation-and-technology#sthash.qqEKodgU.dpuf.
[85]   Shenzhen has a population of 11,378,700 or 88.5 percent of the combined populations of Hong Kong, which has a population of roughly 7.324 million people, and Singapore, which has a population of roughly 5.535 million people. Invest Shenzhen, "Invest in Shenzhen," 2016, p. 2; Department of Statistics Singapore, www.singstat.gov.sg/statistics/latest-data#16; The Government of Hong Kong, Census and Statistics Department, www.censtatd.gov.hk/hkstat/sub/so20.jsp.
[86]   Shenzhen's municipal government does provide tax subsidies and other incentives encourage high tech development in Shenzhen. Understand China, "Investment Incentives: Shenzhen Investment Promotion Authorities and Incentives," July 12, 2016, http://understand-china.com/manufacturing/shenzhen-investment-incentives/.

in 2015 – roughly 47 percent of all PCT filings for all of China[87] – dwarfing the equivalent figures for Singapore (which filed 940 PCT applications in 2014)[88] and Hong Kong (none).[89]

9.5 CONCLUDING REMARKS

In short, both Singapore and Hong Kong have made changes to their respective patent regimes as part of overall and substantial investments in innovation, R&D and personnel development. Both have introduced similar initiatives in terms of manpower development and the promotion of innovation and professional competency. Whether Singapore and Hong Kong succeed, to what extent they succeed and what benefits they ultimately derive from their patent reform efforts, in terms of development of their local IP ecosystems, economies, technological infrastructure, local R&D, etc., remains to be seen.

Hong Kong, which will not be investing in local S&E capability (at least for now), will be unable to enjoy the same benefits as Singapore now can with its in-country capacity. Yet given Singapore's greater emphasis and investment in patent examination – and biotechnology, it arguably needs to succeed with its patent reforms more than Hong Kong does. But government investment can only go so far and, as Shenzhen demonstrates, a city can still become an innovation center even without huge local government infrastructure spending and investment in local patent examination capability.

---

[87] Invest Shenzhen, "Invest in Shenzhen," p. 4.

[88] WIPO Statistical Country Profiles, "Singapore," www.wipo.int/ipstats/en/statistics/country_profile/profile.jsp?code=SG.

[89] WIPO, "IP Facts and Figures 2015," p. 53, www.wipo.int/edocs/pubdocs/en/wipo_pub_943_2015.pdf.

Index

In general, "China" refers to Mainland China. Hong Kong, now a Special Administrative Region of China (HKSAR), is discussed as a separate entity.
Acronyms are used as main headings when the acronym prevails in usage over the full term in the text.

accessibility
  and costs, 47–49, 54, 73, 75
  and duration of utility model protection, 54–55
  empirical research on, 39
  in Germany, 66–67
  imbalances in, 39–43, 77
  of invention patents, 51
  and inventiveness, 35
  and inventive step requirements, 64–68,
  and novelty standards, 60–62
  and patentable subject matter, 55–62
  and patent quality, xii, 42, 50–53, 62–64,
    72–73, 78
  SMEs benefitting from, 35, 46
  and Substantive Examinations, 72–73
  in utility model regimes, 34–36, 47–49, 51
Advisory Committee on Review of the Patent
    System (Hong Kong), 206–211, 216,
    243–244, 246n71
Andean Community, 42n64
APO (Austrian Patent Office). See Austria
Apple, Inc., 175–176
Apple, Inc. v. Motorola Mobility, Inc., 164
appropriability
  and costs, 54
  empirical research on, 36–39
  in EU countries, 54–55, 66–67, 76–77
  and innovation, 32–34, 40–41
  in intellectual property rights, 33–34
  and inventive step requirements, 64–68

and novelty standards, 60–62
and patentable subject matter, 55–62
patent protection as means of, 32–34
and patent quality, 62–64, 78
as patent regime strength, 32n10
and Substantive Examinations, 73
utility models providing, 10–11, 34–36
Argentina, 42n64
Arrow, Kenneth, 33–34
Atlantic Thermoplastic Co v. Faytex Corp.,
    115n43, 115–116
Australia, 38n43, 41, 42n65, 195–196, 206,
    214, 224
Austria
  duration of utility model protection in,
    53–55
  innovation sophistication of, 43–44
  inventive step requirements in, 65–66
  novelty standards in, 62–63, 69, 72
  patentability allowances for, 61
  patentable utility model subject matter in,
    55–61
  patent costs in, 46, 47–49
  patent office of (APR), 45
  patent quality in, 73
  Preliminary Examinations in, 69, 73
  search reports in, 69, 71–72, 74
  as Singapore patent office partner, 237
  as SIPO utility model roundtable
    participant, 45

in the United States, 13
in utility model patent regimes, 55–62
patent applications and filings (China).
 See also Patent Cooperation Treaty
 abnormal filings of, 68
 Action Plan for, 11
 goals set for, 8–9
 increases in, xii, 9n28, 50, 52, 128–129
 invention/utility patent ratio in, 52–53
 in parallel with Hong Kong, 22–23, 190–192
 quality of, 50–52
 rankings of, 1n1, 8, 23n104, 23–24, 128–129, 185–186
 vs. in the US, 9–10
 of utility model patents, 10n35, 10–11, 22–23, 30
 written forms required for, 102–103
patent applications and filings (Hong Kong)
 efficiency needed in, 187
 and first-to-file applications, 224
 formality examinations in, 212
 and innovation and, 177
 low numbers of, 18–19, 25, 189, 193
 OGP enhancement of, overseas, 221
 OGP insignificance in, 223
 OGP promotion of, 219
 outsourcing of, 21
 in parallel with China, 22–23, 190–192
 rankings of, 8, 17–18, 185–186
 ratio of, 187
 recommendations for, 192–193
 for short-term patents, 224
 and Singapore, 243n52
 for standard patents, 185–186, 189, 193
 UK origins of, 2
 of utility model patents, 22–23
patent assertion entities (PAEs), 16, 17, 160n34
patent commercialization, xii, 1–2, 11–13
Patent Cooperation Treaty. *See* PCT (Patent Cooperation Treaty)
Patent Examination Guidelines (China)
 for business methods, 142–146
 for computer programs, 140–142
 for computer software, 146
 and CTI incremental innovation, 146–147
 and CTI innovation characteristics, 153
 and CTI patent infringement litigation, 152
 environmental interests in, 84–90, 96–97
 inflexibility of, 153
 on inventiveness, 134, 147
 novelty requirements in, 68n148

and patentable subject matter, 59
on patent prosecution, 146–147, 150
regarding signals in CTI, 136–140
of SIPO, 133
Substantive Examination requirements in, 72
on technical solutions, 145–146
patent filings. *See* patent applications and filings (China); patent applications and filings (Hong Kong)
patent grants (China), 10–11
 and environmental technology neutrality, 80–81
 goals set for, 8–9
 invention patent costs in, 46
 low quality of, 9–11, 30
 public interest exclusions ignored in, 84–87
 rankings of, 1, 8, 23–24
 in technology, 9–10, 13n53, 13–14n52
 vs. in the US, 9–10
 of utility model patents, 10n35
patent grants (Hong Kong). *See also* OGP (original grant patent) system (Hong Kong); patent applications and filings (Hong Kong); patent law (Hong Kong); Substantive Examinations (Hong Kong)
 increases in, 186
 innovational development in, 17–21
 in the OGP system, 207–208
 patent quality problems in, 226–227
 rankings of, 1, 8
 re-registration as means of acquiring, xi–xii, 2
 of short-term patents, 204–205
 of standard patents, 186, 203
patent infringement. See also *Huawei* v. *IDC*
 Bolar exception to, 6
 in CTI, 137, 141, 142, 152
 doctrine of equivalent principle in, 135, 150–152, 153
 enforcement against, 5, 7, 17, 54, 135, 190, 192
 in environmental protection issues, 99n63
 and FRAND implied licensing, 162
 in Hong Kong, 225
 and IPRs, 225
 legislative strengthening of provisions for, 5–6
 in product-by-process applications, 113–118, 116n54
 and re-registration, 214–215
 and scope of protection limitations, 115–118

For EU product safety concerns, contact us at Calle de José Abascal, 56–1°, 28003 Madrid, Spain or eugpsr@cambridge.org.

www.ingramcontent.com/pod-product-compliance
Ingram Content Group UK Ltd.
Pitfield, Milton Keynes, MK11 3LW, UK
UKHW020336140625
459647UK00018B/2169